# speaking of
# book art

Circle Press

Tetrad Press

Visual Studies Workshop

Rebis Press

Studio in the Sky

Weproductions

Mills College

Paradise Press

Druckwerk

Camberwell College of Arts

Gefn Press

never mind the press

Flying Fish Press

## Speaking of Book Art

Interviews with British and American Book Artists
by Cathy Courtney

Ron King
Ian Tyson
Joan Lyons
Betsy Davids
Sas Colby
Telfer Stokes
Kathy Walkup
Susan King
Helen Douglas
Johanna Drucker
Paul Coldwell
Susan Johanknecht
Alisa Golden
Julie Chen
Karen Bleitz

Anderson-Lovelace Publishers • Los Altos Hills, California

Cathy Courtney was Research Assistant for the Project in Book Art, 1995–97, "The Art of the Book 1960 to the Present." The project was funded by The London Institute and was based at Camberwell College of Arts under the direction of Dean Eileen Hogan. The interviews in this volume were conducted as part of that project. The extracts from the "Artists' Lives" recordings included in this book are used with the permission of the National Life Story Collection. The NLSC is based at the British Library National Sound Archive, London.

Printed and bound in the United States by Thomson-Shore

Anderson-Lovelace
13040 Alta Tierra Road
Los Altos Hills, CA 94022
e-mail: lindalb@ix.netcom.com
Fax: 650-941-0615

The Red Gull Press
Flat 3, 10 Adamson Road
London NW3 3HR, UK

Joanna boldface italics are used in each interview to indicate works by the artist.
The dimensions of the books read height by width.

# Contents

# Illustrations

# Foreword

In June of 1997, in central London, my car was broken into and a package containing a selection of artists' books, owned by Kathy Walkup, was stolen. Kathy Walkup, the director of the book arts program at Mills College, Oakland, California, had loaned them to Camberwell College of Arts for a small exhibition.

When the police arrived to investigate the crime, they asked me to describe precisely what artists' books are—were they books about artists? "What are artists' books?" is a question that has preoccupied me a lot in the last five years. I answered that it was a difficult question, but they could be described as books in which the form was used by the artist both to represent the content and as a vehicle for ideas. The constable wrote down "books about artists."

This anecdote brings together much of the context for this book: the tradition of making books at Camberwell College of Arts, the relationship between Camberwell and Mills, and the desire to develop an underlying critical framework for book arts.

Camberwell College of Arts has been a focus for the making and study of the book for many years through its courses in visual arts and conservation and through The Camberwell Press. The Press was founded in 1984, when Camberwell was host for the First Conference of British Fine Printing. At about this time a link was established with Mills College, with lectures, student contacts, and shared publications. The Camberwell M.A. in Book Arts was inaugurated in 1996 (Kathy Walkup was the external member of the validation panel), and an American gift established the Charlene Garry memorial fellowship to enable a Mills graduate to study on the M.A. Book Arts course at Camberwell. At the same time a research project was funded, titled "The Art of the Book 1960 to the Present," and shared between Camberwell and Chelsea College of Art, with me as director and Cathy Courtney as the lead researcher. Cathy Courtney, co-curator of the 1995 book arts exhibition at the Tate Gallery, has reviewed artists' books for *Art Monthly* for some fifteen years, and recently published a study of Circle Press, *The Looking Book*, as another part of her work for Camberwell's project.

Camberwell's project, which developed both research and practice in book arts, led to the publication of this book, which I believe will enable a great many people, including the two constables at Earls Court police station, to better understand and appreciate book arts.

—*Professor Eileen Hogan*

# Preface

Artists' books attract words. When form and content are indivisible and the message is an exciting one, a journey through an artist's book is a strikingly potent experience and, usually, an intimate one. For a writer, it is natural to want to celebrate this achievement and to draw the attention of others to it. Having discovered the work of some American book artists in New York, in 1983 I began writing a column in *Art Monthly*, largely because there were so few places in Britain—and nowhere publishing regularly—to find out about artists' books and, concomitantly, little general awareness of their existence. I regarded these articles as ephemera. During the decade since then, there has been a mushrooming in this country of exhibitions, book fairs, and conferences and, alongside, an increase in critical writing in the form of articles in journals and catalogues and, more recently, whole books devoted to the subject, sometimes by the artists themselves but increasingly by librarians, critics, and academics. In 1995 a research project, "The Art of the Book 1960 to the Present," was established at Camberwell College of Arts alongside the first M.A. in Book Arts and, for the time being at least, the institutionalization of what had formerly been a marginal activity was consolidated.

The research project and the M.A. were signals of potentially alarming changes. In the days when there was little communication on the subject, book art was often made in a context of relative isolation, coming to life when the evolution of an artist's ideas reached optimum expression in book form. The M.A. course marked the arrival of a generation who very often reversed the process and wanted to make books because they had seen examples in exhibitions and at fairs and were—vaguely or immensely —attracted to the form without necessarily having a clear idea of what content they might build into it. It was the first time in Britain that a group of students signed up to spend a year thinking "artists' books" in a concentrated way, listening to talks from visiting artists who had found the form for themselves outside a teaching context, and interacting with one another as they took disparate paths within the same subject area. Depending on one's standpoint, it was either a development that would lead to weak work which would dilute the impact of the genre or a cause for celebration that book art had "arrived" and was at last being taken seriously. Similarly, the establishment of the research project could be seen as a sign of a coming-of-age—in no other area would students sign up for a course and not be touched by the art history related to it—or a form of hijacking, stifling within a blanket of academic discourse what had been perceived as an highly individual, often anarchic, form of expression.

Whatever one's view, it was clear that there was no turning back; neither the M.A. nor the research project was going to go away. In taking a role in the research project I was, however, anxious to minimize the dangers. It is fairly easy—and enjoyable—to write coherent histories of developments in book art since the 1960s by concentrating only on examples which fit into whatever theory or aspect a writer wants to look at, whether related to movements within the wider visual art world or more general social trends. Texts such as these are healthy as long as there is a plurality of publications from differing perspectives, but, because they very often succeed by ignoring a wealth of material from artists who do not fall within their brief, read in isolation they produce a highly distorted picture. Given that the number of people writing at length on book art is still small, such publications can, therefore, have an authority and influence that, perhaps, exceeds their intention, effectively banishing from history forms of book art that have not met the specialized criteria. For a number of reasons, this circumstance has tended to reinforce the values which have grown up around two major public collections of artists' books, those of the Museum of Modern Art in New York and of the Tate Gallery in London, both of which—owing to financial necessity as well as philosophical approach—have policies limiting the kinds of work they are prepared to admit, exercising an inadvertent form of censorship over artists who use materials or printing methods beyond the chosen demarcations or who produce books that cost more than a fixed sum of money.

Taking into account the fact that the history of book art from 1960 to the present is not only young but still growing and that a key characteristic of the genre is its insouciance toward boundaries and categorization, I regarded it as more important that the research project document developments as broadly as possible than to impose a narrow theoretical framework that would throttle any inconvenient voices. As well as a small seminar group around artist-curated exhibitions within Camberwell College of Arts (designed to bring critics and collectors into informal contact with the artists and their thinking and to help break down the hostility traditionally evinced by book artists toward those who approach the form from a different standpoint), it was decided that an important aspect of the research work would be oral history recordings with practitioners who had a long-term involvement with book art so that a resource could be built as an aid for future generations surveying the evidence of the period. It is from these recordings that the interviews in the present volume have been extracted.

The most detailed recording was with Ron King, part of the process of writing a pocket history of the thirty years' worth of activity at Circle Press, *The Looking Book* (1996), published to coincide with a retrospective exhibition at the National Theatre. This interview was augmented by shorter recordings with other artists associated with the Press. In a separate initiative, recordings were made with Susan Johanknecht of Gefn Press (who took over from Alex Lumley as the M.A. Book Arts Course Leader in 1997) and with Paul Coldwell, a member of the teaching staff at Camberwell College of Arts, whose first book, *Freud's Coat* (1996), was triggered by the research project. In-depth recordings with Ian Tyson, Telfer Stokes, and Helen Douglas, each of whom curated one of the book art exhibitions at Camberwell and led seminars with the research group and with the M.A. students, were funded by Camberwell's research project as part of the National Life Story Collection's Artists' Lives oral history project, which is housed in the special collections library at the British Library's National Sound Archive. The life stories of some artists using the book form were already included in Artists' Lives—for example, Ken Campbell and Ian Hamilton Finlay—and they were, therefore, not recorded by Camberwell. Although the research project was initially funded for two years, there was a reasonable expectation that the work would be extended beyond December 1997, and, had it been, there were many obvious candidates for inclusion, and their absence from this published collection does not in any way imply a value judgment.

The history of book art in Britain since the 1960s is intimately interwoven with developments in America, and it would be absurd to approach the activity without recognizing this. These interviews demonstrate not only the role of the books themselves as ambassadors between the two nations but also the importance of the dialogue between artists on both sides of the Atlantic. It is no accident that the archive of Circle Press is to be found at the Yale Center for British Art or that an important section of Ian Tyson's archive is housed in the collection of the University of California at San Diego. One of the strengths of the M.A. book art course is the relationship between Camberwell College of Arts and Mills College in California, forged largely through the professional contact between Eileen Hogan, who was Dean of the School of Applied and Graphic Arts at Camberwell until 1997, and Kathy Walkup, director of the book arts program at Mills College. Among the fruits of their association was the creation of the Charlene Garry Memorial Fellowship, which annually funds a Mills graduate to come to London and take the M.A. course at Camberwell, and an ongoing exchange between staff and students associated with the two institutions.

Kathy Walkup herself came to give tutorials to the Camberwell students in 1997 and curated one of the exhibitions related to the research project. Similarly, Betsy Davids, a book artist who has also taught at Mills and has been on the faculty of the California College of Arts and Crafts for many years, was a key figure in the symposium which opened the first year of the M.A. book art course and went on to direct the new students in their initial project.

I encountered Betsy Davids again when I attended a symposium and exhibition at Mills in April 1996 in memory of Charlene Garry and on this occasion was able to make a recording with her about her life, her artistic output, and her teaching career. Like many people in Britain, I was more familiar with book artists working on the East Coast of the United States than the West and had much to learn about the evolution of the book art community in the Bay Area and in Los Angeles, just as most of the artists I encountered through the symposium were new to me. One of those people was Betsy Davids's contemporary the artist Sas Colby, whose own recording captures a different perspective on the same period.

America has a much longer tradition of teaching book art than Britain, and the Garry symposium was a valuable opportunity to discuss with Betsy Davids and Kathy Walkup the issues raised by the creation of the M.A. course in Britain as well as many of the topics thrown up by recent developments in critical discourse. Four of the interviews in this book are with former pupils of theirs, Johanna Drucker, Alisa Golden, Julie Chen, and Karen Bleitz. Bleitz came to London as the recipient of the Charlene Garry Fellowship in the second year of the M.A. course and thus provides a bridge between the two cultures, since she is able to compare the opportunities at Mills with those at Camberwell and has served an apprenticeship in London with the artists Ron King and Liliane Lijn.

The remaining interviews collected in this book, those with Joan Lyons and Susan King, were stimulated by the lectures and public seminars organized by the research project as part of the annual London Artists' Book Fair. Joan Lyons gave a lecture at the 1996 Fair and took part in a seminar which centered on her book *Her Mother's Book* and Liliane Lijn's *Her Mother's Voice*, while Susan King's *Treading the Maze* was (in her absence) the focus for the seminar at the 1997 Fair. I was able to record King in December 1997 during a visit to California, when I also made a formal interview with Kathy Walkup.

A child of the computer age, Karen Bleitz (born 1973) is taking her place in a very different book art "community" than existed in 1967 when Ron King (born 1932) began publishing and appalled the fine-press world with his revolutionary use of silkscreen technology. If the spread of interviews in this book documents some of the changes which have taken place in the three decades since Circle Press began, it also captures the extremely broad range of backgrounds and disciplines—literature, painting, sculpture, ceramics, commercial printing, the politics of protest—from which book artists have developed and, consequently, the divergence of intent inherent in the work. Whilst the arguments surrounding definitions of book art will no doubt continue, I hope that *Speaking of Book Art* will go some way toward defending the genre from damage by those who seek to nail it too precisely to the wall.

—*Cathy Courtney*
London, 1998

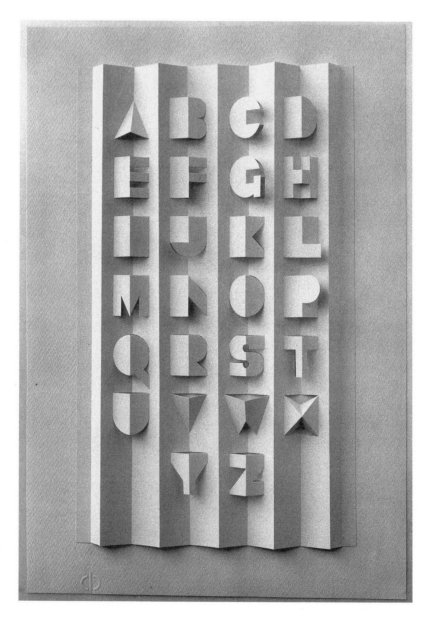

*Alphabet 1,*
cut and creased
roll-up poster,
30" x 20",
unlimited edition,
1983

# ron
# king

This interview with Ron King is extracted from a longer recording, made with
Cathy Courtney between May and August 1996 at Circle Press, in preparation for
a history in celebration of the thirtieth anniversary of the Press, The Looking Book,
which was published in November 1996.

Ron King in his studio, 1996

Photo: F. A. Parisod

*Much of your imagery involves masks of one kind or another. This links to your childhood in Brazil and the annual Carnival there?*

Yes. I was born there in 1932. The Carnival was a three-day event just before Lent and was visually very powerful. I loved the spectacle of the fancy dress, the masks and hobby horses. I spent a lot of time making paper toys and kites. Kites have a tremendous masklike presence, and they have appeared in my adult work; for instance, I used them in my **Antony and Cleopatra** (1979).

*It was as a child in Brazil that you encountered an image in a book which continues to fuel your thinking even now?*

Yes. It's been an obsession. When I was twelve I found a book by my father's bedside which had a horrendous photograph, taken in 1938, of decapitated heads. The book told the true story of the bandit, Lampião, who reached a kind of Bonnie-and-Clyde fame in the north of Brazil in the 1920s and 30s. The book was about an army captain who had tracked down Lampião and his gang and shot them. To prove that he had killed everyone, he cut off the heads of the eleven bandits and their womenfolk and put them on the steps of a church, along with the paraphernalia of their guns, wonderful elaborate hats and clothing, and even objects like their sewing machines. The bandits were highly decorated when they weren't fighting—lace making and tracery had a symbolic meaning for them—and the photograph of the heads looked almost like a wedding table. I was fascinated by the picture, quite terrified, and the image of Lampião has stayed with me all my life as a strange bogey-man figure. He turns up in various guises in my nightmares and dreams and, in retrospect, I can see that many of the images in **The Left-handed Punch** (1986) and **Anansi Company** (1992) are linked to him.

*Coming to school in England in 1945 must have been extremely bleak in comparison with life in Brazil?*

It was more than just a culture shock. The voyage from Rio to Liverpool was just after V. E. Day and was itself a drama-packed tale involving seven boys all going to private schools on a ship full of merchant sailors waiting to be demobbed and a spiteful captain. I hated the school life that followed, and although I've lived in England for most of my life ever since, I've never felt as if I belonged entirely.

*You continued to explore your interest in masks when you were a student at Chelsea School of Art?*

African masks have been a tremendous inspiration to me ever since art school. If I go back to my first sketchbook at Chelsea, I find a collection of studies that I made at the British Museum. I was at Chelsea between 1951 and 1955, and it was there that I met my future wife, the sculptor Willow Legge. I did a fine arts course in painting, which I loved, and I won the Biddulph painting scholarship two years running. The facilities at Chelsea were basic, but the rest of the students included older, demobbed ex-servicemen and the level of work was high. Ceri Richards, Bernard Meadows, and Robert Medley were among the teachers at Chelsea while I was there.

*In 1955 you married Willow and went to live in Canada for five years. What did you do there?*

In Canada I still painted but I made my living as a display artist, an assistant art director, and finally as an art director of a magazine, *Homes & Gardens*. I learned about typography and photography and also illustrated for other publications.

By the time Willow and I came back to England, we had three sons and we settled in a big house in Guildford, Surrey, where our daughter, Jessica, was born. We never lived in Canada again, although I had a one-man show of paintings in Toronto in 1962.

*For you, the path which led you to make books was printmaking. How did that come about?*

I was teaching in the graphics department at Farnham College of Art, and it was there, rather than at Chelsea where the facilities were minimal, that I began to make

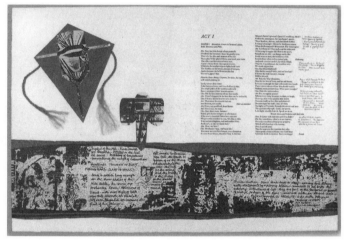

*Antony and Cleopatra* (Shakespeare), illustrated by Ron King, 15¼" x 11¼", 88 pages, edition of 300, 1979

prints and learn about litho and etching. Another member of staff was leaving to go abroad, and I bought from him a very crude silkscreen setup and turned a spare bedroom into a studio at home. I began making monoprints—it seemed an attractive way of getting the color down and messing around with torn and cut paper stencils. A lot of what I was making was still lifes of plants, lichen, and natural growth, and they were quite flat but had a lot of texture to them. I was using paper stencils most of the time and sometimes painting directly onto the screen.

Quite soon after I'd got the equipment, Paul Cornwall-Jones, a partner in a firm called Editions Alecto, was put in touch with me and he bought fifty or sixty of the monoprints for Alecto to sell and asked if I would make editions from some of them. Within a year I'd been given a contract to make larger and more varied prints for Alecto. I was doing editions of seventy-five and using four or five colors. I carried on printing in the spare room for a while, but later I built a studio in the garden and worked in there. The Alecto contract gave me the basis for earning a living, and I stopped teaching around 1964. If I had to make extra money, I did freelance typography or illustration.

*Were you aware of any coherence in the prints?*

I've never been aware of any kind of coherence in my work. I find it quite difficult to understand or believe that people can recognize my work and perceive an obvious individual style. I still see everything I do as completely separate things.

*So the prints weren't a series in any way?*

The prints were an exploration. I always felt that I was doing something that would lead to something else. I never got any satisfaction from turning out one of anything, which is possibly why I moved away from painting (which I virtually stopped doing in 1972), and even an edition of fifty prints was too much focus on one design. That is why the book suits me. A book to me is most often a sequence leading to the idea of a composite, many images that relate to one another and have a continuum. My exploration has been for a satisfactory way to deal with my very obvious leaning toward the development of a theme to a conclusion—in other words, storytelling. The idea for the first book came from a need to put together a group of images that were linked. Chaucer's **The Prologue to the Canterbury Tales**, which I'd studied at school, always fascinated me and, with its company of pilgrims, seemed the perfect vehicle.

*By the time you came to make **The Prologue** (1967), had you seen anything that was like an artist's book?*

Yes. There was a room in the Victoria and Albert Museum that was devoted to artists' books in those days, and some of them had a deep influence on me. Matisse's *Jazz* (1947) moved me tremendously, a revelation in the strength of its color, the economy of its drawing, the exciting presentation of something that had been worked out in cut paper and reproduced by a hand-cut stencil technique in a way that vitalized rather than diminished it. His cutouts were an important inspiration to me, even though I used the practice myself in a way that was far more illustrative. Derain's Rabelais book (1943) was another that appealed to me because it was excessive, which a lot of my stuff is, but I also found some extremely restrained books inspirational, like the deeply embossed work of Etienne Hajdu. I have a vivid memory of Ian Tyson (whom I had met while teaching at Farnham) telling me about a book that wasn't on display but which you could ask to look at, Miró's *A Toute Epreuve* (1958), which, perhaps, had a strong influence on the second book I did, **The Song of Solomon** (1969).

*What was your starting point for the images in* **The Prologue***?*

The Chaucer was very much a print-and-text presentation, and the only thing that made it viable as far as the publisher, Editions Alecto, was concerned was the series of prints that was made independently of the book but using the same images. Equally, it didn't appeal to me just to do the prints of the pilgrims, so I stuck to my guns about doing a book and we bargained quite hard.

At the time I was thinking about **The Prologue**, I had been working on a series of mask prints and I knew this was a solution I wanted to explore for the Chaucer rather than attempting to "illustrate" it. When I began working, I thought in terms of "presences" rather than characters. I was always fascinated by the idea that you could produce the feeling of personality or presence from something which suggested a human face but which wasn't actually a human face. The abstract mask provided the opportunity to express the pilgrims through the merging of symbols—symbols taken from heraldry or the Church, for example—rather than caricature. The Parson, for instance, is not just himself but also a symbol of the Church, just as the Knight is the symbol of ruthlessness and (at the same time) vulnerability but also, in heraldic terms, of the Crusade. The symbol of the Cross was a key to the design of all the characters.

*Did you know much about heraldry?*

No. I picked up rather a good book on medieval costume design and I used five or six of the diagrams, crosses, and fleurs-de-lys. I adapted them in a very abstract way. I used color to put certain moods across; for instance, the Knight is gray, black, and silver and rather rusty, whereas the Squire is bright and gaudy.

*How did the mask relate to the text in visual terms?*

I was working with rectangular shapes opposite the text but I was unhappy with the relationship. I became so frustrated that I ripped up the sheet on which I'd been printing the idea for the Knight, threw it on the floor, and went to the pub. Half an hour later I went back to the studio and came upon the torn remains on the floor, which had fallen in such a way that I saw how to resolve the whole sequence. The way the Knight's "presence" had torn allowed the floor to be drawn into the image and, in the same way, I went on to use the white of the background page inside the imagery, creating much more of a sense of the wholeness of the double spread of the book rather than having rectangular portraits opposite text.

*When you made* **The Prologue** *you didn't have a press of your own. When did this change?*

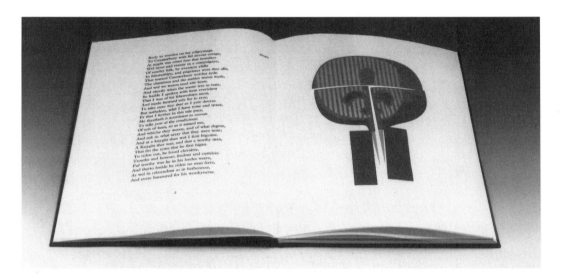

*The Prologue to the Canterbury Tales* (Chaucer),
second edition, letterpress and mechanical silkscreen
with 14 images, 16"x 11", 64 pages,
edition of 5,000, 1978

For the text of **The Prologue** I found a local printing works in Guildford, Seven Corners Press, which in the first couple of years of the Press's history did all our letterpress. They were prepared to bend the rules, so, for instance, a folded half sheet of double-elephant went through a cylinder Heidelberg press for the Chaucer, which was not usual practice. It wasn't until Seven Corners Press became intolerant of my demands that they banished me from the shop floor and gave me an empty paper store at low rent to put my own press into. Ultimately, I bought the building that housed the paper store and added more presses and a proper silkscreen bench, becoming self-sufficient in all the processes other than papermaking and binding. I moved Circle Press to a studio in Notting Hill in London in 1988, a smaller space but better placed.

*There's a theatrical feel to* **The Prologue** *which recurs in your later work?*

Yes. I was unaware of it at the time, but you are quite right. Maybe I'm a frustrated theater designer. It's strange, looking back, how many things I've made that have a feeling of the stage about them.

*When you are working, are the characters in the books alive in your mind as if they were people with voices?*

As characters—not necessarily human beings—yes. Especially in **The Left-handed Punch** and **Anansi Company**, both of which I did with Roy Fisher. When I've given the characters more than one position they begin to live, particularly once Roy's text is done.

*When you were working on* **The Prologue***, did you have a sense of collaborating with Chaucer?*

No, he was too distant. What concerned me more was an avoidance of anything connected to William Morris's Kelmscott Chaucer (1896), which I'd seen reproduced at various times. I don't like that era of English art and find it retrograde.

*Was the need for collaboration one of the reasons for forming Circle Press?*

Although **The Prologue** was initiated through my relationship with Editions Alecto, changes in the structure of Alecto (Paul Cornwall-Jones departed and formed Petersburg Press) meant that despite the sheets being stamped with their logo, I ended up publishing the Chaucer under my own imprint. It was a horrendous situation because I was in a financially precarious position, but I had no option but to go ahead. At that point I telephoned Ian Tyson and Derrick Greaves and said, "Will you join me in something I'm going to form, Circle Press?" A little later Birgit Skiöld joined us too. Birgit was Swedish and had come to England and started the first print workshop in London, in the basement of the house of the painter Adrian Heath in Charlotte Street. I had learned quite a lot about etching from Birgit when I was first starting to make prints. Her whole life was printmaking. She had no children, and her assistants were like adopted kids whom she bossed about. When she did a book with me, it was as if it was her baby and I was the doctor in charge of the birth. She would phone me at all times of the night and day and drive everybody wild while she fussed and worried about things, but her interest in the books was wonderful, so you put up with those things. Circle Press published Birgit's **Chimes** with a Dante Gabriel Rossetti text in 1969 and **Zen Gardens** with a text by James Kirkup in 1973. The last book she did with Circle Press was **The Tao of Water**, again with James Kirkup, in 1979. Sadly, Birgit died in 1982.

*Silkscreening was a method frowned upon by those working in more traditional small-press practices when you began making books in 1967. Your engagement with the book form has led you toward even less conventional approaches?*

Although I was never a wholly traditional printer, I was closer to that standpoint when I began than now, when much of what I do might be described as the work of an experimental book artist. For many years now I have been using materials such as wire, wood, mirror, and stone and exploring the elasticity of the book form itself. In selecting slides for lectures, I'm often aware of how my approach to the book form has developed. From the conventional solution of image and text in the format of the Chaucer **Prologue** in 1967—through pop-ups, mirror books, wire-embossed books with double images, stone books, sawn and laser-cut ones—to the hollow log which I cut earlier this year into forty sections and bound in the inner ring to make four quarter-circle books that fit together into the original log form, is a long way.

*Ian Tyson, Willow Legge, Michael Kidner, and Norman Ackroyd are among the artists who have worked with Circle Press, as well as John Christie, who made his first book with you in 1975 and went on to do a dozen more. Their work varies greatly and there is no "house style"?*

I thought of it as a circle of printmakers who wanted to make books, and I didn't want to make Circle Press exclusive or an elitist group. Obviously, my approach to the book has changed over a period of thirty years and my expectations have as well. "Form" has always been my principal concern. It is amazing how many good and well-known artists produce what I would judge to be "nonbooks"—just a series of illustrations or prints for a text. A good book idea is what I am after nowadays, a work which only succeeds in book form, and where if you take any part of it away, it loses its identity.

*You took on the marketing of the Press list yourself?*

Forming the Press made it easier to go out selling, because it wasn't an ego trip with just my own work—if the person didn't want mine, they could take a book by one of the other artists. The marketing brought the final stage of the business into my act—going out to show the work and being the salesman. I've enjoyed that side of it, particularly in North America—Americans are more relaxed about showing their pleasure, particularly with some of the pop-up presentations I've made. Showing the books came easily to me, although sometimes I would be anxious.

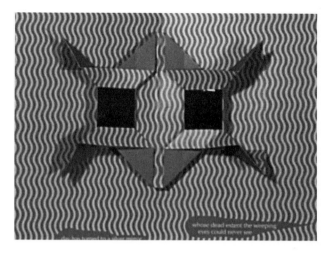

"The Lake of Tears" from *Bluebeard's Castle,* poem by Roy Fisher, pop-up book, 12"x 8", in a perspex box, edition of 125, 1972–73

The interviews I had at the Museum of Modern Art in New York I always remember with a certain amount of horror because of the incredible narrowness of their policy—basically they collect well-known names. When they finally bought **Bluebeard's Castle** (1972–73), it was for ten times the amount I'd offered it to them eleven years previously. Even then it was not bought as part of the museum's main collection of books, but, instead, Clive Phillpot recognized its worth and purchased it for the library.

*Your pop-up version of* **Bluebeard's Castle** *marked the beginning of your collaboration with the poet Roy Fisher?*

It also marked my first step away from the traditional book format. I had begun working with another writer but as the months went by we couldn't make it jell and, when that attempt finally collapsed, I rang Ian Tyson for advice and he suggested I might try Roy, whose work I didn't know at all at that time. The extraordinary thing was that within three weeks of my having sent Roy a mock-up of the book, he had written a text in which we only changed one word. I'd never met him. We discussed the project over the phone and I said that the problem so far had been that the piece had become too much about human emotions. His immediate reaction was, "If you don't want people, why don't we make your sets speak out instead? Turn the castle rooms into the characters for each scene." Instead of having a dialogue between two people, each environment had its own voice. I had marked on the dummy the places where I thought the text could go and Roy was quick to see the opportunity of spreading it through the folds.

*What was the mock-up you sent to Roy?*

It had all the pop-ups but the last one. I remember sitting at a desk and just cutting and chopping and glueing and looking at all kinds of different pop-up material until I turned out the first room, the Torture Chamber. Once I got the idea that to make something pop-up you have to have a symmetrical folding structure, I began experimenting in various ways.

*Did you construct the edition yourself? The portcullis, for instance, is immensely complex.*

I designed the whole thing, and making it was incredibly masochistic. Absolute hell. The difficult thing about a work like **Bluebeard's Castle** is to translate the dummy into something that can be manufactured or constructed in an edition. I had never in my life used cutting formes before but I was introduced to a professional, saw how the operation was done, and came away and designed my own formes. The structure of the portcullis helped solve the other sections, because I continued to develop the egg-crate system, slotting parts into one another, but there was plenty of anguish along the way. A lot of people helped me put **Bluebeard's Castle** together. I'm quite good at working out what people can do, but not so good at having the patience to do it myself. I had students who helped me, I had housewives who helped me.

*What governed the size of the page?*

I'd acquired a vacuum-topped screen bench and that determined the size. I used paper that didn't mark too much when folded. The sections had to be long strips that folded so that I could hide the workings of the pop-ups inside.

*The colors in **Bluebeards's Castle** play an important role?*

The color is predominantly printed. It was silkscreened, the only way to achieve the intensity I wanted. I intended to produce strong, flat color and to get away from some of the textures I'd been using, for instance in **Macbeth** (1970).

*What was the response to **Bluebeard's Castle**?*

I was in the province of what is normally accepted as being a children's book area, and it was extraordinary how many people were prejudiced against buying it because as adults they couldn't allow themselves to enjoy it. It was exciting to use the form in a more sober way to express strong

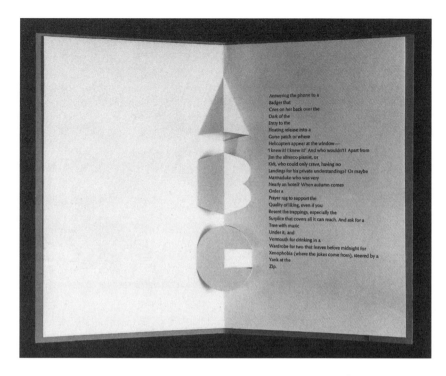

Answering the phone to a
Badger that
Cries on her back over the
Dark of the
Entry to the
Floating release into a
Gone patch or where
Helicopters appear at the window—
"I knew it! I knew it!" And who wouldn't? Apart from
Jim the alfresco pianist, or
Kirk, who could only crave, having no
Landings for his private understandings? Or maybe
Marmaduke who was very
Nearly an hotel? When autumn comes
Order a
Prayer rug to support the
Quality of liking, even if you
Resent the trappings, especially the
Surplice that covers all it can reach. And ask for a
Tree with music
Under it; and
Vermouth for drinking in a
Wardrobe for two that leaves before midnight for
Xenophobia (where the jokes come from), steered by a
Yank at the
Zip.

*Scenes from the Alphabet*,
first of alphabet series pop-ups, letterpress,
poem by Roy Fisher,
12" x 8", 4 pages French fold,
3 editions to date, 1978

feeling. Over the years the final edition of 125 has sold out and I have only personal copies left.

*When you finally met Roy Fisher, what was he like?*

Very English in the best sense. A bit phlegmatic, an understated person. Just the opposite from being over the top like me, which is what has made our collaborations work. He's very amusing and also very gentle and not self-centered in a way that quite a lot of writers and artists are. On one or two occasions we've spent a couple of days together but mostly it's been measured in hours and, usually, our communication is by telephone or post. We seem to accept each other's solutions without any problem. Once we've decided on a collaboration we feed off each other well. For instance, when I was going to do a series of alphabet poems, he sent me his **Scenes from the Alphabet** (1978), which I complemented with an A B C structure down the gutter of the page, and he was so pleased he said, "Why don't you do the whole alphabet?" That's how we often work together, a bit like playing jazz, where we improvise and play off each other's tune.

*Anansi Company, Jack Mantora, the "listener,"* 1 of 13 removable wire and card puppets, text by Roy Fisher, 15"x 11", 15 unbound sections, edition of 120, 1992

*Your alphabet series has gone through many permutations?*

Yes, and there are still one or two to come. The Crafts Council gave me a grant of £2,800 to develop the alphabet series (the only grant I've ever received for myself). I just sat in the studio and snipped away with scissors and a knife and worked out the whole alphabet. **The White Alphabet** (1983) was the most difficult production I've ever tackled and is perhaps the purest of my book-form ideas. The poster, **Alphabet I** (1983), still sells well, the Tate Gallery alone selling about 150 of them a year. I would like to do a large one in steel.

*The Left-handed Punch and Anansi Company were major publications, again using texts provided by Roy. Punch involves paper puppets with movable limbs, while the wire and paper puppets in Anansi can be taken out of the book. Were these books stages on the journey toward the near-human-scale sculptural bandits you have been working on since 1994?*

**The Left-handed Punch** and **Anansi Company** are the two most elaborate books Roy and I worked on. **The Punch** is my favorite of all the books I've done; it holds together better than **Anansi** and has more dimensions. **Punch**'s movable puppets, on-stage descriptions, the large chunks of the original Cruikshank version of the text, and the drawn Victorian tableaux scenes (spoofs of famous drawings and paintings) all fit together easily, and the photo montages and collages are relieved by the inclusion of the poet's (Roy's) handwriting to strong effect. The **Anansi** book is more spectacular with its removable puppets made of wire and card—the whole book is like the Brazilian Carnival scene as I knew it, lots of noisy music and revelry coming from all directions. The elements are hardly containable even in the large box I designed for them, but they are like that on purpose and I intentionally avoided the compact quality of **Punch**. The origins of the **Anansi** story are African and form a central part of West Indian culture, which I felt connected to when I moved from Guildford to the epicenter of the Caribbean Carnival scene in Notting Hill, at a time when it was probably one of London's most active drug areas.

As far as the bandit sculptures are concerned, I'm still too nervous and lacking in confidence about my installation ideas to know what to say about them, but you are probably right in connecting them to the **Punch** and **Anansi** puppets. The latter move and can be taken out, whereas the bandits are free standing but nevertheless are capable of being folded and packed away. The bandits are a kind of portable sculptural edition—forty of them, laser-cut and assembled—but each with a different mask. I plan for them to be seen with a dozen or so life-size carved heads. Again, the series links directly to the Lampião photograph I saw as a child.

*You have begun research on a book that has been germinating in your mind for a long time about the printing history of your own family. Again it will involve Roy Fisher?*

Printing has been in my family for seven generations. I didn't know that until recently, since my father was separated from his father when he was two and followed a career in banking and wasn't aware of the real family history. It turns out that I have printing in my genes (and also painting on my grandmother's side). The Gutenberg Museum held an exhibition to celebrate twenty years of publications from Circle Press, and during that time I gave a lecture and mentioned that I'd recently discovered that the King family history covers over two hundred years of printing. Through a route of extraordinary chance, that reference led the museum's director to present me with a box of wooden type from Lymington in Hampshire, which had been used by the King family firm of printers. The type will be used, and its genealogy celebrated, in the next Circle Press production, which Roy and I are just beginning to work on.

*A lot of changes have taken place since you began to publish books thirty years ago. At that time there were not many artists working in the field in Britain and you quickly became a figure that others came to for advice?*

Ian Mortimer, who went on to become a highly skilled printer, was among those who came to Guildford, as well as the artists Natalie d'Arbeloff and Anne Brunskill and, later, Jane Rolo and Pella Erskine-Tulloch when they were nursing the idea that later became Book Works. One of the first who came to me was Eileen Hogan, who was sent to me by one of the staff at the Royal College of Art, where she was a student. She brought with her the first book she made, *The Dream of Gerontius* (1975), laboriously printed with hand-cut lettering, which I bought and still have. By that time I was beginning to buy other people's work.

*What else did you have?*

I already had an extensive collection of illustrated books, old and new. Among the books I bought by artists was Eduardo Paolozzi's *Moonstrip Empire News* from Editions Alecto, and I also had a lot of Ian Tyson's books, which I either bought or swapped with him. I had some of Derrick Greaves's books and some of Birgit Skiöld's, besides those she had done with me. I also began to buy smaller books by people like John Furnival, Tom Phillips, and Hansjörg Mayer, and also some concrete poetry that was being produced at the time and in which I was very interested.

*Where did you find the concrete poetry?*

By then I had been going to the Frankfurt Book Fair and had begun to find a lot there. In the 1970s I had also visited the Coracle Press Gallery in south London and I bought a number of their books, including work by Simon Cutts. I have quite a collection of Ian Hamilton Finlay's early books, many of which I found at Coracle or in America.

*How often do you look at your collection?*

Quite often. At least three or four times a year I really go through my shelves, spending a day pulling books out and looking at them again. Of course, I find my attitude has changed and there are things I no longer like, whereas perhaps I begin to see new things in something I have disliked. I tend to be impulsive about buying things.

*Compared to 1967, there is now much more activity in Britain associated with book art. Where do you situate Circle Press within that community?*

I feel Circle Press books as a whole have more form and content to them than books done by most of the other small presses around. You can go into our books for longer and come back to them for more. Certainly I try to make my own multifaceted. **Punch** is a good example of what I aim for. It needs studying. If I am to criticize other works, I would say that, too often, one look through is enough! That does not mean that I can't enjoy that "one-look" type of book; not only do I have a large collection of them, but my own wire-printed productions, **Turn Over Darling** (1990) and **Echo Book** (1994), are books of that nature. However, with the increasing number of book fairs and book art exhibitions there seems to be a disproportionate number of "one-look" books, all too often ill conceived and badly printed. For my part, I try to make even those "one-look" books tactile and pleasing to handle and the printing relevant to the content. As in a good speech, the message is not enough, the quality of delivery is vital.

*In the last few years book art has begun to be taught formally within British art schools. Do you regard that as a good development?*

This is a difficult question. I can find a parallel to this in the reservations I hold in my attitude to the printmaking degree-courses that were foisted on students a few years back. I am old-fashioned in wanting to see more hands-on opportunities in a general creative sense in art education and wanting young people to grow into areas of specialization as and when they are ready. Printmaking and book art courses should be there in a subsidiary role initially. The B.A. and M.A. courses are too often taught to students too early in their process of development—which is probably why there is so much superficial work around.

COLOR PLATE IA:
Ron King, *Acrobats,*
laser-cut and hand-painted bookwork,
9"x 6¾",
edition of 50, 1996

COLOR PLATE IB:
Ron King,
*The Left-handed Punch,*
screenprints with fold-out puppets, 15"x 11",
72 pages, edition of 90, 1986

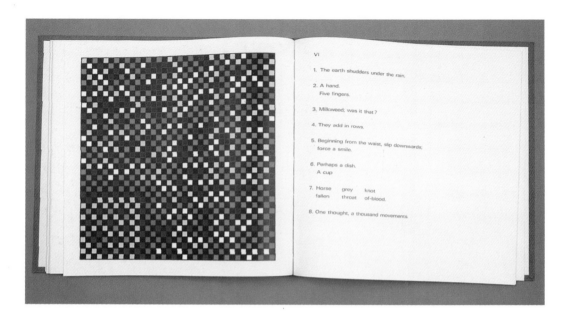

COLOR PLATE 2A:

Ian Tyson, *Sightings I–IX & Red Easy a Color,*
text by Jerome Rothenberg, letterpress with 10 screenprinted
images, 14"x 14¾", 14 pages, edition of 120,
published by Circle Press, 1968

COLOR PLATE 2B:
Ian Tyson,
print from *The Pronouns—
40 Dances for the Dancers—
Feb. 6–March 22, 1964 ,*
text by Jackson Mac Low,
letterpress with 8 screenprinted
images, 25"x 20",
edition of 75,1998

**COLOR PLATE 4A:**
Susan King,
*New York City*
*(My Mother Told Me),*
laser print Japanese screen,
11½"x 48", one of a kind, 1998

**COLOR PLATE 4B:**
Sas Colby, *Shrine,*
wood, canvas, acrylic, found
object, 20"x 16"x 9",
one of a kind, 1994

COLOR PLATE 5A:
Susan Johanknecht,
*of science & desire*
(installation view),
CD-ROM and book,
6"x 6", 32 pages,
edition of 150, 1995

COLOR PLATE 5B:
Susan Johanknecht,
*WHO WILL BE IT?*,
letterpress, 3½"x 4"in archival box,
edition of 50, 1996

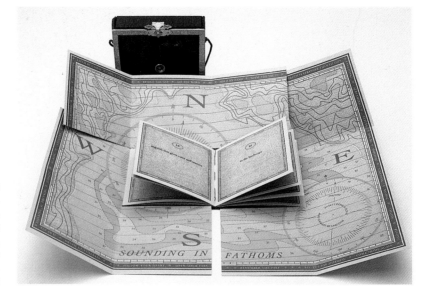

COLOR PLATE 6A:
Julie Chen,
*You Are Here*,
letterpress printed from
polymer plates,
4"x 4", expands to
11½"x 15",
edition of 100, 1992

COLOR PLATE 6B:
Julie Chen, *Ste Ostrich in Manhattan*,
letterpress with linocuts,
8"x 6", expands to 8"x 90",
edition of 125, 1990

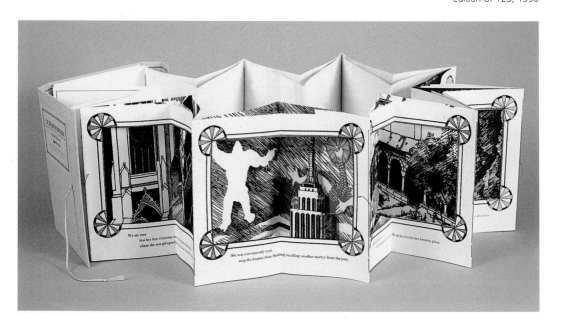

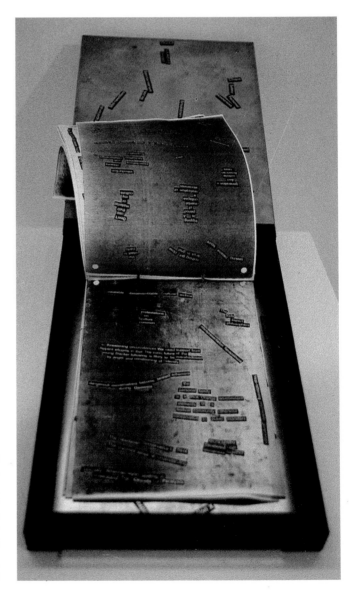

COLOR PLATE 8:
Karen Bleitz,
*Redefining,*
metal pages, magnets,
screenprinting,
photocopies,
13"x 10½"x 2″,
add-on pages,
one of a kind,
1997

Print from *The Pronouns–
40 Dances for the Dancers–
Feb. 6–March 22, 1964,*
text by Jackson Mac Low,
letterpress text with
8 screenprinted images
25"x 20",
edition of 75, 1971

# ian
# **tyson**

This interview with Ian Tyson is extracted from a longer recording Cathy Courtney made in London at various times between February 1997 and April 1998.

Ian Tyson, 1998

Photo: Matthew Tyson

*For the last twelve years you've divided your life between homes in east London and the south of France, but you were originally from the north of England?*

I was born in April 1933 in Cheshire. The house I lived in for the first part of my life was in Upton, in a commuter belt just outside Birkenhead that emerged during the depression of the 1930s, built for people like my parents, both of whom worked in the Midland Bank. Looking back, it was a suburban nightmare, but, as a small child, I also spent quite a lot of time with my grandparents and I have vivid memories of life with them near Wigan. There, I would wake early to the sound of steel-capped clogs on the road outside, the miners going on shift. The sawmill that made the clogs was nearby, and my grandfather and I would walk there and to the colliery, where the miners worked under very difficult conditions. It was all hewn coal at that time.

During the 1930s there were a lot of vagrants, people who could only get refuge for one night at a time, so they walked from refuge to refuge and existed on a very genteel form of begging. My grandparents were compassionate and would always find them something. I don't remember my parents ever discussing this directly, but the legacy they tried to pass on to me was the idea of a safe job, like going into a bank. My mother would refer to people who lived nearby in slightly larger houses with lace curtains—perhaps a lawyer or a Liverpool cotton broker—saying, "Of course, he's a thousand-a-year man, you know." They felt there were very ordered strata of society.

*What early books do your remember?*

I vividly remember Beatrix Potter's books. The pictures fascinated me and the stories seemed to come from somewhere else, from the voice that was reading to me. Those books were important in that sense of providing a picture with a text almost subservient to the image.

*Did you do anything in childhood that approximated making a book?*

I don't think so. My aunt did watercolors and she showed me how to paint. I liked drawing. I was very interested in the theater—particularly the way it worked—and by the time I was about twelve I had made a model theater and scenery. In my early teens I went to the Liverpool Playhouse quite often and, eventually, when I was at Birkenhead School of Art, I went backstage and did a lot of drawing there.

*Did you write?*

I tried writing plays.

*Where were you educated?*

I was one of the first wave of children to be educated completely by the State. At one point I was at school in Wigan, which everybody thought was a lot safer during the war—I can remember standing in the back garden and seeing the whole of Liverpool on fire because the Germans had hit the oil containers on the River Mersey. Later I was sent to my father's old school, a grammar school with pretensions to tradition. I disliked it from the first day I went there.

*What was the art teaching like?*

After the war, a young man came and took over the art room. He marched in one morning and said, "I have just restored the *Victory of Samothrace* to its original condition. It is now in several hundred pieces at the bottom of the rugby pitch." He had taken all the plaster casts and thrown them away, so that was the end of drawing from the cast until I encountered it again at the Academy Schools. This particular teacher encouraged us to paint what we felt about a subject, so our paintings could be quite abstract. Sometimes he would take a simple still life and ask us to interpret it, at the same time showing us reproductions in books of paintings by people like Juan Gris and Picasso. He lent me one book, Wilenski's *The Modern Movement in Art*, which opened my eyes to another world. I have a copy of it now.

*There were not that many art books in those days?*

Very few. One would have relied on black and white to a large extent. Phaidon did books on modern artists, and Penguin Modern Painters started around then. Color printing was beginning to re-emerge after the war, but it was a time of great hardship.

*How did you react to the reproductions of Gris and Picasso?*

They were exciting. There was a nagging feeling that they were cocking a snook at society, this terrible middle-class miasma that one lived in. You can't imagine how shocking it was. My parents were very upset that I should be exposed to this nonsense. I think it was at this time I also started listening to jazz seriously on AFN (American Forces Network).

*What happened after school?*

I went into the shipyards as an apprentice engineer for two years, but without going to night school and doing maths I couldn't get anywhere and, as I had no understanding of maths at the time, I realized I had to do something else. I had been making drawings and paintings and, thinking that perhaps I could one day teach art, I went to Birkenhead School of Art and showed them what I had done, and they said, "OK." I was there for about two years.

*And then you came to London in 1954?*

I went to the Royal Academy Schools for four years, which was wonderful. Figure and still life were what really interested me, particularly drawing, and the Academy Schools were very strong on that. From the middle of my time there I was looking for a way forward, for a voice of my own. I was beginning to be concerned about landscapes and the structure of the land and I did a lot of straight landscapes, which gradually began to change into something else; I was very interested in Paul Nash and the way he transformed natural forms anthropomorphically. I used to go to the Natural History Museum and look at fossils, and my straightforward drawings of them led to abstracted paintings derived from them. The natural history connotations took me to Thomas Bewick, the eighteenth-century engraver, whose images of birds and animals became a lasting passion for me. Bewick revolutionized wood engraving, amalgamating woodcut and engraving techniques in a way no one had done before, and he remains unique in that he was a journeyman who took the craft into another personal and innovative dimension.

*Had you learned any printing techniques yourself?*

I went to evening classes to do etching and lithography.

*When did you encounter Ron King?*

Immediately after I left the Academy Schools I had a job as a technical assistant in the printmaking department at Camberwell School of Art and Craft for about a year. Then a job came up teaching lithography at Farnham and, after I'd been there for a year, Ron came to run the foundation department. He wasn't making books then—he was painting, working on an exhibition he was having in Canada. Soon after, he acquired some screenprinting equipment and started cutting stencils with paper. My work was still organic in conception but the edges were getting tighter and tighter and he said, "Cutting a stencil is ideal for the flat shapes you want to use, why don't you try it?" So I went to his studio and started screenprinting. The first experiments I made were screenprints with handwritten Japanese haiku alongside the image, made to go on the wall. Then I went on to make the **Six Extracts from the Zenrinkushu** (1966), the first word-image piece I made where the text was printed rather than handwritten. It was a folio, six prints and six two-line aphorisms and, again, I was responding to texts that were relatively enigmatic. The images were the first really geometric pieces I had made, perhaps a natural response to the text.

*Would you have seen anything by then that you would, in retrospect, have called an artist's book?*

I would have seen the Max Ernst collage books in reproduction—probably in an art magazine—but I wouldn't necessarily have thought of them as artists' books. It was quite a long time before I saw the original Ernst books and only about five years ago that I saw the actual collages in Germany. The first time I remember the excitement of handling a book was at the Victoria and Albert Museum around 1966, when I asked to see Paul Eluard's *A Toute Epreuve* with its Miró woodcuts. It was a great privilege to be able to hold that: handling it was essential to the experience of the book. *A Toute Epreuve* changed something in my life. I also looked at Matisse's *Jazz* and that was very influential.

*Would you have seen Ed Ruscha's books?*

I can't remember exactly when I first saw them, but it must have been the very late 1960s or early 1970s. I bought the *Thirtyfour Parking Lots in Los Angeles* (1967) somewhere in London, together with *Various Small Fires and Milk* (1964). I thought the *Parking Lots* were visually interesting in the same way as other aerial groundplans are, but the *Small Fires* have a marginal existential interest for me. (The original 1964 edition of *Small Fires* was limited to four hundred, presumably because it wasn't thought it would sell. I have one from the second edition of three thousand.) None of his books figure largely in my collection, and I find it difficult to understand the seminal status they have acquired.

*You went on to make your first book at Circle Press using a text by the American poet Jerome Rothenberg. That was the beginning of a collaboration which is still continuing?*

Because Ron's *Prologue to the Canterbury Tales* was successful, he asked if I'd like to do a book and this led to **Sightings I–IX & Red Easy a Color** (1968). By this time I was teaching at St. Martin's, where typography was taught by Des Jeffries. Des was an enormous influence on the development of my approach to typography as a very important part of my work in a much more sophisticated way than just page layout. He introduced me to new typography, particularly German and Swiss of the early 1960s, which didn't crowd the page, and which impressed me greatly.

It was probably Des who taught me to use a grid to divide the page into sections, using a rectangle divided into equal parts that is placed on the page in relation to its edges. This grid is placed on each page in the maquette and from that, I can hang the whole design of the book. Each part of the text, therefore, relates to every other part of the text.

*The principles behind the grid have been fundamental to your practice since* **Sightings***?*

It's just a practical layout device. It got more complex for me later on when the proportion of where the points on the grid were in relation to the page became crucial—the numerical relationships became important.

*That focus came from using the grid in a practical way rather than from an intellectual appreciation of its implication?*

That's difficult to say, because there was a lot of art that I liked beginning to impinge on my consciousness that had to do with that way of constructing images. The reason why I imposed the rules on my own practice was that I had reached a stage in the work I was doing where I never knew if it was finished. Paintings would hang around for months and I would constantly alter them, feeling immense frustration because I had no idea whether they were complete; I couldn't ever reach a conclusion. I felt that, if I had a set of parameters to work within, then, for better or worse, I could say, "This is finished." I used the grid in a primitive, naive way to start with, but it wasn't too long before I realized I'd opened up the doors on something much more complex that anything I had envisaged. The frustration of not knowing when a work was finished was supplanted by knowing there were infinite variations of whatever mathematical progression I was using. Often I've tried to evade that by moving into informality, but I've always ended up disliking those pieces. You spend a lot of time finding out what you don't want to do.

*Numerology underlies several of your collaborations with Jerome Rothenberg?*

We've done three books, **Six Gematria** (1992), **Surimono 2** (1992), and **DELIGHT/ DELICES and other GEMATRIA** (1998), using the ideas that underlie the gematria. In Hebrew there are no numbers, but there are letters of the alphabet that have a numerical value so, theoretically, you can transpose any Hebrew text into numbers. About twenty-five years ago, somebody in the States transcribed the first five books of the Old Testament into numerical form, *The Spice of Torah*. Jerry has a copy of this and has used it to compose poems over the last twenty years; it's not the main body of his work, but it is a consistent element. His approach married well with my own use of the grid system.

Other books I've done with Jerry have centered around a mutual interest in archetypes, atavistic sources, and arcane word games. In **Songs for the Society of Mystic Animals** (1978) it was the visual poetics translated typographically that interested me, whereas in **The 17 Horse Songs of Frank Mitchell X–XIII** (1969–70), a total translation Jerry had made from the Navajo, the texts were the corollary to the images, giving a sense of "going through," a response to the songs recounting the shaman entering the spirit world. **Millenium (sic)** (1982) made a counterpoint of text and image in a more formal way. In our most recent collaboration, **DELIGHT/DELICES and other GEMATRIA** (Ottezek) we changed our way of working; I gave Jerry the number sequences and he composed the texts from them. My part involved coming up with five finished pieces that have only three elements within the grid of each one. I didn't know what the results would be; they depended largely not just on the placing of the three squares within the grid but on what color the squares are and their relationship with the black background, which is itself set against a white page. The nuances of the colors may or may not refer to the words on the parallel text but the two have to relate to each other visually. It is a very intricate composition: the structure of the words and the structure of the images rely very much on each other.

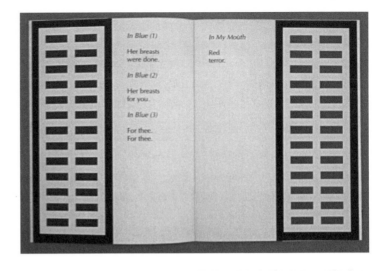

*Six Gematria*, text by Jerome Rothenberg letterpress text with 6 screenprinted images, 13¾" x 10⅝", edition of 100, 1992

*How did Tetrad Press come to be founded?*

In 1969 I went to the States and taught design at the University of Wisconsin for several months, which was when I got to know Walter Hamady. He was teaching printing and bookmaking and ran Perishable Press. From him I learned a tremendous amount about the technique of printing and papermaking. Although I didn't print anything myself in the States, it was while I was there that Jerry gave me **The 17 Horse Songs of Frank Mitchell**, and I immediately made a lot of images in response. When I got back to England I

*The 17 Horse Songs of Frank Mitchell X–XIII,*
text by Jerome Rothenberg and Richard Johnny John,
letterpress text, 4 screenprinted images,
11½" x 9¾", 5 pages in a box,
edition of 250, 1969–70

decided to publish them and formed Tetrad Press in order to do so. (Although it says 1969 on the colophon, **The Horse Songs** was actually published in January 1970, the launch of my press.) I could have gone on publishing at Circle Press, but I knew I was taking risks in working with contemporary poets and, as I didn't see the sales rolling in, I didn't want to involve anyone else financially. I was searching for writing that had an astringency that paralleled what I was interested in visually and I wanted to have a total rapport with the poets, not just take a text and use it. I chose the name Tetrad because I wanted it to relate to Circle but to be opposite; there was a Square Press already, so I chose the Greek equivalent.

**The 17 Horse Songs of Frank Mitchell** is a loose folio of five pages contained in a gray cardboard box, conventional left-hand text, right-hand image. The text was set by Des Jeffries, and the images were screenprinted at Kelpra Studio because they were reputed to be the best and I had come back from America with some money. It was the first time I met the printer Chris Prater, who, with his wife, Rose, ran the Kelpra Studio. The difference between Chris's screenprinting business and most of the others was that he did very little commercial printing and worked almost exclusively with artists. Nobody before him had seriously considered screenprints and he was responsible for part of the resurgence of interest in printmaking. One of his major projects of that period was Eduardo Paolozzi's *Wittengenstein* series and *Moonstrip Empire News*. Technically Chris was superb. I worked with him subsequently and we remained friends until his death in 1997. His archive is in the Tate Gallery.

*Tetrad had a name but no equipment. When did that change?*

Around 1978, when I got my Vandercook SP 20 cylinder press from a printer in the City. It was a proofing press from a firm of typesetters who, as many of them did at that point, were getting rid of their hot metal equipment and converting to photosetting. Over the life of Tetrad Press I had a platen press (Model No. 2), which is still in use by my son, Matthew, and a FAG, which eventually went to Ken Campbell.

*You've said that **The Pronouns** (1971) is one of the Tetrad books you feel very happy with. How did it come about?*

I was in New York in 1969 and met the poet Jackson Mac Low at Jerry's and went to a couple of readings that he did. As I liked his work, Jerry suggested Jackson give me a manuscript. The full title is **The Pronouns—40 Dances for the Dancers—Feb. 6—March 22, 1964**, a series of texts that can be danced as well as read. I used the basis of this idea to set up the proportions of the grid for those particular images. It was a seminal book for me because it was the first where I felt that if each page were a transparent sheet, placed one above the other, they would read as coherently from top to bottom as from page to page. It was the first time I did that consciously.

*What were your images?*

They were a grid of nine rectangles with black outlines filled with flat color. The color and its disposition were taken partly from the text and partly from the way I wanted to compose it.

*You were the first person to publish Tom Phillips's **A Humument** (Tetrad Press, 1972). Had you always intended to publish other people's work?*

Yes. Tom Phillips lived next door to me in Camberwell, where I'd moved in 1966. The basis of **A Humument** was a novel bought secondhand, *A Human Document*, which Tom "treated" in different ways. I often saw him working on it in the evening at the kitchen table with pen, ink, and watercolors. It was fascinating (he's still doing it, using other copies of the original book that he's found or other people have sent him) and I thought it would benefit from a wider audience. As it was 364 pages, I couldn't finance the whole work, so we decided to do it in installments, an arrangement which also gave him leeway to continue to change it as he went along. We published ten volumes over approximately five years.

There were three distinct ways in which Tom treated the pages. One was using gouache, which had a lot of opaque color; another was where he tended to draw and crosshatch and cross things out, and this was generally black and white; the third was where he did something between the two, using watercolors. I thought we should follow with the printing media whatever he was doing on the pages, so the opaque gouache pages were screenprinted, the drawn ones were relief printed, and the watercolors were lithographed. Along the route with this we published **Ein Deutsches Requiem After Brahms**, a series of six lithographs plus a title page printed by a firm in Camberwell.

*You didn't physically print* **A Humument**?

I was the middleman between Tom and the printers. The sheets were sold in boxes of pages by medium rather than in sequence. Chris Prater did volumes one, two, and three, which were screenprinted. Volumes four and five were letterpress, volumes six and seven were lithographed, and so forth.

*How did you market them?*

We had subscriptions. I had a brochure printed and I sent it round to libraries, museums, and collectors. They went to some interesting collections; the Gemeente Museum in the Hague put on a big exhibition of **A Humument** and there was also a big exhibition at the ICA in London. (The Museum of Modern Art in New York subscribed to volumes one to three and asked if I would donate the rest, a request I declined!) Eventually sales were generated by Tom's growing reputation. In the end I sold it to Tom and his dealer. Ultimately it was published, via Hansjörg Mayer, by Thames & Hudson.

*Who else has Tetrad published?*

I started Tetrad to do both books and prints and I published **The Falls Tracer** by Glen Baxter in 1970 and **Spare Parts** by Richard Pinkney in 1971. Pinkney also did two of the pamphlets in the **Tetrad Pamphlets Vol I** series and one in the **Vol II** series. The pamphlets were volumes of ten (Vol. I, 1971) and eight (Vol. II, 1973) broad sheets, 30 cm. by 25 cm. They were text-and-image pieces with either a poet/artist collaboration or using the artist's own words. Vol. I was an edition of 500 and Vol. II an edition of 125. Derrick Greaves did two pamphlets in **Tetrad Pamphlets Vol I**, and Tetrad published Greaves's **Also** (1972) with a text by Roy Fisher.

*James Hugonin was another artist with whom you worked?*

I saw a folio of prints he'd done in Sunderland, near where he lives, very reduced, pale, minimal work with a strange beauty about it. He wanted to work with a Basil Bunting text, **Ode**. I did the letterpress printing and designed the book, and the images were printed by Advanced Graphics because Chris Prater had virtually stopped by that time. (That book was published by "imprints," the publisher/gallery for selling and publishing

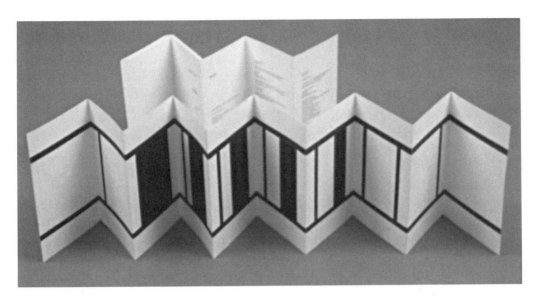

*Millenium (sic)*, text by Jerome Rothenberg, letterpress text with screenprinted images, 9"x 6", 12 pages folded into 6, edition of 100, 1980

artists' books, established in 1984 by my son and daughter, Matthew and Hannah Tyson, and now run from France by Matthew Tyson and Isabella Oulton.) In 1988 James and I did **Two Extracts from Briggflats** together, again from Basil Bunting's text alongside two screenprints, an extremely beautiful book.

*You've also had a long working relationship with the painter Julia Farrer?*

Julia and I met at Wimbledon School of Art, where we both taught. She had made a book at the Slade, *Les Prunelles de la Libellule* (1978), when she was a student and showed me a copy when I did the British Artists' Book exhibition with Silvie Turner in 1984. We included the book in the show and it reawakened Julia's interest in making books. Julia and I did **Temple** in 1987 with text by Jonathan Griffen. Julia made four etchings, which she printed and put together with the letterpress text for Jonathan's eightieth birthday.

*What was the British Artists' Book exhibition?*

It came about through conversations I had had with my son Matthew and with Silvie Turner, the owner and editor of estamp, the company which publishes books on printmaking, papermaking, and related matters. (She was also coeditor with Birgit Skiöld of *Papermaking Today*.) The Atlantis paper company in east London had a big warehouse and gallery and it seemed logical to approach them to do the show. Our policy was inclusive rather than exclusive. As long as the artist was making books as a serious intent and was going to make more, we took them.

*In other words, there was no division between livres d'artiste and artists' books?*

No. For instance, we had the massive *Canterbury Tales* by Elisabeth Frink and one of Jake Tilson's Xerox books. They were both made by an artist and, therefore, each was an artist's book. Isn't livre d'artiste translated "artist's book"?

The other important fact was that we supplied cotton gloves and all the books could be handled.

*If you were doing the show again, would you do it the same way?*

Yes. I dislike the way the book scene has changed.

*How has it changed?*

The tendency to compartmentalize the kind of books artists make I find unacceptable. The criteria used are confused, and therefore only add to a lack of understanding as to how or why artists make books. If an artist has had a direct hand in the production of a book, it is an "artist's book" (or any translation of those words). The history of the artist's book shows change and proliferation for well over a century and it is helpful to look at them in that context.

**Partworks** (1994) *was a collaboration with Julia Farrer and perhaps could not have happened if you hadn't known each other and worked so closely together for such a long time. How did it come about?*

Wimbledon School of Art received money for research and members of the faculty were able to apply for grants. Julia and I applied to collaborate on making books and were given an award. The problem was how to proceed, and the solution was that Julia sent me a drawing on the middle of a piece of paper which, to me, suggested a proscenium with a stage behind it. I wanted to get onto the stage, so I responded by collaging some pieces of paper into the drawing and returned it to Julia, who drew again, reestablishing what she'd already drawn and adding some more. She sent it back, whereupon I cut the whole thing up and reassembled it on another sheet of paper and posted it to her. She altered it again, by which time we'd reached saturation point. The piece of work wasn't very good, but it had given us a modus operandi and we started on various ideas.

Julia conceived a book structure she wanted to use and, in discussions, we thought we would like to make a pair of dedications to two artists we admired, Donald Judd and Witold Lutoslawski, both of whom had died in

1994. We started in the same way as the initial experiment. Julia did drawings—proposals—which I then altered and gave back. At different times we also worked on them together. Of all the books we did for **Partworks**, these are the most difficult to say who actually did what. The medium was handcolored drypoint with acquatint, and the text was printed letterpress by Ian Mortimer. They were bound and put in a slipcase as a pair, **Dedications 1 & 2**. The structure is an accordion-fold in three sections and interspersed within each section is a single sheet that holds the text and supports an image.

That was the beginning of **Partworks**, although because they took such a long time to produce, they were not in fact the first books that came off the production line. The first to be produced were **Motet 1 & 2**, which were printed offset litho and were based on the idea of counterpoint between a very simple basic structure that I designed and an overlay of transparent sheets that Julia had drawn corresponding to the structure underneath.

At first we had the ideas and did them. Later, the books evolved and, toward the end, we were doing separate parts related to what the other was making. We might decide a size and proportion for a book and each make one; they would be quite different but they would relate. **Comedia 1 & 2** is a good example of this—handcolored acquatints where Julia did one and gave it to me and I did another in response. They were an edition of forty. Our uncertainty about one

*Motet 1 from Motet 1 & 2,*
*Partworks* (with Julia Farrer),
offset, 13"x 9¾", edition of 50, 1994

of the books, just before it was due to be printed, led to two others as, by one o'clock in the morning, we had taken the initial book apart and redesigned it to form three separate new works, one of which was **Sainte**, using a Mallarmé text, in an edition of fifty.

*What was the benefit of this way of working?*

It allowed me to see the possibility of using more complex ideas without the imagery necessarily being more complex. Julia's work is more intricate than anything I would ever do and she made me think much more about the hidden geometry of things. After we'd collaborated, I could take images I'd done and though they would remain basic, the way they were used had a more complicated thought process behind it. From Julia's point of view, I think she simplified a lot.

We did ten books in eighteen months, not counting collages, drawings, unique books, and prints. It was an enormous amount of work, a very fertile collaboration. Until recently there was no one place where all the books could be seen, but the special collections library at the University of California at San Diego now has all the edited **Partworks**. They have also been shown together in Tubingen in Germany, at the Gallery Buch und Druck, and at the Eagle Gallery in London. **Partworks** is finished now, except for one final work, **Partworks 2000**, for the millennium. Our only regret is that Wimbledon School of Art seemed completely indifferent to what we had achieved.

*Between 1993 and 1994 you made a series of unique books?*

They came about because I had started to look for different ways to use the book form and they were a means to experiment. I used pieces of paper I had left over from different projects. There was no involvement with texts. Those books are difficult to describe in any terms other than as objects; each is an object that looks like a book and has pages and a cover and is bound. The

*Dedication 1. For Don Judd, Partworks* (with Julia Farrer),
6 drypoint aquatint images, hand colored, 13"x 6", edition of 15, 1994

bindings differ and are cut up in different ways to fold in on one another and form different images, and the pages, which are folded and cut paper, sometimes overlap so that as you turn them they, too, begin to form different images. They are varied in color, some dark blue made with offcuts from a book, **two lines** (1995). One is from blue paper made from jeans, which had an interesting variation in tone. Each is unique.

The main development that came from the series was a large book I did in 1997, a long, narrow leparello made with black paper (untitled), which was ingeniously bound from the center page by Charles Gledhill. Inside each page is a strip of cream paper and, collaged onto that, are four squares—red, blue, yellow, and white. It's an extremely simple book. Somebody said that what they liked about it was that it was perfectly, absolutely, and mysteriously obvious. That pleased me enormously.

*Why did you eventually get rid of your presses?*

I enjoyed printing very much, but it ran its course. I had the presses from 1978 to 1990 and, although I appreciated the machinery and miss it, I would never have a press again. I didn't want to be a printer, but I was finding that in order to reach the standard of quality that I wanted, I needed to be printing all the time. I would, for example, paint or make sculpture for several months, then I would decide to do a book and it would take at least a week just to get into the feel of being able to print properly. It was becoming very nerve-racking, and after finishing a book I would be totally exhausted. I would have designed it, made the images, set the type, printed it, sometimes even bound it, and these are all jobs usually done by separate people, all to an exacting standard. Even something like proofreading was a strain; I could print the whole book and someone would find a mistake and I would have to reprint it. Another reason for getting rid of my own presses was that I missed the feedback from working with other printers. Also, I became less and less interested in using texts.

*Has Tetrad stopped? Is that the same as getting rid of the presses?*

Yes, in 1995. I wanted to do other things more than to publish. I formed another imprint last year, ed:it. It is based in my home in France. The first publication will be a book called **A.B.C.**, in memory of Klaus Mollenhauer, a friend of mine who died this year.

*Will there be more from ed:it?*

I hope so.

*My Mother's Book,*
offset, 9"x 6", unfolds
into 9"x 18", 48 pages,
edition of 800, 1993

# joan
# lyons

Cathy Courtney interviewed Joan Lyons in London on November 18, 1996, during the London Artists' Book Fair.

Joan Lyons in her studio, 1998

Photo: Elizabeth Lyons

*When were you born, and in which part of America did you grow up?*

I was born in New York City in 1937. I was an only child and had a lower-middle-class childhood. I grew up in Brooklyn with the feeling from an early age that I was going to leave. I didn't know what "out" meant, but I was going there: out of the neighborhood, the family, the familiar environment which, I guess, I must have found depressing. I was a child in the 1940s, when things were quite gender oriented and my parents tried very hard to get me to grow up to be an appropriate little girl. This met with some resistance.

*What was on the walls of your parents' apartment?*

There were a couple of pictures, a strange art deco painting of an elegant woman in a diaphanous white dress playing with greyhound dogs. There was a deco imitation bronze head on a pedestal and there was a portrait painting of my father as a young man. My strongest early memory of a painting was a Maxfield Parrish print in my grandmother's house, one with nymphs playing in a garden beside a lake. I remember it by candle-light because I associate it with Friday night dinners at my grandmother's house; she was an Orthodox Jew and lit candles.

*Did you know art galleries existed?*

Probably not, but I remember taking a Saturday morning class at Brooklyn Museum when I was ten or eleven. I was a compulsive image maker from the time I was a small child. I did a lot of drawing—portraits, caricatures, what I saw out of my window. Later I got interested in fashion drawing, as adolescent girls do.

*Were books important in your childhood?*

Books were important and I read all the time. My mother had a real reverence for books and taught me how to handle them properly at an early age. I was a pretelevision baby. I read the entire children's section in the local library and got special dispensation to graduate to the adult section and proceeded shelf by shelf, starting with the As. I read volumes and volumes of Charlie Chan mysteries because they happened to be on the bookshelf at home. There were ceremonial books in the shelf, too, the kind with leather bindings that were probably bought for decoration. I read them as well.

*Did you write?*

Not very seriously. I remember starting a diary a couple of times.

*When you were a teenager, what was life in the city like?*

When I was growing up cities weren't considered particularly dangerous, so by the time I was eleven I was allowed to take the subway from Brooklyn to Manhattan by myself. By the time I was in high school I would go to Greenwich Village and pretend to be bohemian with the other children from Brooklyn and the Bronx. You'd put on your black outfit and go and drink coffee. City kids were able to live several different lives and I had three or four different groups of friends and as many personas.

*Did you have dreams for your future?*

I graduated from high school when I was barely sixteen. Ever since I was a small child, I had the feeling I was going to be an artist. Maybe that was a form of rebellion, a way to get out. I was going to be one but I wasn't quite sure what it was.

It was expected that I would go to university in the city because my father didn't want me outside of his reach, but I was determined to get away. I found a listing in a college handbook of a little school in upstate New York that had an art program, Alfred University. I applied because it was far away. I got on the train one day, never having been out of the city in my life, and at the end of eight hours I got off and picked up a bus and was taken to an extremely rural place. I was deposited in a little dormitory in this tiny town and was rather terrified. I had never been in any place where there were cows in fields and no lights at night. After a couple of weeks I really loved it. It was real culture shock, which everyone needs to experience at that stage of their lives.

*What did you love about it?*

I was left alone, which was nice. There was a serious work ethic and that was quite wonderful. Although it was a college of ceramics, you didn't do ceramics for the first two years. It was a good foundation program, painting, sculpture, two-dimensional design, art history. It was a time to begin to understand what growing your own work was about.

I was in college in the mid-50s, so the models were the Abstract Expressionists, a very male world. There were no female role models, and I aspired to be associated with men and would make my paintings as macho as I could. I'd get the biggest surface I could afford—a door or window shade—get some house paint and big brushes and start throwing paint around. Although the art schools had more women students than men, they weren't taken terribly seriously, whereas the male students were. I had only one woman teacher, a person in her late sixties and close to retirement. She was marvelous but was treated as a charming grandmother by the rest of the faculty, even though she was a good artist and a passionate teacher. (Ten years after she retired, the women who were then students discovered her and started flocking to her home to take classes with her.) One of the male teachers, John Wood, did take women seriously and didn't discriminate on the basis of gender. He worked across media as a printmaker, graphic artist, and photographer and he had an interest in books. I remember making a first book that was a series of cardboard etchings. We were starting to think about sequence and series, probably because of the photography we were looking at.

*Were you taking photographs?*

I did get a camera but I don't think I did anything with it other than document my other work. At this time I met my future husband, Nathan Lyons, a student who had gone back to school after a number of years in the military during the Korean "non-war." He was a photographer himself, wrote a lot of poetry, and was politically very active at a time when not many people were. He was editor of the school newspaper and was constantly making little revolutions. It was a terribly cynical and apathetic time, and college magazines weren't dealing with political issues, so Nathan's energy and activism were pretty interesting.

*Were you politically active yourself?*

I was fairly active in high school because it was the McCarthy era and some of my favorite teachers were being fired. I remember going to rallies at city hall and protesting. I was horrified at the fearful stance in response to the Communist witch-hunting of some of the adults I respected. In New York at that time a Communist wasn't such an oddity and almost everybody you knew was at least a liberal Democrat or a Socialist, so we were not aware of conservative politics until the McCarthy issue came up.

*What happened at the end of college?*

I graduated in 1957 and took the path of least resistance, going to graduate school because I got a nice assistantship at Mills College in California. Mills was another culture shock, a West Coast women's college. I was teaching freshmen classes and was rather traumatized because the students were eighteen and I was only twenty myself. They were smart women but docile and totally willing to accept me as the authority, which freaked me out a little bit.

I was treated very well at Mills and had a fabulous studio and was still struggling with painting canvases and making ceramics. There wasn't a great visual art scene in the Bay Area at that time but the beat poets were just hitting San Francisco, so I went to readings by Allen Ginsberg and that group. Just the style was refreshing. The 1950s were uptight and everything was regimented and formal and poets usually wore jackets and ties to give readings, which the Beats didn't do. They were experimenting with combining poetry and jazz, trying to open up some of those areas in between. It was very exciting.

I didn't stay at Mills long because my father died and I had to go back to New York to be with my mother. I wanted to see whether I was capable of working in the real world, having been at school since I was five. It was very competitive and I didn't have a graphic design background or portfolio, but only my little photographs and my avant-garde typographic experiments. I managed to get a string of entry-level graphic design jobs and found the classier the place you worked, the worse the job was. The best was working for a man who published pulp detective magazines, three a month, and the whole staff consisted of him and me. I could design all the magazines and do wild typographic things and picture layouts because he didn't care what the thing looked like as long as it was done. The covers got farmed out because I kept trying to clean them up and couldn't make them gory enough.

*Did you learn about print and production?*

Having a crafts background, I realized a lot of the graphic designers I was working with didn't know anything about printing. I decided to learn and went to work for a job printer. It was hard because they definitely did not want to hire a woman and, as they would not let me near a printing press, I worked in a prepress department. I learned a great deal about the offset printing process, how to handle film, how you translated an image into a printed piece. It seemed to be worthwhile because I had an interest in print, printmaking, typography, design, and books, but the job itself was tedious and the other people working there were unhappy guys with chips on their shoulders, always angry and screaming. At some point I had worked enough to collect unemployment, so I went to Mexico for a few months.

*Your first free time?*

Exactly. I could travel—I couldn't get to Europe, but Mexico was very cheap. I experienced more culture shock, which was wonderful. There was a real difference between Mexico and America in the 50s, especially where women were concerned. I traveled the way you do when you are very young, totally gutsy and oblivious to danger. After a while, I settled in an area near a village potter who made blackware. The way I had learned ceramics was technical and complicated, but she was marvelously simple in the way she proceeded. She allowed me to sit and work with the people there. Eventually I ran out of money and went home.

*What happened next?*

I married Nathan and moved to Rochester. He was working at the George Eastman House International Museum of Photography and had been hired as an editorial assistant on their magazine and was also working on exhibitions. It was difficult for me coming into Nathan's life because I felt disconnected. I got some design and printing jobs to earn money but nothing particularly interesting. Nathan was part of a community of photographers and was also spending nights going through the incredible photographic and book collection at Eastman House. The people we knew were all photographers and all men. To them I was Nathan's wife. It's not easy to be somebody's wife. I probably spent a number of years being angry and not showing it as much as I felt. We had three children in five years. Suddenly I was wife and mother and caretaker of photographers. In the 60s women everywhere were experiencing the same kind of thing, not knowing what was wrong and not knowing it was a shared experience. I didn't know many other women with children. But later I discovered that isolated women everywhere sort of invented a personal women's movement for themselves.

Even with three children, I kept making work. Nathan was very supportive and wanted me to do my work (as long as everything else had been taken care of). I was connected with a gallery in Rochester, run by a woman who would show my work. I was still painting but not splashing on doors. I was introducing a lot of fabric collage into the paintings and also doing drawings, pastel, collage, and some screenprinting. Then, around the late 60s, I started working with photographic images.

*Why?*

I knew a few artists in Rochester but not anybody I felt a real connection with and, by this time, Nathan was curator at Eastman House so there was a lot of photography around me. I was excited by the ideas that the photographers were starting to deal with, similar to those I was looking at in my work. It was mainly the idea of sequence—not in the sense of the way painters were making series that were variations on an image, but working with groups of images that were sequential conceptually. The other aspect was that I was working with collage and frottage, things that I now think of as approaching photography because they concern imprinting. And, of course, I was printmaking—mostly screenprinting at that time.

Looking back, I was totally inept at the big macho paintings. There was a feminine content to my work. In the summer of 1968 I made an intensive series of forty or fifty drawings that were almost automatic drawings. They were ideas and gestures that got stated and restated and recombined. The color was more restrained than the color I had used before and, even though they were drawings, they were related to photographic ideas. I put a show of them up in a theater lobby and noticed that women really responded to them and spent a lot of time with them, whereas men would run past like there was somebody chasing them. I think there was some kind of sensuality that the men didn't want to see or relate to. That was the first time I was consciously able to start thinking about work in terms of some kind of feminine content that was developing. I began to know who I was speaking to and where the work was coming from.

Untitled (self-portrait) from the portfolio *Presences,* offset lithograph, 24"x 18", edition of 15, 1980

*Was there any feedback from Nathan?*

Nathan and I don't talk about each other's work a great deal but we communicate well through work and images. I think he understands my work and I think I understand his. It was around the time of my exhibition in the theater lobby that Nathan left Eastman House.

*This was the moment the Visual Studies Workshop was founded?*

Nathan had started a graduate program in photographic studies at the Eastman House, affiliated with the University of Buffalo. It was a moment in the late 60s when there was an openness and energy and when unusual programs were being considered. When he left Eastman House in 1968, the graduate program left with him. Thirty students arrived in September and helped renovate an old loft he had rented. That was the start of the Visual Studies Workshop.

I wasn't directly involved at the beginning but by 1972 I was studying there myself for a master's degree because I thought I needed the credential. I was also doing some teaching. We bought out an old print shop and I did the letterpress photography portfolio with the students because I was the only one who knew how to print. Soon after that we got an offset press, a wretched old thing held together with rubber bands, and I started running that.

*Had you seen artists' books by this stage? Would you have seen Ed Ruscha's books, for example?*

I didn't know the term "artists' books," but I probably had seen Ruscha's— I have a vague recollection of thinking they were neat and fun, but they hardly changed my life. I certainly knew people who made books and I was very aware of small-press publishing. I knew of the historical livres d'artiste and I owned a facsimile of Matisse's *Jazz*. I would have seen livres d'artiste at MoMA and, in New York, I used to hang out in George Wittenborn's book shop; Wittenborn had published "Documents of Modern Art" by Klee and Kandinsky and others and he also had small-edition books made by the abstract expressionist painters in the 50s and 60s. I would have been aware of Moholy-Nagy and of the Dadist and Futurist publications. I was impressed by the Bauhaus books and by Man Ray. There were also artists' magazines that made an impression on me and I was aware of concrete poetry. All the poets were doing mimeographed things and sending them to their friends and relations. Concrete poetry was to the 50s what photography became to the 60s and, maybe, what books and videos were to the 70s.

In personal terms, I knew people out of the Chicago Institute of Design tradition who made books. I met Keith Smith there in 1963 when he was starting to make one-of-a-kind books. Sonia Sheridan was teaching at the Institute and started a program, Generative Systems, working with machines. She was always involved with art and technology and, earlier, when she was teaching screenprinting, had her students make books. She got involved with the early copy machines and was very much immersed in collaboration. In fact, the late 60s and early 70s were very much a collaborative time—we did collaborations with other people where you sent a page and they sent a page—and there were a lot of ideas around about books, but I don't think they'd have been called artists' books at that stage.

The first VSW books started more in relationship to the photographers' need for book activity than to artists per se. Most photographers in the

1970s followed the venerable monograph form and produced books that looked like portfolios between covers, but there were signs of change— Robert Franks's *The Americans*, for instance, or the Oklahoma photographer Gaylord Herron, who included paintings, snapshots, and autobiographical texts as part of his book. Offset printing began at Visual Studies Workshop as one way of extending ideas about what photography was as well as thinking about books. The students made some individual and a number of group books in the early years. The first project with outside artists was when a media collaborative called the Video Freaks approached me with a book proposal in 1972. An artists' press soon evolved. Visual Studies Workshop has gone on to produce over four hundred books.

*Were you still painting by this time?*

I stopped painting very deliberately in the late 1960s. It was a conscious political and aesthetic decision.

*When did you begin to produce books of your own?*

It was around 1972. I had started working with an old Haloid-Xerox machine, which I loved, and which I went on to work with extensively for fifteen years. It was a copy camera that I could manipulate by hand. In contrast to my print portfolios, which were elaborate, labor intensive, and probably took around six months, the first books I made were quickly done. At around this time Sonia Sheridan came to Rochester and got the 3M company to bring the first color copier to the VSW, where it stayed for a week. We invited a group of artists to come and use it. Sonia persuaded me to get up on the machine and she made copies of me. It used a marvelous dye transfer process that produced lots of waste material, which I swept up and used to make offset plates for a book alongside my own text in letterpress, **Self-Impressions** (1972).

As well as investigating what the offset press could do, my work also addressed feminist concerns. With **Wonder Woman** (1974) I transformed a woman at an ironing board into my favorite childhood heroine. In 1975 I made **Bride Book, Red to Green** using a "found" bride (looking very unhappy) and explored what I could do with the plates on the offset press if I turned the ink off and kept running paper through. The "bride" faded. When the pages were run through in reverse order overprinted with a negative image, she slowly re-emerged in negative in a new color. Many of my books at this time were concerned with ideas that evolved out of the process of making them as well as being based on feminist/political ideas.

*Seed Word Book,*
from the Natural Book Series,
6"x 4", edition of 6, 1975

In the mid 1970s I started an ongoing series of natural books in which I planted seeds or let nature intervene to make an image. There was, too, a series of blank books that I buried and left in the ground for a season or a number of months. I also made **Seed Word Book**, an edition of six, made by cutting up a dictionary and sprouting seeds in the pages. This was based on my discovery that "word" and "seed" have the same etymology and that wet paper is a fine medium for sprouting seeds.

*How involved were you with feminism?*

Very much in terms of the evolution of my understanding of the world. I spent most of the 1970s working on extended portraits of women, mostly self-portraits. I wasn't interested in them being pictures of me as much as archetypal representations of women. I needed to look at women and to see how they looked when they were represented by a woman instead of by a man. It sounds clichéd now, but at the time it was difficult because autobiographical work wasn't being done. I was a compulsive worker and, as do a lot of artists, you work to try to understand what you are thinking about. You work intuitively without quite knowing what it is about and then later—five or ten years after—you see why it was interesting. I worked on that series for over ten years, but I was doing other things too.

*What was the other work?*

I did a series that had to do with patterning, with repetitions and plant forms. It related to book decoration and to a kind of art making that I didn't understand—decorative art—another "minor" art form associated with women's work such as weaving, needlework, and flower painting. There was also a series of works that began in the 1960s when I did a print portfolio called **A Family Album**, screenprinted photographic snapshots. The next portfolio was trompe l'oeil representation of fabric—personal power objects such as the shop rag I used when I was printing, an Indian shawl that was a family heirloom, or the tatty bag my son used when he was a paperboy. Fabrics are defining for a lot of women and I had realized that bits of cloth and fabric had real importance in my life.

Later I made a six-print piece, **Prom**, which was very autobiographical. My daughter was about fourteen and was at the stage when she was very self-conscious about her body. She was going to her first prom and needed a dress and we went through the trauma of searching for one when nothing was right, so finally I wound up making the damn thing for her when I wanted to be making my own work. I was feeling cross until I realized there was no reason to separate making the dress from the rest of what I did: women can't separate their work from their life. After the prom, I took the dress and color-separated it into pieces. Each piece is printed on a separate sheet of paper and, if they are hung in order, it makes a life-size dress. It's the trace of a rite of passage. It took incredible courage to make something so blatantly sentimental—the dress was pastel and flowery in color—and that commemorated a personal event, everything I was taught as a student to avoid like the plague. I assumed I couldn't show it to anyone and then I thought, "This is what my life is about. Cloth and recipes are what women's lives are measured in. This is culturally significant and I'm going to get it out there."

*Is your life still measured in those things?*

Less so. Fabric is still important. I have made six photographic quilts in the last several years, printing onto fabric. There is, of course, a strong quilting tradition in the States that is a little different from the English tradition, which is more appliqué. Quilting is traditional women's work and I like working in that tradition, although my images are unconventional. One quilt has to do with landscape, one has three layers of image in a tumbling block pattern. The first quilt I made for my granddaughter was about five generations of women in the family. Making quilts strongly relates for me to making books.

*How does that link with* **My Mother's Book** *(1993)? Which came first?*

I was working on them both at the same time, because I started the quilt when my granddaughter was born and I interviewed my mother shortly before her death in 1990, by which time the baby was maybe one or two.

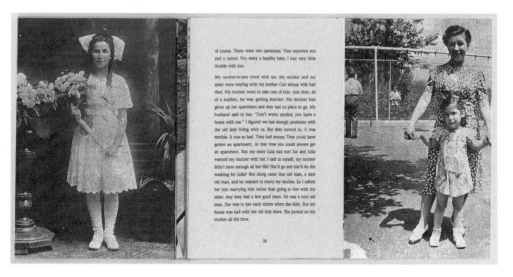

*My Mother's Book*,
offset edition, 9"x 6", unfolds into 9"x 18",
48 pages, edition of 800, 1993

*Would you have done the book if your mother hadn't died?*

Yes. I started interviewing my mother simply to get the stories because I knew very little about her family. After she died I acquired a box of photographs and that's when I knew I was going to make a book. It was lovely doing it, not traumatic at all. The stories are told in my mother's voice and illustrated with generational snapshots. Originally it was to be a private edition for my children but I realized how generic the pictures and stories were and decided on a broader publication. Memories don't happen in a linear form, so I structured the book with two opposing openings so the time line can be rearranged. Memories, I think, are not chronological.

*Is* **The Gynecologist** *(1990) also a personal book?*

It is based on extended research as well as personal concerns, and I spent months in medical libraries digging through gynecological texts and medical journals and amassed a huge amount of material. The book is a juxtaposition of a doctor-patient conversation and ancient anatomical representations of women. It's about the control that—until recently—the male medical professions, by virtue of the authority of their position, had over women's bodies. Even as late as the 1980s major gynecological texts were published that are absolutely brutal in regard to women's bodies and totally uninterested in their feelings. I didn't want to be scholarly or didactic, so I presented images and text and left the readers to draw their own conclusions.

*Isn't that the same as in other areas of surgery?*

Medical histories are full of images of passive, supine, scantily clad young women being "worked on" by older, fully clothed men. These surely illustrate power positions.

*Do you think women approach books in a different way than men do?*

I want to be careful in responding here. Women have been drawn to the book form because it is a private, intimate form. They are comfortable dealing with an audience of one. Related to this, the women's movement has been largely responsible for giving permission to bring personal content into work and this kind of content has informed bookmaking—books made by men as well as women. I don't think men would be making this particular kind of work if it hadn't been for the feminist movement. It's a sticky issue. Can you look at work and always tell the gender of the person who made it? Definitely not. Can you often tell? Definitely yes.

The stories women were beginning to tell in the 70s were not only different in content from men's, they required new structures. I remember reading the poet Adrienne Rich's book *Of Women Born* (1976), in which she dared to bring her personal voice into a scholarly book and her scholarship into what was a memoir. She was one of the writers who broke ground for others to freely combine theory, research, and personal experience into their art practice. Visual narratives, sequential and serial images, found or written texts, multiplicity and juxtaposition were all in the structure of such work. Although such work is strongly influenced by feminist practice, it isn't gender specific.

*What do you feel about the flood of autobiographical work that is appearing in book art now?*

Much of the autobiographical work bores me. Although what I do grows out of my experience, generally I don't make directly autobiographical work but something generic that will resonate with other people's experience. Life needs some translation and transformation to become art. I've always visualized the point at which personal consciousness encounters the phenomenal world as an experiential screen or filter that separates the interior from the exterior, the personal from the public space. It is very much like a garden I once visited with a great lawn and tidy rows of annuals that hovered eight thousand feet on the edge of the Rocky Mountains. The place where garden and wilderness meet is the place where creative work is born and where work exists.

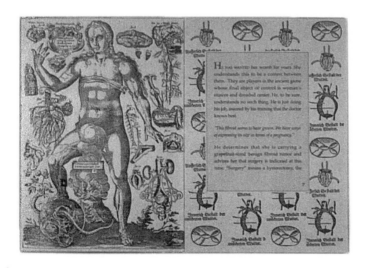

*The Gynecologist*,
offset, 9"x 6", 32 pages,
edition of 1,000, 1989

*This interview has been done in London because you were here for the London Artists' Book Fair, at which you gave a lecture. What view did the trip give you of the state of artists' books in Britain?*

It's astonishing how much support structure there is here, how much is being published and written. There's Stephen Bury's book, *Artists' Books*, there's Tanya Peixoto's *Artist's Book Yearbook*, there's the history of Book Works, there're your own *Art Monthly* reviews and your book on Circle Press. It feels as if there's a network of people—Telfer Stokes, Helen Douglas, Clive Phillpot, Simon Cutts, and Erica van Horn are definitely part of the book community—but I don't feel they're separate from the book community in the States.

*What role did Clive Phillpot play in America from your perspective?*

He was sensitive about being the spokesperson for MoMA, but I never thought of him that way. He had two functions: he was the librarian at MoMA and bought books, which was marvelous and important, but outside that was the writing he did and the lectures he gave. His activities and concern about the artists' book community were of major importance. His position at MoMA allowed him to look at a lot of stuff. It was a major collection, a focus. By the same token, I think maybe his position there meant he became a little too influential. When I published **Artists' Books: A Critical Anthology and Sourcebook** (1985) I had to be careful to counter his views with those of others.

*What was it like working with Telfer Stokes at Visual Studies Workshop?*

I had the pleasure of producing *Real Fiction* at Rochester with Telfer in the years when we had money for artist residencies. No one has explored the nature of the page more thoroughly than he and Helen Douglas. *Real Fiction* considers the book as an architectural site in construction, progressing page by page. I was surprised to learn that Telfer doesn't make anything but books. He came out with the material ready to be printed and was fun but efficient. I have the feeling that on his home turf he's a bit of a hermit when he's working too.

*Is there anyone you'd like to invite from Britain to work at the VSW?*

There are any number I would like to invite. Unfortunately, we haven't had much publishing money and generally the artists are paying for the books so, in that sense, my attitude has been to encourage bookmaking. If somebody approaches me and says they'd like to make a book, I'll say, "Let's figure out how to make it possible" and sometimes I may be able to find a little money. I'll contribute some of my time, the facilities, and a place to stay and they'll often pay for most of the edition. My emphasis has always been on encouraging artists to make books rather than on building a title list for VSW Press that includes the hottest titles and the most polished editions. We have a great workspace, a supportive community, and lots of production experience. My attitude about facilitating work is rather democratic and now even with limited funds, digital technologies are opening up incredible new areas for artists' publishing. But this is another discussion for the next twenty-five years.

*Dreaming Aloud Book Two,*
laser printed with video/
computer-generated images,
7⅝"x 11", 132 pages,
edition of 141, 1989

# betsy
# davids

Betsy Davids was recorded by Cathy Courtney at the artist's studio in Berkeley
and at Mills College, California, on April 10 and April 13, 1996.

Betsy Davids, 1998

Photo: Jaime Robles

• 55

*Where were you born and where did you grow up?*

I was born on the Fourth of July, 1939, in the Midwest, north of Chicago, in Appleton, Wisconsin. I grew up in one of a string of small industrial cities, mostly paper industry, along the Fox River. It was about a hundred thousand population, total. There was a college in the town. There was some industry, some culture (music, dance, theater), and a fairly narrow class structure—nobody very rich and nobody very poor. It was not a small town in the sense that one knew absolutely everybody but there was a considerable sense of community.

I discovered in the mid-80s that my father's uncle had been a letterpress printer. He'd founded a newspaper and later a printing business. Virtually everybody in my father's family—my father, my grandfather, and my aunt—had all worked there at one time or another. I was not aware of that during the entire time that I was doing letterpress printing.

*Do you think it's just coincidence?*

I don't think it's just coincidence. I don't know that I have the language for it, but something that was inherited, or suggested by whatever of that culture was still present in my father, has been reactivated in me.

*Is your father alive?*

No, he died when I was twenty.

*What do you remember him doing professionally?*

He was a physicist who was doing research and development work in the paper industry.

*Did you grow up knowing about paper in that sense?*

Yes, machine-made everyday paper. My current interest in everyday paper in the books that I make derives partly from that. I grew up surrounded by the paper industry and most of the adult males I knew were involved with that. As a child, they took us up to the paper mills on school field trips pretty regularly. I mostly remember large machines and being impressed by the sound, the activity. What those machines form is a long stream of paper emerging very quickly, a belt of paper. The place where I have found something similar to that in my adult life has been watching large offset presses.

*Your father would bring paper home?*

Yes. My earliest memory of involvement with paper was drawing on it during the preschool period when I did a fair amount of drawing before I learned to think that I couldn't draw.

*At what age did you learn that?*

At school, age six. We were asked to draw something or other and the teacher went around the class identifying the drawings that looked like what they were supposed to look like, and I was not identified among those good at drawing.

*And that was it?*

Yes. For twenty years or so.

*What did you do with the paper instead of drawing on it as a child?*

I did write. The first thing I can remember that I would identify as an attempt to make a book was when at about the age of ten I read a novel (I was quite a reader at this point), something I had gotten out of the library. It was a novel written by a fifteen-year-old English girl about a group of teenagers putting together their own theater production. I really loved it and didn't want to give it back to the library—I wanted to have a copy myself. I undertook to try to type the text of it, a project which didn't last very long, of course. But that got me started and I began a novel of my own about a family of orphans.

*What was on the walls of your childhood house?*

There were various prints or reproductions, but only a few of them meant much of anything to me. One is a reproduction of a Winslow Homer marine scene. What did that mean to me? The image of a boat in water sums up something; maybe it's a soul metaphor for me.

The visual art culture in my hometown was very thin and under-informed. I was not really seeing much art until I got to Northwestern University, where I met Ken Davids, whom I later married, and he directed me toward art history—I took to it right away. Then I was looking at a lot of art at the Art Institute in Chicago, a wonderful museum with a very strong Postimpressionist collection. Later I spent a lot of time in museums during a year in Europe.

*What were you studying at Northwestern?*

I had gone to a program in journalism for high school students and figured that's what I was going into. You ask yourself if you want to write, what do you do to make a living—"oh, journalism." I headed for the journalism school but by the time I had been there a couple of months, I understood I really wanted to major in literature.

*You didn't complete the course?*

Ken and I got married after he graduated, which was at the end of my sophomore year, and we came to Berkeley for the next stage of our education. Berkeley was wonderful for me. I immediately felt at home, among my own kind of people in a way I had never felt in my hometown; it was very freeing. I majored in English, which meant English and American literature and I took a great deal of art history and history as well. After I had finished my B.A. and done one year of graduate school, we took a year off and went to Europe. The most memorable reading experience of the year was probably *Ulysses*, which I read sitting next to a radiator in the only cafe in Granada with any heat.

*Did you come across any livres d'artiste in France or have any idea that they existed?*

No.

*Her Her/Her & Her/Her vs Her/Her-Her,*
text by Betsy Davids and Carole Peel,
cover drawing by Carole Peel,
letterpress, 13¾" x 9", 15 pages,
edition of 150, 1974

*When did you begin to draw again?*

At a watershed period in my twenties, when the 60s, with all that that meant, were really happening in the Bay Area.

*What did the 60s mean to you?*

Most centrally, the 60s were about releasing subjectivity and feeling. It was the permission to speak in one's own voice, including about what one felt. That got expressed in the public sphere in the Free Speech Movement, but for me it carried deeply into implications for any kind of speech and for writing. The 60s also meant, of course, the music and the drugs, all of the altered states of consciousness that came along with that, the heightened experience of inner images.

By 1967 I came to the end of the line with my graduate school experience. I figured I wanted to be teaching and to be teaching at a small school rather than at a university, where I could engage in a more direct and interpersonal style of teaching than lecturing. I wanted to be doing creative writing rather than a dissertation and I wanted to be writing in the first person.

I got a job teaching at CCAC—California College of Arts and Crafts—in 1968.

*What were you writing at this point?*

There were about five years of writing mostly poetry, and that led directly to bookmaking for me. The pathway was that after I had developed a certain body of poetry I wanted to see it in book form, and that's part of what the book is for me—the goal of writing, the form that writing wants to be in. By that time my marriage had broken up and I was living with a poet who was trying to get his poetry published by mailing off poems to editors he didn't know. It looked like a frustrating process. I could see around me the kind of books that were coming out of small presses and the possibility of making a book oneself seemed attractive. Telegraph Avenue, the street near the Berkeley campus, was a hotbed of 60s activity and there was a poetry reading series at Shakespeare and Company Books, and a lot of little mimeographed books for sale produced by individual poets and collectives. In addition there were other letterpress-printed books like the Black Sparrow books in the book stores. And at CCAC I was surrounded by artmakers—so why not make a book?

*Was the first book you were involved with publishing done at CCAC?*

Yes. After I'd been there a year there was an experimental interdisciplinary program with ten teachers—both studio and humanities faculty—and a hundred students thrown together in one chaotic unstructured program called the Pilot Project. There was a group of students who wanted to put out a magazine or journal and I and another faculty member undertook to put together some printing equipment—there was a member of CCAC's Board from the Knowland family who owned the *Oakland Tribune*, so we hustled some type and a little letterpress equipment from him. I bought a book, *Printing as a Hobby* by J. Ben Lieberman, and that was my instruction on how to print. So we jury-rigged a little tympan-and-frisket system on a simple flatbed cylinder tabletop proof press, and that's where I did my first letterpress printing. Having taught ourselves to print, the whole group of us put together a magazine in a can, **CCAN**, a play on CCAC. It was a bunch of single sheets that were poems or printed images in various combinations. The first book that was mine alone was made from proof sheets of the poem of mine that was included in that anthology.

*That was **Blue Elephants**?*

Yes. I gathered a sequence of pages that tracked the poem's evolution from manuscript to typescript to first printed proof to a good proof from the edition and then beyond into multiple printed proofs that dissolved the poem into a verbal shimmer. The poem was about dream memory, how dream images dissolve, and it involved a metaphor of a self-fermenting letter. The pages weren't bound; they were enclosed within an envelope that was collaged to look like a mailing envelope.

*So it was rearrangeable?*

I would say I was not at that level of planning or organization, of taking into account the possibility that it would get rearranged.

*Would you do the same thing now?*

No, of course not.

*You bought a press?*

Yes. I made my first bound book on the jury-rigged proofing press at CCAC and then I took a deep breath and bought a reconditioned Vandercook SP 15, a major investment and the largest single purchase I had ever made. It went into the basement of the house my boyfriend and I were renting and then when we were evicted and I moved to an apartment of my own, it went into the garage there. Within the space of a year it was in the garage of a house across the street from a group house where I was living briefly. It then moved into the garage of a house I shared with Jim Petrillo for five years, where we built a complete letterpress studio. Jim was a faculty member at CCAC and one of the ten teachers working on the Pilot Project. He was coming from the visual arts and had been to Pratt and had done multimedia work there.

*You formed Rebis Press when you bought the Vandercook?*

Yes, in 1971, and Jim Petrillo became my partner in the Press shortly thereafter. Rebis is an alchemical term that came up in Jungian reading. The press mark is derived from a fifteenth-century alchemical text with an image of the Rebis, a sort of hermaphrodite, a Siamese twin–like figure in which one half is female and holding a moon and the other half is male and holding a sun. It's a symbol of transformation and union of opposites.

*The first book you did at Rebis Press was **Double Rising Eyelids Rolling Blue**?*

That was a book of collaborative poems between myself and Ed Moore, an ex-student. It also included images by Ed and me. The book looked like literary letterpress. There was some rather free-form typography on the cover—the beginning of my typographic work—that was influenced by Dada and de Stijl and Russian Futurist typography. I still have a lot of affection for those poems, but in terms of words and images living together on a set of pages, the book was very preliminary. In terms of the materials, they were really standard good American machine-made paper. Almost immediately thereafter, the Rebis books started being involved with a wider range of material culture and stepped beyond what was traditional.

*Collaboration was firmly part of your working process?*

The traditions of publishing and small presses had some effect on how we worked and also the fact that my bookmaking emerged from within a teaching and learning project that was functioning mostly collaboratively.

*In Britain until very recently artists working with books did so very much on the margins. Was the climate much different in America?*

Bookmaking was not being taught by and large in colleges and universities. There were little pockets of letterpress printing here and there around the country, but basically I was able to start it happening at CCAC because that context was small enough and malleable enough to introduce what I was doing into my teaching life. Not only did it emerge out of my teaching life, but I was able to institutionalize it. In 1972 Charlie Gill, the printmaking chair, invited me to co-teach a class called creative writing with printmaking, a combination of letterpress printing and creative writing. Next year it will be twenty-five years since I first started teaching letterpress there.

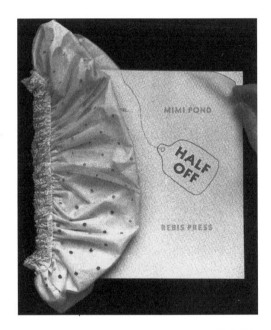

*Half Off*,
text and illustrations by Mimi Pond,
letterpress, 8½" x 8½", 24 pages,
edition of 115, 1981

*There must be a lot of people you've sent out into the book art world. Is there a network among them?*

Some of them, yes. The first person who went on with bookmaking that came through my classes was Johanna Drucker, who was in the very first letterpress class I ever taught and who subsequently worked with Rebis Press. We did one of her books

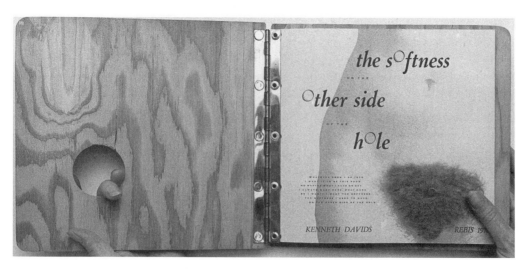

*The Softness on the Other Side of the Hole,*
text by Kenneth Davids, illustrations by Jim Petrillo,
offset, letterpress, and silkscreen in wood cover,
9"x 10", 94 pages, edition of 325, 1976

early on, **As No Storm or the Any Port Party**, in 1975.

Then there was a group of students in the 80s who got to know one another and who are still involved with bookmaking, including Val Simonetti, Alisa Golden, and Beth Herrick —that's probably the most interconnected group. And Anne Schwartzburg, who was from a later period, has just finished doing a collaboration with Alisa Golden. And Michael Henninger. I try to build connections and create a network.

*How did Johanna Drucker come to work at the Press?*

When we got our first National Endowment for the Arts publishing grant in 1975, we invited her to do a book with the Press. She was remarkably gifted as a writer and artist and the book seemed her natural form. She worked with Rebis through several books and performances.

*What are the other key Rebis books of this period?*

**The Softness on the Other Side of the Hole** was published in 1976, a short novel by my ex-husband, Ken Davids, set in two adjoining bathrooms in a cafe (loosely based on the Caffe Mediterraneum on Telegraph Avenue). An erotic relationship develops through the hole between the bathrooms between two men who think they are a man and a woman, but finally learn that they are father and son. The book has plywood covers with a hole, behind which is visible some pubic hair, and when you open the cover there's a body image on the interior. All the way through the book there are sub-textual images that are abstractions from photographs of body parts.

There was also a Mimi Pond book, **Half Off**, in 1981. She was an ex-student who went on to do a good deal of cartooning work in magazines. **Half Off** is often referred to as "The Shower Cap Book" because it's bound into a shower cap, and that alluded to a whole range of cheap plastics that were in the imagery of the text, a series of stories from a day in the life of a waitress (which was in fact what Mimi was doing when she wrote the book). That book got around a good deal and was in the AIGA—American Institute of Graphic Arts—annual award book show.

In terms of the books in which I was functioning as author, there was **Bathtub** in 1975, in which the images were done by John Wehrle and the bookmaking was mostly done by Jim. It was an old favorite from early poetry readings, a surrealist narrative that begins with an image of a bathtub and imagines where the bathtub might go if it were following its own inclinations. And there was **Her Her**, a collaboration with Carole Peel, a CCAC faculty colleague. We wrote and drew and talked together, a lot of women's talk, and played word-and-image games together, then gathered the best of it into a letterpress portfolio that was big and white and elegant in a simple way. And **Books & Changes**, which was derived from a Rebis performance piece. The text was a dream meta-narrative I constructed from fragments of a dozen dreams, which we reenacted and Jim photographed for the performance. The book version is a heavy flat board that's like a stretched-out book spine with stiff cards on it that you flip up like turning pages.

*How did you distribute the books?*

We developed our own mailing list and we took the books around when we were doing performances. Jim and I and Johanna did a good deal of performance work in the 70s and we would take the books with us and that generated some visibility as well. The performances were mostly storytelling performances with slides as the principal visual component.

*How much of a book art community was there in the Bay Area in the 1970s?*

When I started there was a fair amount of networking, a community gathered around fine printing and literary small presses, and there were events, gatherings, conferences, and newsletters. In the fine printing and fine binding end there were things like the Roxburghe Club, a dinner meeting club with a speaker, lots of collectors and librarians, men only at that time. "Artists' books" was not even a term and there was nothing in the art world to connect anyone who had been making books with anyone else. By the middle 70s there had started being some exhibitions of artists' books in the Bay Area and the term had emerged. I remember an exhibition at the Union Gallery, San Jose State University, which I think didn't use the term, but the next year, in 1977, Ralph Reed organized an exhibition at Mills College and he did use the term. The term was a little bit current among those people who had begun to identify themselves through those exhibitions.

*Was it a less controversial term in those days?*

It was fraught with difficulties, but primarily for other traditional book-arts-oriented bookmakers, binders, and fine printers and literary small-press people who would query whether "artists' books" were even books. That was a common attitude at the time. By the mid-80s there was lots of crossover and that's certainly the state of things now. There are still fine-print people who would like to growl at artists' books, but it's not part of what happens very much in public meeting places any more.

*When did the Pacific Center for the Books Arts happen?*

There was a group of us that got together to plan it, starting in 1977 or 1978, and the call for members probably went out in 1979. PCBA came out of a traditional book arts world but that whole collection of people was not boundary oriented; the idea was to develop an organization that was broader. We were hoping to sponsor lectures, events, and exhibitions. There was also a desire for space where workshops could be held and until this year that hadn't really happened. It's now about to happen with the formation of the new San Francisco Center for the Book. PCBA is mostly run by a volunteer board. There's been a biennial members' exhibition that has been very good, traditionally held in the San Francisco Public Library, which draws quite a few people. Lots and lots of lectures and events where people visiting from other parts of the country or Bay Area people have presented their work—at a typical event you might get twenty to forty people attending. The membership is currently over four hundred. It's national and there are quite a few libraries that carry a membership to receive the newsletter, *The Ampersand*. It's a networking point. It has been for me a way of feeding my students into a larger world of book arts.

*Can you tell me about the Woman's Building in Los Angeles?*

The Woman's Building was a remarkably generative center of artists' book work starting from the mid-70s. A number of people were involved in its formation, including Judy Chicago and Sheila de Bretteville, who emerged as the leader after the first year or so. I would not be the best historian for the first year because I wasn't there, but Sheila was the leading force by the time I became aware of it. The Women's Graphic Center had already emerged and Susan King was already connected with it. I found out about all this at the time that Judith Hoffberg and Joan Hugo arranged a large artists' book exhibition in L. A. called "Artwords and Bookworks" in 1978. I saw Susan's work in the show, liked it, called her up, and we met, and it was then I learned about the Woman's Building. It was already a place where artists' books were being produced, both letterpress and offset.

*It was heavily political?*

Sure. It was politicized in the way that a lot of organized feminism was politicized at that time. I felt both linked and separate. Another thing I should say about politicization in general was there was a very intense 60s experience in this area of politicization of our lives that I participated in and withdrew from. I came out of the 60s not wanting to have my creative life agenda heavily influenced or managed by a collective political thinking.

*Does the Woman's Building still exist?*

In a much transformed way. The Women's Graphic Center I believe still exists pretty much as a women-run business. That transition happened maybe in the middle 1980s, but there was quite a long run of the Women's Graphic Center as a community-based facility that was accessible to women who wanted to be printing or making books.

*How much to-ing and fro-ing is there between San Francisco and Los Angeles?*

For me, for example, there was a time when I got down to Los Angeles at least twice a year. That's no longer the case, although I wish it were.

*The phrase "Bay Area artist" crops up often. Do you see yourselves as having a regional identity?*

There is a strong regional identity. In the traditional book arts, San Francisco has a continuity that we're all aware of and Southern California also has one, but it's somewhat distinct.

*What is the starting point for that tradition?*

Probably John Henry Nash around the turn of the century. And the Grabhorn brothers. The immediate heir to that tradition in its full-blown form is Andrew Hoyem. These were letterpress printers who did luxury editions that were finely handbound, often literary classics with illustrations by notable artists. That's the core of the San Francisco tradition.

*How do you see yourselves in relation to East Coast book artists?*

Jim Petrillo and I made a tour of the country in 1978 doing lectures about West Coast bookmaking and Rebis performances and selling Rebis books, and met a lot of people at that time. Since that time I have known a bunch of people in the Midwest and in the East whose work I have been following, so I see work from those regions with a fair amount of regularity and am in touch with people elsewhere. But in this region, as in every other region, there are numbers of people who are not in touch with what's happening elsewhere in the country. There's a fair amount of separation.

*What about the Center at Minnesota?*

MCBA (Minnesota Center for Book Arts) was probably the second major book arts center with a space and full range of programs. The Center for Book Arts in New York was the first. Another one that is important is Pyramid Atlantic in the Washington, D.C., area. There are also publishing press facilities like the Visual Studies Workshop in Rochester, New York, and Nexus in Atlanta. There are now quite a few colleges and universities around the country that have a significant teaching function. The University of the Arts in Philadelphia has a book arts graduate program and the University of Alabama has a more traditionally oriented graduate program, too. Mills College had a good one until it got canceled. We have an organization of people who teach book art in colleges and universities, the Council of Book Arts Programs, and we have conferences every couple of years.

*Can we look now at the way your own books have developed during the 1980s and 1990s?*

The 80s consisted of basically two books that were a long five-year project. By then Jim and I were not working together as much. He started learning video work and I was very much in need of doing **Dreaming Aloud**, which was a 250-page text based on my dreams. If I could have done only one book, that would be the one, the one I had to do in order to feel fulfilled in my life. It was developed from my dream-journaling practice. The life experience of dreaming and the mystery of it are really core content for me. A lot of us who keep dream journals or work with dreams over a long period of time are aware how dreams seem to build a life of their own that is parallel to and connected with waking life but has its own distinct characters, events, images, places, experiences. I was always wanting to see anything that would represent that long-term experience of a dream life, and there's so little. There was what is written in the literature of psychology, which is mostly written from a case-study point of view and uses very lim-

*Dreaming Aloud Book Two*,
laser-printed with video/computer images,
11"x 7⅝", 132 pages,
edition of 141, 1989

ited verbal resources to narrate brief, dry versions of dreams. The book I came to want to do was one which would give a sense of the longer trajectory of a dream life.

I started out trying to create longer texts by selecting related dreams and putting them together. I found that was not giving me the kind of coherence I wanted to see. So this particular project involved a fairly intense period of dream-journaling with the aim of ending up with the book. I was incubating a book of dreams. It ultimately became issued in two books, **Dreaming Aloud Book One** and **Dreaming Aloud Book Two**, which because of the length of the text moved me out of letterpress printing into electronic bookmaking methods. For **Book One** I developed the images and did the printing on copiers, after setting the type on Visual Studies Workshop's photocomposing equipment. By the time I was doing **Book Two** in 1987, I had gotten a Macintosh, so it's entirely desktop publishing. The images were scanned from a video camera right into the computer and the type was directly entered on the computer, and I printed the first edition on a laser printer.

*Turning Into A Pumpkin,*
assemblage with photos, post cards and paper bags,
8¼" x 7¼", 16 pages plus inserts,
one of a kind, 1994

*A very different way of working?*

It seemed much more disembodied to me—this is the retrospective view of it. And ultimately it made me realize how important it was to me that the process of making a book involved my body in a fuller way and that the book is for me in many ways an embodiment of spirit. The book itself is a body metaphor. I don't want the book or the process of bookmaking to become disembodied. The immediate aftermath of the computer book was that I went into some very handmade books for the next five years. It was the first time I was doing one of a kinds: the bag book series.

*What is that?*

This is a series of books that are composed of paper and plastic bags bound together. The one I'll describe is the one that is most developed, **Turning Into A Pumpkin**. It's half a dozen paper bags, each one folded in half, and they are stapled together, mostly at the fore edge, sometimes at the spine with one slightly larger bag serving as the cover. The bag openings create pockets, compartments, in which things can be put that can be pulled out and read or handled, and the bags also create page surfaces. In **Turning Into A Pumpkin**, the first and last bags are American, gathered from the Bay Area, and the bags in the middle are from Greece. The book incorporates material not only from a round-the-world trip when I first went to Greece but also from two subsequent trips to Greece. There's a text on the surface of the bags that is fairly short and accessible and that is about transformation. There are three moments of transformation that are textually identified; one is when Cinderella's coach turns back into a pumpkin, one is when the dream dissolves and the sleeper awakens, and one is when the traveler returns home. Then there are a series of images which are mostly photographs of Halloween pumpkins that I carved first before the trips to Greece and then after the trips, using images from dreams I had relating to the trips. Those pumpkin images form a visual sequence. In the pockets are other texts about what those trips mean to me—which was linked with healing and ancient dream incubation practices at Epidaurus—also my attempts to recapitulate the experience and the dreams that evolved out of that and how I brought the whole experience home and learned to identify its true locus as being at home rather than elsewhere. Part of my thinking is that there's a fairly accessible, not too personal, experience that anyone can engage in on the page surfaces and a more private story, an inner life story, that is inside the pockets.

*Are countries other than Greece important to you?*

Yes. The Greek experience was the one that claimed me first and as a consequence has been the most fully developed. There's a very important one that I have only begun to deal with that was in India and extending into Thailand. France and Italy have meant a lot to me and what I have absorbed from several trips to England and Wales is important also.

*Requiem*,
wood, scrim, wax, and
found objects,
7½" x 5½",
one of a kind, 1994

# sas
# colby

*Sas Colby was recorded by Cathy Courtney at the artist's studio in Berkeley,*
*California, on April 19, 1996.*

Sas Colby, 1992

Photo: Kelly McKaig

*You grew up entirely in America, but your grandparents came from Europe?*

My father was born in Italy and came to America in 1910 at the age of five. My mother is first-generation American and her family is Swedish. I was born in Massachusetts, in 1939, into an idealistic family who believed in the American Dream. My father was the youngest of thirteen children, all of whom came to this country and built prosperous businesses. They believed in hard work and individualistic endeavor, and yet had great community spirit. My mother served on school committees and set me the example of activism as a way of life.

*Did you feel part of the community?*

I did. It was the 50s and life was simpler. Fathers worked and mothers generally stayed at home taking care of children and running the household. There was a regularity and seasonal pattern to life. Every year we went to the Memorial Day parade, held Fourth of July cookouts, raked leaves in the fall, and went sledding in the winter. Dinner was served at five thirty every night without fail. My mother was active in Girl Scouting when I was growing up, which did not interest me. I always knew I was an artist and I was interested in the theater and self-expression early on.

*Did you rebel?*

I was a conditioned good girl, directed not to make waves. My mother ruled the house and was extremely rigid, so strict that I could not leave anything on top of my bureau and, if I did, I would have to buy it back from her for a nickel.

*What was on the walls of your house?*

There wasn't any art that I can remember. We had one gilded framed picture of an alpine house, a wedding gift to my parents. There were a few embroidered homilies. In the attic there was a picture of a blond nude, kneeling over a candle. Thinking back, I remember it as a tasteful girlie magazine image in black and white. Its significance is that it was in the attic, as if one didn't hang a nude in the public rooms of the house. I never asked about it. We lived near Boston and my mother was good about taking us to museums, and we did a lot of cultural things but nothing really sticks in my mind except the Isabella Stuart Gardner Museum in Boston, with the hanging vines of nasturtiums. One of our neighbors was involved in local theater and I was really drawn to her life and literary interests. And my high school music teacher seemed to embody a kind of passionate art life. At that age I took the bus to Boston on Saturdays to take classes at Massachusetts College of Art. It seemed a daring thing to do, leaving the protected suburbia where I lived and riding a bus to the city to be in the bohemian environment of an art school.

*What did you read as you were growing up?*

I was more involved with colorful things, plants and flowers, than books, although I do remember reading Françoise Sagan in high school. We were taken to the library every week, and I browsed in the stacks selecting whatever appealed to me. Comic books were suspect and we were encouraged to read "real" books. (For a different reason, I've never been interested in comics, but that's because of my vision. I can only see out of one eye and if a page gets too busy I can't look at it. Comics and video art affect me the same way.) We had subscriptions to *Readers Digest*, *The New Republic*, and *Life* and *Time* magazines. Later I got myself a subscription to *The Saturday Review of Literature*. My mother liked naturalist magazines. I was always fascinated by the printed page and I loved the pictures and was curious about the people in them.

*Were you encouraged to write and draw?*

I did a lot of coloring as a child and also wrote the neighborhood newspaper. By the time I was in junior high school I had sixteen pen pals around the world. It was a way to extend small-town boundaries and bring the world to my door. I loved the foreign postage stamps, the feel of the air-mail paper, and the exotic handwriting. There was always something to look forward to in the mailbox. My impulse to write took the form of letter writing.

Sewing and making things came naturally to me. I also made books. There are two crude books made when I was about fourteen. One commemorates my brother's homecoming from the hospital and pictures his leg in traction; the other is a recipe book for my mother. I taught myself to type and liked anything to do with words, and I was influenced by the drawings of houses that I grew up with—my father was a contractor and built houses. (We lived in a succession of new houses built by my dad. By the time I was nine years old we'd moved four times, each time to a better house, until we stayed in the house on the tree-covered hill.) I grew up thinking I wanted to be an architect but I wasn't good at math.

*Were you involved in your father's work? Did you see how the drawings were turned into houses that were built and used?*

As a youngster I was allowed to hammer a floor, collect scraps, and hang out at my father's work sites, which were usually in the neighborhood.

Once I reached puberty, the sexist division in our household became apparent. Even last fall, when I visited my parents, my dad would not let me hammer a nail to fix his garden fence. There was just no changing his attitude that this was not the proper work for girls. However, despite that, I was very influenced by the process of building, the fact that you could have an idea and make it happen. When I show slides of my work, half are of textures and fragments of buildings, because I think a lot of bookmaking is like building. That kind of layering, when you see inside something and understand its makeup, is very booklike and buildinglike.

*Where were you educated?*

I went to grammar school in Massachusetts and graduated from high school in 1957 before going to Rhode Island School of Design in 1957–59. At RISD the freshman foundation program is a general two- and three-dimensional design and drawing course with some liberal arts. It was a firm grounding in the basics of seeing—perspective, figure and nature drawing, studying color. In the second year I majored in painting. I was interested in textiles because I loved sewing, and I was influenced by the apparel design and textile departments.

I left school after two years to get married. It was not exactly my choice, but I had gotten pregnant and had to get married. I guess if I ever rebelled, that's how. I broke the rules and had sex before marriage and got caught. It was a time of stress; my mother stopped speaking to me. Even if I didn't wear my shame, she certainly did. I married my college sweetheart, who was a very creative and inventive guy. We had an apartment in Boston and immediately set about fixing it up. We painted one wall a deep orange and back then paint was not available in those amazing colors. I recall adding pigment to a kind of tractor orange to get the effect we wanted. My husband had a job installing marine electronics, and I spent my time learning to cook and making things. He had a job and I could sew all day. We were waiting for the baby's arrival and then for my husband's military career to begin.

*Had you wanted children?*

I hadn't even thought about it. I didn't have a clue. It was biology as destiny. Now I'm grateful it happened that way because I have two amazing daughters and that sense of continuity and connection that having children brings. But when I left art school in 1959, already pregnant, and wasn't able to return in the fall for my junior year, it was hard. Fortunately my husband and I were in love and into the adventure of being together. He knew he wanted to be married and have children and that made a difference.

My husband went into the air force and we moved to Georgia and Alabama. By the early 1960s I had become a young air force officer's wife with two babies, and I wore white gloves and hats and went to teas and fashion shows. My husband went to Vietnam in 1964, leaving me alone with the kids. I thought it would be a good time to go back to art school, but it wasn't possible. There was no such thing as day care,

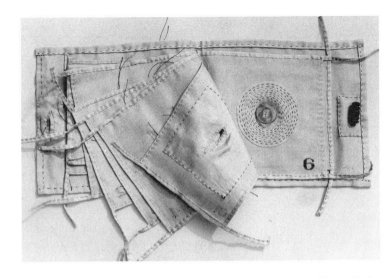

*Step-By-Step Bound Buttonholes,*
hand-stitched silk with rubber stamp printing and buttons,
6"x 13" full spread, one of a kind, 1977

and the attitude of the times was "you should stay at home with your children." I was twenty-five and had been out of school for five years. I felt frustrated because I wanted to finish my degree.

*Did you become political?*

I got political to the extent of being horrified by my husband's air force pals. In those early days no one had heard of Vietnam and there wasn't a war yet. Pilots would tell of getting rid of ammunition on isolated villages, and seemed to be unaware of the impact of their actions. I experienced first-hand the government's lack of morality, and seemingly there was no plan for the men they assigned. I was very disillusioned to think my life was going to be controlled by this. Most of the air force wives I knew encouraged their husbands to return to civilian life.

*Did your husband get out?*

Yes. He became an airline pilot flying out of New York. We moved to Ridge-field, Connecticut, where I started taking classes at the Brookfield Craft Center and met people with similar art interests. There was an explosion of interest in the crafts in the late 1960s and early 1970s. Soon I taught classes at Brookfield and began exhibiting my work in wall hangings, banners, fantasy garments, and masks. I made wild pieced-work satin and velvet capes with pictures and words on them. I made group garments for three or more people to wear. My work was shown at the Museum of Contemporary Crafts and the Fairtree Crafts Gallery in New York and at the Egg and the Eye in Los Angeles (which became the Los Angeles Craft and Folk Art Museum).

*When did you start adding words?*

I rarely made anything without incorporating words. I've always had a strong feeling for letter forms, almost a mystical relationship to them, as well as to the sounds of words. I like wordplay and nuance, the poetic associations conjured by a word or sound. I'm fascinated by word origins, and relate words directly to the use of my voice. It's physical as well as mental and I've always sought the company of writers.

Around the time I was showing my garments and my work began attracting attention, I met the Connecticut Feminists in the Arts, a group of artists and writers who got together in the early days of the women's movement. We were close to New York, a center of feminist activity. It was an extraordinary thing for suburban women to get involved with. I had the freedom to stay home as a mother and take care of my children, but I also could devote a lot of time to my work; to come together with these other creative women, who were also starting to take a larger view of their own lives than had been possible before, was very exciting.

The CFA was quite a radical group, and I wasn't part of the first wave of consciousness-raising. One of my masks was pictured on the cover of a book, *Unmasking*, which documented that time. It's hard to explain just how much effort it took for women to break out of traditional roles back then. It wasn't about being against men or marriage, but more about the necessity of changing your perceptions of what a woman's life could be. When I started to look, I realized I thought of myself not as subjugated but nevertheless in a subsidiary place. I think my husband felt threatened by the recognition my work was receiving—for example, as an exhibiting and professional artist, I wanted to have my name on my checks and to get my own bank account. Our marriage did not survive; we were divorced after fifteen years.

*Was it an inevitable part of becoming an artist?*

No. It was an inevitable part of an early marriage and my urge to change and grow and create a life as I saw it for myself. I wanted to explore as many things as I could. Through the CFA, I met Anaïs Nin and, through her, other writers and artists. The divorce was devastating, but through it a new life emerged.

*For example?*

My work blossomed, and I was free to accept offers to teach. I liked creating ways for people to come together. It was a time of incredible expansion (what is referred to as the 60s also happened in the early 70s). Because my husband was a pilot I could fly anywhere for practically nothing, so I developed a bi-coastal art life, which continued after the divorce.

*What was Anaïs Nin like?*

I found her expansive and open. She must have been seventy when I met her, and she adored connecting artists and writers, being part of a network of creative people. She responded to my masks and capes and invited me and my friend, Susan Boulet, to show slides at some of her college lectures. Susan would show her paintings and I'd show my capes and we'd stage processions with the audience trying on the capes and masks. Anaïs was generous like that. She enjoyed a rich fantasy life and that kind of surrealistic play. Two of my friends from the Connecticut Feminists in the Arts, Valerie Harms and Adele Aldridge, formed Magic Circle Press, and their first book was *A Celebration*, a record of a weekend featuring Nin and her circle, including Frances Stelloff, the founder of the Gotham Book Mart in New York and an important figure in the New York literary world.

I made my first book because of my association with Anaïs and the writers in the CFA. At the time I was working in textiles, and one of my friends, appealing to the frustrated writer in me, suggested I make a fabric book. It was called **Silky Book** and I made it in 1972 or 1973. It took the form of a sophisticated children's cloth book with zippers and buttons and hidden pockets containing brief cryptic messages. The text was not written per se, but came forth, kind of like automatic writing, during the making of the book. It was stitched, typed, or appliquéd onto the pages. I was surprised when the book was purchased by the owner of a Madison Avenue craft gallery. It was an experimental piece and opened the door to a new way of working.

*Had you seen anything which you would in retrospect call an artist's book?*

No, but living in Connecticut, I was very aware of the avant-garde festivals that were happening in New York with the Fluxus people. I was far from that world, though drawn to experimental and marginalized art forms. My impulse was to make art an extension of life, or rather for art to be completely integrated into daily life, for it to be participatory.

*How quickly did books become an important part of your practice?*

It took maybe two years. By the time I made the next book I had gotten divorced (1975) and moved to Berkeley, California. California in the 70s

Clockwise: *Foot Care, Do Not Disturb, Storage Suggestions, Under Wraps*, color Xerox, approx. 3" x 4", editions of 25, 1979–80

was a wonderful place to start a new life as a single parent and an artist.

*What did you find there?*

Freedom. There were many constraints on people in New England, and California was wide open. A good place to start over.

*Did you feel you quickly became part of a group in Berkeley?*

Not immediately, because I didn't know where I fit in. I connected with people involved with fiber works, but I gradually moved closer to an art community that included performance, mail art, and artists' books. I stopped working in textiles altogether and moved into mixed media, mostly books and photography.

*Were the textiles and the mixed-media books mutually exclusive?*

No, but I remember stitching books and feeling it was like a step out of time. The handstitched books took forever, and meanwhile I had a sense of the world going on and I wanted to be out in it, not isolated in my studio. Around this time I began working in color Xerox and produced a series of envelopes-to-assemble. They were original collages in the shapes of envelopes, which could be cut out and put together and mailed. I sold many of them. In the late 1970s and early 80s I made four small editions of Xerox books, **Foot Care**, **Storage Suggestions**, **Under Wraps**, and **Do Not Disturb**, with found text and images from mail-order catalogues. These books were small, maybe three by four inches, printed on cover stock in editions of twenty-five. Working with Xerox brought me out of the studio and into the Krishna Copy Center on Telegraph Avenue in Berkeley, where other artists were also in line waiting for the color Xerox machine. And the process of Xeroxing was very much like performance, because you had to work quickly, arranging spontaneous collages on the platen. There was also an element of chance and discovery. I also used color Xerox to make paper copies of my fabric books. The pages were stitched together and I added buttons and other found objects. All of these sold immediately.

Working with mixed media brought me into contact with a group of experimental artists, and in 1976 I met Susan Wick, the first other artist I knew who made books. Through her I met Betsy Davids. Susan was already exhibiting books and had a show at the Annenberg Gallery in San Francisco (which no longer exists) in 1976. They were one-of-a-kinds, mostly purchased journals with collaged correspondence, envelopes, and records of her travels abroad. In 1979 Susan and a group of artists rented a shop on College Avenue, the Aart Store, and I became part of that group. Our philosophy was to make art available to everyone in a kind of living store/gallery. Prices ranged from fifty cents to fifty dollars. The displays were constantly changing, and performances and events were also scheduled. The neighborhood loved us. You could pick up some art along with your wine, bread, and flowers on your way home from work! Later I ran a similar project, Art Space, which was rented to artists by the week. These public art projects put me in touch with both artists and the community and were valuable public relations and marketing experiences for me.

*Photography has played a role in your work?*

Yes, from the beginning. I've always wanted my slide shows to be entertaining as well as to picture a way of seeing, so I've always had a reason to roam the world with my old 35 mm. Olympus. Also, I've made a large body of work with a 1939 Brownie camera (made in the year I was born). I'm a completely nontechnical photographer and although I've worked in the dark room, it doesn't interest me. I have also made art about the camera (which became an icon for me, a little black purse), so it has been both the tool for and the subject of books. One series of Brownie books combines photography, collage, and fabric and was stitched together on the sewing machine. The covers are shaped paintings of the camera, and the books have two layers: the camera and what the camera saw. In some there is a handwritten stitched text which becomes the voice of the camera. Another body of work is based on enlarged Brownie snapshots and appropriated images which are blown up so the image breaks down, with paint and collage added. There are two photographic books made for the wall, **The Ear Book**, twelve feet long, and **Be, Do, Die**, seven feet long. In each the photographs are treated more like fabric. The unmounted prints have been stitched and they hang freely. As the temperature and light change in the room, the corners of the photographs curl up, creating wonderful effects with shadows. These two books were made in 1986, when I wanted to get some distance from the intimate small-scale work I'd been doing.

Photography was a good medium for me when I had a full-time job and less time for making art. Something about the process of taking pictures seemed quicker. I could pick it up and get back into it faster than with other media. For a while I was exhibiting mainly in the photography world and producing fewer books. In 1986 I had a show at the Photographers Gallery in London, curated by Zelda Cheetle, where the work was miniaturized photographs, printed the size of stamps. I'm always working on my slide show, so photography remains an integral part my work.

*Were you involved with setting up the Pacific Center for the Book Arts?*

That started in 1978 and, no, I wasn't part of it. Some time in the 80s I was invited to speak to the group by Alistair Johnston, one of the founders.

*Did you begin to feel part of a wider book art community?*

There were many national and international exhibitions during the 1980s, and I felt part of that community. But because my art making did not include printing, binding, and papermaking, I always felt outside the mainstream of book art activity. There are many book worlds around San Francisco. There are the small-press people, involved primarily with writing and poetry; there are people whose main interest is in the crafts of binding, papermaking, and printing; and there are those like myself who do work that doesn't fit into these categories and probably mostly make one-of-a-kind books. I do almost exclusively one of a kind, not because I don't want to do a multiple, but because I've never been part of the artists' presses which produce them. I also make paintings, assemblages, and constructions.

*Have you ever been involved in teaching book art?*

Yes, the book world has given me a creative home and place to teach, even though I've felt somewhat outside it. I've taught classes at most of the summer craft schools, including Penland, Haystack, and Anderson Ranch, beginning in 1978. In 1991 I taught in Australia, at the Graphic Investigation Workshop, a part of the Australian National University in Canberra, and in Wollongong and Brisbane. It was exciting to have this kind of exchange on another continent. My classes emphasize unifying form and content in the book and lately have examined the use of metaphor in text and symbolism in visuals.

*The Brownie Book of Paintings* and *Dark Room Secrets,*
watercolor, snapshots, collage, and stitching,
approx. 8"x 12" (full spread), 8 pages,
one of a kind, 1981

I have an idea that books are made by shy artists, those who are terrified about making their writing too public. The enclosed space of the book makes them feel safe. I relate to small things and to the intimate scale of the book. I like the handwork involved in making a book, the feeling of constructing it, and the use of layering to reveal and conceal and to inform the reader gradually. The book contains a powerful, potent voice in a small space. I see the passion my students bring to their books and it's something I've been thinking about as I've read Johanna Drucker's *The Century of Artists' Books,* especially where she discusses the book as a fetishized object.

My work in the book form evolved naturally from a physical, sensual approach to art making. I think of books as a holistic form because all the senses come into play in both the making and the "reading." The text to me is pure voice speaking, sometimes in a whisper, sometimes in a shout. The pages act as passageways or barriers, depending on the material used, and they reflect our thought process, developing over time. This is how books come alive.

*More recently, you've been making canvas books?*

In 1990 I moved to Taos, New Mexico. I put aside everything but paint and canvas. For one thing, I was tired of being marginalized as a "book artist," in spite of all the other work I'd done. I made a number of strong collages and realized they could just as well have been made as books instead of two-dimensional pieces, so I began making books out of new materials and worked through a series of ideas over a five-year period. The books range in size from six by ten inches to twenty by forty, and the canvas weight varies from finely textured linen to crude canvas. They're sewn together with a simple pamphlet stitch in linen thread. I became aware that I was creating a tactile object that people wanted to touch, so I paid a lot of attention to the surface of the canvas and prepared it as I would a wall I was going to paint. Some of the page edges are folded smooth and some are left as rough canvas edges, and there are three-dimensional objects—symbolic metaphorical objects—inside. Without actually directing the viewer to handle the books, I added handles or tabs at certain points to indicate possible approaches through the work. (I've always loved the implied command in books.)

The text is often cut out of canvas and applied to the page and then painted over to appear embossed. I write my own text, always simple, often only a single word. The latest book, **Psychic Research** (1995), has more text than the others, with chapter headings in canvas letters and a subtext typeset and glued in.

*What are these books exploring?*

They are really layered paintings, bringing the viewer into close contact with paint and canvas. They can be regarded as filmic, as paintings that move. They are meant to be seen over time so that a page can be turned every now and then and a different relationship of color to form to space can be experienced. The most complex books have a French-door binding with pages and text that overlap and interweave. These books are mysterious objects and difficult to categorize. Their scale is beyond that of an average book. And they throw the viewer off because they are paintings, which we are unaccustomed to touching. They read best when supported on a slanted shelf that is hung on the wall above waist level. Most galleries don't know what to do with them. No one in Taos had ever seen an artist's book, and I was lucky to find the Fenix Gallery, whose owner, Judy Kendall, decided to show the books. She put them on pedestals, like sculptures, and found that visitors stayed longer in her gallery because they weren't just standing at the door passing their eyes around the room. When I came in a few days after the show had opened, she said, "Even the mailman's reading your books."

Because they are made of canvas I no longer worry about their deterioration from touch. A five-year-old book looks like a five-year-old book that's been handled a lot, but it doesn't look destroyed the way it would if it were paper. Lots of people have touched the canvas books, and I've dragged them everywhere.

*Books to Read and Write*,
acrylic on canvas, 16" x 42" full spread, 20 pages,
one of a kind, 1992

*The cycle of making canvas books
is completed for the time being?*

I've begun working on a series of paintings combined with objects and boxes. The organizing principle is a set of words in juxtaposition. For instance, a black painting of the word "devotion" is paired with a box that says "desire." The box is installed on a shelf directly underneath the painting, so they are seen in relationship to each other. The viewer will naturally want to raise the lid of the box and is confronted with another juxtaposition to ponder. The palette is simply black and gold, and each piece is richly presented.

*The book, for you, can become a form of fetish?*

Yes. They become total works of obsession, and the process of making them is outside time. That's not so different from making a two-dimensional painting, but it's the layering and the sequencing, the working out of the complex interrelationships that is unique to making an artist's book. One small book, **Requiem**, was made as a prayer for a sick friend. I sewed a whole page of buttons, and each button is a prayer. Making this book, like making a shrine, was an active meditation, transforming materials and energy. Books mirror our way of thinking in layers; they allow for a mood to develop over time. Some of the strongest pieces are made from a deep personal voice that expresses a transformative wish.

"Fig. 1" from *Passage,*
offset, 7"x 4½", 128 pages,
edition of 1,000, 1972

# telfer
# stokes

This interview with Telfer Stokes was recorded with Cathy Courtney
in London between November 5, 1997 and January 29, 1998.

Telfer Stokes and his
son, Laurie, 1998

Photo: Helen Douglas

• 85

You were born on October 3, 1940 in St Ives, Cornwall, where your parents were part of an artistic community that included Ben Nicholson and Barbara Hepworth, Patrick and Delia Heron, Naum and Miriam Gabo. Your father, Adrian Stokes, was a writer and painter, and your mother, Margaret Mellis, is an artist. While this background meant you were rooted in the art world, it was also a context you needed to escape?

Yes. I wanted to make my own way. For example, I was at Bryanston School with the sons of Kit Nicholson, William Scott, and Robert Buhler and Derek Hill's nephew. We knew we had vaguely important antecedents but we had to find out whether we were artists in our own right I was quite happy playacting at being an artist as a schoolboy. The ultimate for me then was seeing the publication of work by Pollock, Rothko, de Kooning, and Clifford Still in *Life* magazine in the late 1950s. We all started working on the floor of the art room and throwing paint around. I was already interested in knocking down old values. The reaction to home was the paramount part of it.

*Did you feel a link with any of the painters in your father's world?*

The one island that I always related to is Alfred Wallis, and I feel secure about what he represents to me. He is an example of independence from tradition. We had a vast collection of his work because my mother had bought from him and my father cleared out his house when he died. Adrian rang everyone he knew and said, "If you want a Wallis, come and collect it." We were left with what wasn't taken away, which was most of it. Wallis had a quality that wasn't anything to do with representation at all; he never painted from anything in front of him, which was important. He was trying to re-create something that wasn't there anymore. He is neither representational nor abstract. One canvas had been given to Wallis by my father (a rejected painting by Adrian himself), and Wallis adapted the pink and green of my father's painting and incorporated it as part of his own. He would also use odd-shaped bits of cardboard to work on. When he showed things, he apparently would hammer them up on the wall outside his house with enormous nails sticking out of his paintings. There were many elements about Wallis that were extraordinarily sophisticated in a way that is absolutely abstract. I associate him with abstract art in every sort of way.

*You went to the Slade as a painting student between 1958 and 1962, where the prevailing attitudes were no more to your liking that those at home?*

I rejected the Slade partly because I hadn't gone there through my own choice—it was through my father's friendship with William Coldstream and the other Euston Road painters who taught there—and partly because I rejected the idea of representation that was prevalent and also the dominant influence of Bomberg. In 1962 I went to America because I was so disillusioned with all the things I had been pushed into. I wrote in my notebook that this was the opportunity to prove to myself whether or not I was an artist, irrespective of my background. It was a great success; the fact that I had set it up for myself, what happened in New York, and the work I did, were terribly important to me.

*How was it different to be painting there than at the Slade?*

It was immediately an enormously different environment. New York in 1962 was the most invigorating, powerful place. There was an atmosphere that was enough to change anybody. I made work that was important to me. By chance, I met Barnett Newman, who took a detailed interest in my work. It was also the beginning of my building "expertise," because I had to design a loft space so that no one knew I was living in it because it was illegal to do so. I shared the space with an English painter and we would have endless conversations about being ants in this very big city. We understood the relation between art being done there, the link with the pioneer spirit, and the gigantic continent, unencumbered by tradition. The scale the American painters worked on related to the city landscape and to the enormity of the country. In Europe people were making paintings that would hang on the wall of a small room, but the American canvases were things you could walk into. It was an infinitely more expansive place than Britain. When I got back to London I tried to re-create the atmosphere in the East End and it was a total disaster. The studio was small and I had to do the paintings in sections to get them up and down the stairs or out of the window.

*You were still painting at this stage. When did the notion of making a book occur?*

About two years after I got back from New York, in 1964. I was introduced to someone named Arthur Lacey, who said he was going to write a novel. When I asked him to describe it, he said, "I'm not going to write anything. I'm going to use a camera. It will be a visual book." I remember that even though I didn't even have a camera, the idea made me feel jealous. At the same time, another friend came back from Reykjavik and talked about having seen an exhibition of books by a crazy man. It must have been Dieter Rot.

The second occasion when I thought of making an image-oriented book was when I was back in New York in 1971 with Martin Attwood, who had been one of my students when I was teaching graphics at Corsham

Court in the late 1960s. Martin came to rent part of a house I had bought in Kentish Town and we became friends. On our way back from New York he suggested we do a book about our trip. He had taken a lot of slides in America and had a camera that kept going wrong and superimposing images one on top of the other, which he felt would be part of the book. As it turned out, Martin was too busy to work on the book because he went to the University of East Anglia, which is where he met Helen Douglas.

Although he didn't actually work on *Passage* (1972), in the end Martin was terribly necessary to me as the link who could work out practically how things could be achieved. I had no idea how to work a camera or find a printer. All these things I owe to Martin. I would say, "How do I print this?" It was on Martin's initiative that I began to use Joe Weldon, a jobbing printer in Kilburn High Street, who printed the first five We-production books.

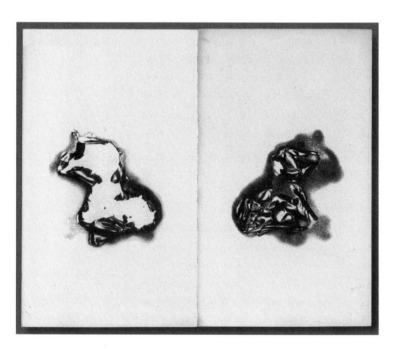

"Burn" from *Passage*,
offset, 7"x 4½", 128 pages,
edition of 1,000, 1972

*How did you begin work on* **Passage**?

In a sense I had been working toward something that whole summer before going to America, which I had spent on a beach in England taking photographs and writing. Going to the beach was the result of an enormous failure, a big exhibition I had at the Serpentine Gallery in 1971 of constructed reliefs that had writing in them. I felt angry about that exhibition and was ready to make an important change. Oddly enough, two of the photographs I took on the beach that summer are going to be included in the book I'm working on at the moment, **Song of the Thrush**.

With **Passage** I was attempting to show the physicality of the book itself. For instance, I assembled a section of pages, lit a match, and burned a hole through them. I then separated the sheets and photographed each front and back from the first to the most receding burn mark at the end of the sequence. Having completed that photographic cycle, the images were put into the book in exactly the same sequence so that one could see how the pages had been affected by this action. I used photographs of both sides of slices of bread in a similar way, so that when a page turned it formed a sandwich at the end of the sequence. I was making the slices of bread analogous to the pages of the book.

*Had you seen the work of Ed Ruscha at this stage?*

Yes, I saw his work early on at Compendium Bookshop in London, but the only one I ever bought was *Real Estate Opportunities* (1970).

*Ruscha is often credited with being the initiator of a certain type of book art. Do you go along with that?*

I think I am responsible for getting that idea put forward. It was certainly taken on by Clive Phillpot. He asked me who I thought was important, and I said Ed Ruscha. I do think Ruscha made a contribution that was unique. I also admired the fact that a lot of people who were not interested in art understood what he was doing. When I went to Los Angeles in 1972, I discovered there was a wider social context for that kind of work than you could find in Britain. L.A. in the 70s was full of puns, there was wordplay on everything. For instance, people would go around with cars for sale but the notice would say "FOR SAIL." Everybody was probably stoned out of their minds, but the cultural underground was overground. In a certain way, Ruscha's work appealed to me very much on that level. I went to L. A. partly because I wanted to meet Ruscha. I put a copy of **Passage** through his door, but he never responded.

*Wordplay has always been very important to you?*

It's gotten me lots of places but it's never an end. It's a beginning. It got me fascinated in meaning.

*In what context did your conversation with Clive Phillpot take place?*

Clive was the first person to review **Passage**, and he wrote completely out of the blue in Studio International in about 1972. Then he reviewed **Foolscrap** (1973) and **Spaces** (1974). When Martin Attwood was organizing a show of book art for the British Council (Artists' Bookworks, 1975), he asked me who would be a good person to write the catalogue and I suggested Clive.

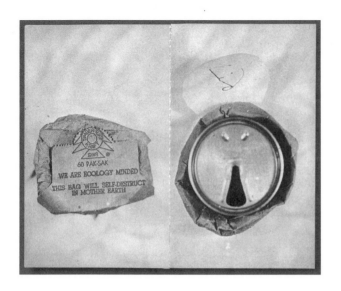

"A Tin Teardrop" from *Spaces,*
offset, 7"x 4½", 158 pages,
edition of 1,000, 1974

I expect that was the context of our conversation. After that Clive wrote the catalogue for the Arts Council exhibition of books (*Artists' Books,* 1976), which was before he left England to live and work in America.

*Why is Ruscha important to you?*

He didn't relate to any tradition. His work leaves something in the mind that you can't take out of the book. It leaves a very strong concept. You can only refuel by re-looking at the work. I was also interested in him as someone who took photographs. I liked the detachment of his photography. I chose to use the camera partly to have a way of communicating that avoided drawing. I thought, perhaps wrongly, that people understood a certain truth in photography.

*What do you think of his work now?*

I don't think about Ed Ruscha's books. Perhaps what people should do if they are going to write about his books in retrospect is relate them to everything he's done since. What he did with his books has not been equaled by what he has done subsequently.

*Duchamp was another artist who interested you greatly at the time you made* **Passage***?*

Again, he found a way of breaking with tradition. He was a helpful trigger, someone I could relate to when I was launching myself. Nowadays I don't think of Duchamp at all. He was important to me at one point, just as Samuel Beckett was at another. Someone to step off from. The chair/ladder in **Spaces** has a Duchampian element to it in that I was animating a dead object. It was a small stepladder that folded into a chair, and I photographed it where I found it in the loft where I was staying in New York in 1973. The Duchampian element wasn't where the greatest appeal lay, it was the possibility of using the ladder to confirm the three levels that I had established about the paper in the book. The levels were "in the paper," "on the paper," and "over the paper." I set a beer can on the ladder and, as the ladder folded into a chair, the can fell off and got caught, which made me remember an article I had cut out of the the *Guardian* newspaper about a woman captioned Miss Mousetrap, who was retiring after forty years as manager of the box office at the Ambassador's Theatre, where Agatha Christie's *Mousetrap* had been running. As I was photographing the ladder trapping the beer can, I realized I could join the two things together and reprint parts of the article in the book.

*The beer can is used again in what you call the "Tin Teardrop"?*

If you take the tab off a beer can to open it, it leaves a void in the shape of a tear. I made that vacant space into a solid within the process of making the images for the book in the sense that in taking and preparing photographs, you are dealing with reversals all the time—negative to positive, positive to negative. I've been using that concept derived from working with film ever since I started making books. In making a solid out of the void, I was trying to make something from nothing. All art, ultimately, is giving value to something that's valueless.

*Does the idea of the beer can as the mouse link with the HMV dog that appears later in the book and also with the cat on the cover?*

The HMV record player was something I was allowed to play with as a four-year-old, so there was a personal significance, but the mouse, the dog, and the cat were also a connection with Herriman's cartoon *Krazy Kat*. I indulged deeply in all these iconographic levels, working out my own connections. I admire enormously the use of language and image in cartoon. (The sequence with the ball in **Spaces** relates to the way a cartoonist might transfer an image across consecutive frames.) I had also read *Oz* and *Ink*, which were underground papers in the 1960s, put out in a fairly unconventional way with a lot of overprinting and where, although the word played an important part, a lot of the printing was image based. They were concerned with the current culture, particularly in relation to music, but also with what from the

"Miss Mousetrap" from **Spaces**, offset, 7"x 4½", 158 pages, edition of 1,000, 1974

80s became called "lifestyles," never a term used then. I like various subcultures, things that have been underground. They form an important basis to something very real. I want to make statements about that sort of thing and it is one reason why I'm a book artist. If I continue to make books, it will be as a kind of catalogue of what has gone on.

*Did you expect readers to pick up the references, for instance, to Krazy Kat?*

No, not at all. I was such a formalist at that point that it was a question of trying to avoid content as much as possible—there was so much content in everything. I was very suspicious of content for content's sake.

*But content was inescapable. In the end you had to work with it and not fight it?*

What I did was play with it. When Helen Douglas and I began to collaborate on **Loophole** in 1974 and the series of books we did after that, we would argue about composition and also subject matter because I always wanted to make the subject matter very, very subsidiary to the formal way in which it was presented. She would say, "But I'm very interested in subject matter." We proceeded with the paperback series with her interest in subject matter and my lack of it.

*How did you come to work with Helen?*

Helen came to rent a room in my house in Kentish Town in London, and we started doing what we were to do for the next twenty-five years, which is that we talked and talked and talked until I said, "We should do a book." I was very conscious of being isolated and I wasn't too sure whether what I was doing appealed to anyone at all, so it was very important to find someone who shared the ideas. Interacting with people had always been an ingredient of the work. For instance, the title and the idea for **Loophole** came from talking to a girl I knew who said her life had gone in the shape of a loop.

*For **Loophole**, as for some of the sequences in the previous books, you built models or sets, which you photographed in order to achieve the degree of illusion you needed in the books. The action of building and tearing down becomes an analogy for the architecture and spaces within the book. Building has been an important activity for you not only in the London house but also in Deuchar Mill in Scotland, where you currently live with Helen Douglas and your son, Laurie?*

The houses I have lived in have been sites for making work in. The house in Kentish Town, which I still have, has remained in an incomplete state. A lot of artists tend to end up living in what are almost building sites. Sometimes the idea of finishing a house for a particular purpose means that life is going to be pinned down in a particular way and there is, in contrast, an attraction to the idea of a transient and changing environment, which you adapt to the way your life is changing and your new requirements. It means that human relationships become more pointed, more secure, because the environment is somewhat unresolved. The physical building work gets put aside as other things have to be continued.

The work on the Kentish Town house did become fairly creative and it fed into the sequences in **Loophole**. I was feeling trapped at the time—I had done three books while I was based in that house, during which two marriages had come and gone. The investment in the house had reached a point where there was nothing I could do to change it and it was becoming history. I was trying to break out by symbolically making a hole in the wall that we built as part of the set for **Loophole**. It's significant that Helen and I left and went to Scotland at this point. I had been caught in a situation and it was very important for me to find somewhere else to live.

*Did you go to Scotland because it was where Helen had grown up?*

One of the incentives was to get money from the Scottish Arts Council to do **Chinese Whispers** (1976). Our plan was that we would then move on to Wales and apply to the Welsh Arts Council, but we ended up buying Deuchar Mill in the Yarrow Valley. **Chinese Whispers** relates to the game in which a group of people sit in a circle and one whispers a word to the person next to them and it gets passed round the circle until it comes back to the original person, by which time the word has usually been transformed by mishearing into something quite different. Having looked at the loop in our previous book, our concern here was the spiral or circle, which determined the sequence of **Chinese Whispers**. There is first a prelude and then the building within the pages of what becomes a corner cupboard, playing on the idea of the spine of the book. The Chinese whisper isn't a whisper in the verbal sense, it is there in the visual sense of the cupboard undergoing transformation from shelf to shelf. We established the idea of the three levels of shelves within the cupboard, the idea of under the ground, in the ground (growth), and over the ground, and Helen's interest in objects was then important in determining what appeared on the shelves. The countryside content was much nearer to Helen's sympathies. We also introduced the first text to the books, part of which I had actually found on a gravestone in Highgate Cemetery: "Life's an open book." An enormous amount of pressure was taken off me with Helen's collaboration, and I remember feeling very relaxed when we got to Scotland. **Clinkscale** (1977) and **Stells**

(1978) both occurred while we were building the mill, which meant we did shorter, more concise books. **Clinkscale** is an accordion book that uses an image of a musical accordion and includes my hands holding the instrument—the fingers are ingrained with dirt, which was because of the building work I was doing. When the work space was ready I bought a Vandercook proofing press, on which I printed **Back to Back** (1980), and around 1982 I bought an offset press, on which I printed **Spin Off** (1985).

*You tend to see your collaboration with Helen as splitting up into three phases?*

The first stage was on the paperback series; the second was in the 80s when we did **Mim** (1986) and **Real Fiction** (1987); and then we stopped working together for a while before doing **Yarrow Cooks** (1992) and **Water on the Border** (1994). The character of the collaboration was different at different times. Helen was almost a helper on the first book and that was more or less completely reversed by **Water on the Border**. I didn't notice at the time, but most of the photographs for **Water on the Border** were Helen's, which were right for the book as it evolved, whereas I was using the camera differently, photographing on the hoof with a lot of images blurred and out of focus. I was the person who did the darkroom work, putting the images onto film, and then we put the book together between us.

**Yarrow Cooks** *brought you into conflict with Printed Matter in New York?*

**Yarrow Cooks** was a cookery book that we did in collaboration with local schoolchildren. It was a community project. Printed Matter wrote and said they weren't certain it was an artist's book. I was astonished they should react like that. I argued there's got to be a point where people have got to be able to go in whatever direction they want. To say **Yarrow Cooks** is not an artist's book because it uses children's drawings is nonsense; the material for the book was chosen by us, irrespective of who drew it. It had to be seen in the context of the history of all our books as part of our development. They apologized and did sell the book and certainly accepted the next book without any qualms. Neither **Yarrow Cooks** nor **Water on the Border** sold as well in America as our others have done. I've come to the conclusion that no books sell in America unless they're about or relate to America or were composed or thought out there.

*You've published three books in America?*

Clive Phillpot put our names forward to Riva Castleman at the Museum of Modern Art and they commissioned **Young Masters and Misses** (1981). Through meeting Joan Lyons at a conference in Boston at which Clive was speaking, I was invited to print **Real Fiction** at the Visual Studies Workshop. Brad Freeman was the press man there, and I formed an important connection with him. Afterward, I set up a new darkroom at the mill with a water supply and a process camera, and that was modeled on the one at the VSW.

The other place I worked at was Nexus in Atlanta, Georgia, which is part of a large arts center. I printed **Desire** (1989) there, having done the preparatory work in Scotland. **Desire** is a book dealing with the senses—peering, looking, feeling, and smelling—and in which I was stacking and layering color, which was a development for me. I had to find a device that went through the book to stop the colors floating away and used an image of fencing wire running through the pages as a fixer keeping them in place. The text was another thread running through, which was taken from a series of tape recordings in which I blocked out various parts to take out its original sense, leaving certain words which amalgamated with the wire and the layered colors. It was essential to establish a ground color to make it clear that it was printed color rather than colored paper; the left-hand pages were the ground color with images layered on the right-hand side. Because of a strike at Nexus, only half the book was printed before I had to leave, which was a disappointment.

"Slicing the Earth Cake with Chardin's Knife" from *Chinese Whispers* (with Helen Douglas), offset, 7" x 4½", 176 pages, edition of 1,000, 1976

*The next book was **Ajar** (1991), which uses color in a different way?*

You can't pretend that color is something that fills an image. It is something on its own. There is image and there is text and there is also color. With **Ajar** I was no longer establishing a ground color and then printing images on top of that; I was stacking colors again, but there were different images in each layer. It was a complicated process because I was printing things, rejecting or accepting certain configurations, and then reprinting.

The images were from a hardware catalogue and various newspapers that I had accumulated.

Although I have a strong attachment to the mill and am very happy with my studio there, I am aware that I have to go elsewhere to find my material. The last few books have involved going to different countries. I am fascinated by dominant cultures—America, Russia, China, and India are all countries I have visited. My visit to Russia coincided with my interest in Cyrillic script and, through seeing some of his work in a gallery, I met the poet Vsevolod Nekrasov. He gave me the Russian text for his poems with an English translation. By this time I had already half printed **Ajar**, but I took words out of the poems and put them into the double spreads. I had no idea what the Russian meant—I was using letters that were attractive and that I imagined would make a nice sound.

*What spurred your visit to India?*

I was hoping I would find material to make a book. I went to Bombay to see the Buddhist caves. Bombay was a sobering experience, a bit like hell on earth, with three to four million people who have nowhere to sleep, nowhere to live, and nothing to eat. The text for the book I am working on at the moment, **Song of the Thrush**, comes from conversations I had with an Indian who stopped me in the street and said, "You are wearing sandals. I thought the English introduced slippers to India." He said, "Would you like to come for a drink" and later he said, "Would you mind paying for it?"

*Song of the Thrush*,
left-hand page backed
onto right-hand page,
offset, 7½" x 5⅘",
148 pages,
edition of 400, 1998

There followed a series of meetings in bars where he gave me a great deal of advice. I never thought these conversations would work their way into the book because there is a highly politicized part to it, but we did talk about the poverty of India and the book has ended up being about poverty.

*Which images from your summer on the beach in 1971 will go into your 1998 book?*

One is of the tent which I lived in in a hollow in the sand dunes. It falls into the preliminary part of the book, **Covers**, a series of covers bound in before the book proper—**Song of the Thrush**—starts. There is even a photograph of my mother in the **Covers** section, one that I took last summer. Neither image is there for autobiographical reasons. In each case there is a disparity between the image and the title that it's been given. Sequence plays an enormous part in understanding what is going on.

*You like to juxtapose image and title in an uneasy relationship to each other?*

The only way people really look at an image is if there's no attempt to make the caption relate. What I am trying to do is make the image equal to, if not more important than, the caption. I'm trying to reverse the trend that newspapers use. Words do not sum up images.

*What technology are you using for **Song of the Thrush**?*

I am using a computer and have done sections of layered images and then scrubbed through them. The computer has made a difference to the way I work, and I think it will become more important. So far I have only used it very primarily and there is a lot more for me to learn. I will still be printing the book on the offset press.

*Why is it called **Song of the Thrush**?*

It is a musical book; the text is a little like music with images clumped together the way you read music. The bird was one I heard at the mill and the title was written in my notebook long before I went to India.

*Since **Water on the Border** you and Helen have been making books separately?*

To keep a collaboration going, you have to avoid breaking things down as to who did what, but there is a point where it is necessary for people to move away and start doing their own things and at that stage you need to know who contributed what. We have survived the period of separation, although at one point I didn't think we would. Helen has now finished her book *Between the Two* (1997), and when I have produced **Song of the Thrush** I think that process will be complete.

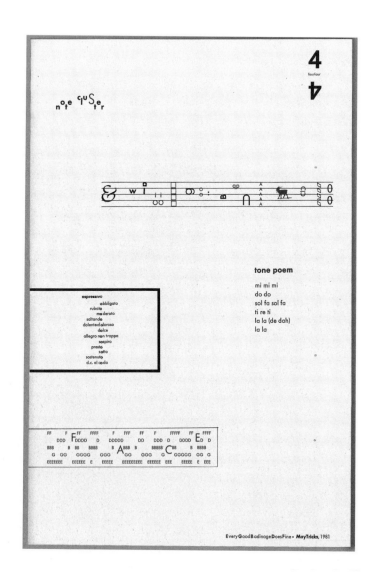

*Every Good Bandinage
Does Fine,*
letterpress, 18"x 12",
edition of 6, 1981

# kathy
# walkup

Cathy Courtney's interview with Kathy Walkup was recorded at her home in Menlo Park, California, on December 16, 1997.

Kathy Walkup with students, 1998

Photo: Jaime Robles

*You've lived in the San Francisco Bay Area for nearly thirty years. Was California a big contrast to the place where you grew up?*

I was born in Portland, Oregon, but I grew up in a rural environment in western Pennsylvania, a combination of coal mining and small dairy farms. We lived in a tiny town of eight hundred people, probably the only non-Germans in the entire community. My mother's mother lived in the town, an American who had married a British mining engineer and lived with him in Ireland for many years before moving to America. She was a pianist, entertaining the troops during the First World War in England and France. My grandfather died before I was born. I spent an enormous amount of time with my grandmother, and she introduced me to a kind of life that didn't exist elsewhere for me—classical music, opera, antiques, "tea-time" every day at four. She was extremely religious and very involved with the WCTU (Women's Christian Temperance Union) and, although she had art books around the house, she would carefully slit out any prints with nudes in them.

*What was your own family home like?*

My father was a high school teacher and my mother, who hated housekeeping, worked on and off as a journalist. There were four of us born in five years; I was the oldest. Our home was total chaos, no privacy and no space at all. We had tons of books, not terribly good ones, including a series of children's classics in standard format, which I hated. We also had the *Golden Books*, cheap, thin picture books, heavily illustrated, with cardboard covers and shiny golden spines with no printing on them; you'd be hard-pressed to find an American child of my era who didn't have contact with that series. I can recognize that books represented an enormous escape for me, but there was something more active than that. There's no question that the material object of the book was as important to me as the content, even as a child.

As there was no library in our town, a bookmobile would come once a week. I was a voracious reader and, when I was about twelve, we turned our dining room into a library with books from the bookmobile and I would loan them out to the rest of the local kids. I ran the library for a couple of summers, making little cards for the books, fining people a penny a day if they were late bringing them back. I was allowed to wallow in all these books and help the other kids in town choose their reading.

*Did you write yourself?*

Quite a bit. I kept diaries, but it was hard to keep those private. My brother especially would dig them up and expose them and, even though he thought it was funny, I found it humiliating and stopped writing in them after a while.

*Did you draw?*

The idea of creating art in my household was literally paint-by-numbers. I was told from the earliest age that I had no drawing talent whatsoever and that I was very clumsy. By the time I was older, I was so traumatized by the idea of using a pencil that I used to beg other people in my junior high art class to do drawings for me—I'd have the ideas, it was totally conceptual art!

*Were you taken to galleries or theaters as a child?*

No. You cannot imagine how isolated my hometown was, even though it was only thirty-five miles north of Pittsburgh, which at that point was not a stellar city. It's ironic that thirty-five miles is the distance I drive every day now to commute to Mills College, whereas we maybe got to Pittsburgh once a year as young children. I'd never set foot in a gallery until I was in college.

*Were you brought up with a degree of political awareness?*

Yes. My mother was considered practically a Communist in our town because she was a left-leaning Democrat. She was my political conscience. She didn't think of herself as a feminist, but that's what she was. She always felt less than equal in society because she didn't have a college education.

*Was a college education automatic for you?*

My parents told me very early on that they would have enough money to send only one child to college and that it would not be me because my brother would have to go. My grades were better than my brother's and I was supposedly smarter, so they said I was going to have to get myself to college—which I did. I ended up being an emancipated minor, which means by the age of seventeen I was self-supporting.

I wanted to go to Northwestern in Chicago, but it was too expensive, so I went to Temple University in Philadelphia, a very undistinguished school. I was an English literature major.

At that time they called Temple "the white cancer on the black breast of the city." It was a huge commuter school, smack in the middle of north Philadelphia, a very intense black neighborhood. The resident population at Temple was about 85 percent Jewish; I had never even eaten a bagel. I was totally lost and had no idea what was going on. I must have looked about thirteen. I came with a wardrobe of four handmade dresses and a dictionary.

My prize possession was a hairdryer. To make it worse, because I had applied late, they didn't have a dorm for me, so they shipped me a mile north to the nurses' dorm. I had never been on a city bus and had no idea what to do, so I used to walk back and forth. It was a total learning experience. I didn't do particularly well as a student, but I learned a hell of a lot about urban living. I began to think about things like tolerance and discrimination.

*How were you received?*

I was like a little koala bear that had just stepped off some alien planet. I was Exhibit A. I was never victimized. For example, I could go into a black church and be the only white face there and it didn't bother me a bit. Also, my friend, Renée, who was African American, introduced me to art. She was a photographer in the visual arts school. I began to learn not so much the objects of art but the way an artist sees the world. I learned to shift the prism a little and to visualize things differently—not step back, but step more into them. I began to think about the materiality of whatever in the moment might be captured in a photograph or a painting. It maybe validated some sense that I had that there were more complex and transformative ways of looking at things.

*Did you think you might get a camera?*

No. I saw photography as what other people did.

*Were you still writing?*

I got trounced in a creative writing class at college, so I pretty much quit.

*What were you reading?*

Milton. Restoration literature. All the grand old men of literature. Very little twentieth-century. The best classes I had were in the street; the second best were in comparative religion, where you could read more broadly.

*What were you doing to support yourself?*

Waiting tables, filing jobs, running a switchboard at the dorm, doing freshman orientation for the incoming students. Everything.

*You left college in 1967.*

Yes. Then I went into the Peace Corps and was sent to Turkey to work in an isolated orphanage on the Mediterranean Coast. I lasted there a little under a year. I came back and drifted. I had no skills. I had a couple of friends and some relatives in Boston and went there, thinking I would go into publishing because that's what English majors did, but when I looked at it, all the women were in the typing pool. While I was bumming around and waitressing, I stumbled into a place called the New England Free Press and saw all these presses with women running them. (Through my mother, I'd been around a lot of newspaper presses as a child, but that was always a male domain.) The project the New England Free Press was printing at that time was a book, *Women in Their Bodies*, a version of which still goes on, called *Our Bodies, Ourselves*. It was printed on cheap newsprint and done by a collective. The Press was also printing anti–Vietnam War literature and feminist stuff. Although I was pretty antiwar, I didn't even know what feminism was.

I wanted to work at the Press, but they didn't need any apprentices. Instead they introduced me to two men who wanted to start their own press. Five of us, three men and one other woman and I—formed a collective and started an offset press. We all pooled money and the poet Denise Levertov helped fund it. We bought some army-surplus printing equipment and moved into an abandoned warehouse and called ourselves Hovey Street Press. We needed to wire the shop and an electrician traded services—he came after hours to help us and we went out on his jobs with him as assistants. As a consequence, I learned wiring and ended up doing an entire warehouse in San Francisco when I moved there.

We had one offset press, a dark room, and a giant horizontal camera. We did posters, business cards, letterheads—whatever we could get paid to do—but we also did antiwar work and political work for the community. We published a book about George Jackson, one of the most famous political prisoners of the time, who was killed by guards in jail. Every week we were out protesting the war, tearing out the railroad tracks, taking over buildings, sleeping in tent cities in Washington, D. C.

*Were you a natural printer?*

Yes. I didn't know a ratchet from a hole in the ground, but I was willing to learn. I knew I really liked it.

*How crucial was it that there was the integration with political protest? Had you been printing railway timetables, would you still have been hooked on printing?*

I like the physical work and enjoy working the machinery up to a point, but what attracted me to printing was absolutely that integration. I was working hard physically and mentally at the same time.

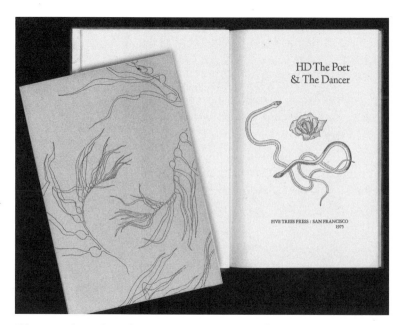

Title page and cover from *The Poet & The Dancer*,
text by HD, illustrations by Jaime Robles,
letterpress with zinc engravings and linocuts,
8¼" x 5½", 44 pages,
edition of 600, 1975

*Did you become a feminist?*

Yes. By the time I left Hovey Street Press, after two years, I was very strongly attached to a feminist agenda and came to California with a sense of wanting to pursue political feminism.

*Had you by this stage seen anything which, in retrospect, you would term a book work?*

No, definitely not.

*You came to San Francisco in 1971?*

Yes. I got a job in the offset trade right away, with a Korean small business owner who wouldn't let me run the press because he thought women's reflexes were too slow, but I did everything else. We were printing mostly business cards and I was paid a relatively decent wage for the first time in my life, but it wasn't feeding my soul. I started making the rounds of the small presses out of the phone book and one Saturday stumbled into Cranium Press, which was run by Clifford Burke. They were working with funny little metal letters and I had no idea why. I thought, "Don't these people know you can do this faster?" I guess Clifford had seen about four thousand people come in that door all starry eyed and asking to work there. I was sent immediately to the basement to clean galleys, probably his standard trick. I got violently ill because there was no ventilation and I was breathing in solvent fumes. I staggered out and was told later that Clifford said, "I guess that's the last we'll see of her," but the next Saturday I was pounding on the door at nine o'clock.

Holbrook Teter had his linotype machine in the basement and Clifford and his family lived upstairs. They were printing Gino Clays Sky and Keith Abbott and all these highly regional, hippy and beat-type poets. I kept going back and doing minor chores and that's how I met people like Jaime Robles and Cheryl Miller.

*What did you discover about the letterpress world in San Francisco at this time?*

That there was a very vibrant life there. That they were doing a lot of limited-edition publishing of original poetry. That there was a schism between the literary fine-press printers of the classics and those who were interested in small-press publishing. That there was a very strong male printing community.

*Five Trees Press was established in 1973?*

We—Jaime Robles, Cheryl Miller, Cameron Bunker, Eileen Callahan, and I—were the new girls on the block. We were all working out of Cranium. We formed Five Trees Press with the idea of publishing others rather than ourselves; the only person who was publishing her own work was Jaime. We bought a platen press and rented a storefront in Noe Valley in San Francisco. We named ourselves after the Celtic myth recorded by Robert Graves, five trees for five muses.

*Did you have a policy?*

No. I came out of the collective environment—which means you don't pee without a policy, you have a policy for everything—so I was expecting to. I think there were too many different interests among us and that if we had had a policy we would have been dead in the water. The way it worked was haphazard. Each of us would be in charge of a book and see it through production and the others would all support the endeavor. It was relatively slow paced as it was all part-time. We published small chapbooks of poetry. A lot of the distribution was me pounding on library doors. The librarian at Stanford University loved Jaime's work and immediately bought our books and gave us a show, which gave me a lot of courage.

I was very interested in publishing women's work and wanted desperately to publish an essay by Tillie Olsen, *Silences: When Women Writers Don't Write*. I courted Olsen, literally from San Francisco to Boston, trying to get her to release it to me, but she kept saying she had to edit it. Ultimately, the essay was put out by Feminist Press, which was headed by Tillie's daughter, and became an icon.

I was lucky to have the opportunity to produce a book by HD, **The Poet & the Dancer.** This manuscript was given to us by Eileen and Robert Callahan at Turtle Island, who miraculously, since HD's literary executor wasn't letting anyone publish her poetry at that point, had gotten permission to reprint it. I knew nothing about HD, and can hardly believe that I printed that as my very first "real" book.

What I really learned at Five Trees was how to think about book design. Cheryl and especially Jaime mentored me; I am amazed to this day about how patient they were with me. Even with my printing experience, I was a complete novice in the world of design and typography, and I brought to the press all my old fears about my inability to create anything. In many ways I still have that same fear, but at least I've managed to work around it with more or less success a few times now.

Eventually, because I wanted to devote more time to Five Trees, I cut my other work to part-time and sank into fairly abject poverty. We had moved to a warehouse with a women's offset press, Jungle Press, and with Clifford at Cranium. Cheryl Miller and I founded Peartree Printers, strictly for job printing, and worked from the same premises. (This was the one I wired. When the inspector came he just looked around and shook his head, but he passed us.) Most of the available printing jobs went to members of the Roxburghe Club, which was strictly male, so we were fighting our way. There hadn't been a women's letterpress job shop in San Francisco since the Women's Co-operative Printing Union folded in 1901.

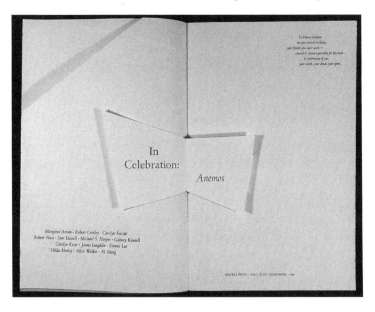

*In Celebration: Anemos,* letterpress with pop-up title page spread, text by Alice Walker, Robert Hass, Al Young, Carolyn Kizer, et al., 12"x 8¼", 38 pages, edition of 150, 1983

*You've now done a great deal of research into the history of women's involvement with printing?*

I have. I'm not sure how I got started, except that it may have been when I came across the work of Jane Grabhorn. She was such a renegade, and I was immediately attracted to her wild stuff, things like her Valentine's poem which ends, "And this has been an awful winter/Oh god it's hard to be a printer." I wrote a tribute to her, a long piece of doggerel, which I set very stiffly in, I think, Caslon. (Cheryl Miller convinced me to at least give the title, which was about fifty words long, a bit of typographic life.) In the early 80s someone also put out a book about women printers that was so astonishingly inaccurate about Five Trees that I began to wonder where this kind of information comes from. I've been doing research since that time. My recent focus has been on the nineteenth century. I got very interested in the intersection—or perhaps I should say collision—between the artisanal craft of printing and the industrial trade and how women fit into that. My research has been primarily in England, so my main findings are based there at least for now. I find myself increasingly interested in a class analysis of all this and would like to find the time to write a book on it, if not an overview of the entire history of women and print.

*By the time you formed Five Trees how much book art had you seen?*

I was not even remotely aware of the mail-art movement and the Joan Lyons type of books. The first I knew was Holbrook Teter and Michael Meyers's off-the-wall oeuvre, work that was combining a wry sense of humor with astonishing fine-line visual images. An important experience for me was my encounter with the *Gary Snyder Pine Nuts*, which I came across while buying cigarettes at a Chinese grocery store near Cranium Press. Snyder had just won the Pulitzer Prize for *Turtle Island* and what I encountered were small plastic packages of half a dozen pine nuts, stapled at the top with a large red label saying *Gary Snyder Pine Nuts, as Eaten in Turtle Island*. That was the only comment on it. Each packet had a hole punched through the label and they were all hanging on racks in the shop. I had never thought about using the medium of letterpress in that way.

A little later I was exposed to the work of Betsy Davids and Frances Butler, which I began reviewing in the magazine *Fine Print*, of which I was an early editor. I loved the vibrancy of their work and the personality of it and the fact that these were visual books taking a different perspective, pushing the envelope in a way I had not seen books doing. They also reminded me of my childhood fascination with pop-up books.

*How did Mills College come into your life?*

At Five Trees we got a call from Mills asking us to take on a student apprentice, which we did reluctantly, and out of that came the opportunity to teach there. Mills at that point was an undergraduate liberal arts college for women. It had had an operative press since 1930, the Eucalyptus Press, but by the 1960s it was moribund. It was revivified when Clifford Burke was

*Science? Imagine! A field guide to science for girls*,
illustrations by Owen Martin, letterpress, photographs,
photocopies, and hand drawings,
13½" x 9⅝", 92 pages, one of a kind,
1996

hired to come in and teach. Following Clifford was Betsy Davids and, when she left, they asked me.

I began there in 1978 and started teaching a half-unit letterpress printing class. At that point the students were mostly English majors, attracted largely for the same reason I was—you didn't have to be able to draw, but it was the chance to make something with your hands and you could work with your love of words.

*Is that also when you began Matrix Press?*

Yes, it is. There was a natural evolution of the various partnerships formed around Five Trees and Peartree Printers; both presses ended in 1978. I started Matrix Press at that time with a couple of small projects and a couple of large ones. With my assistant, Connie Thorpe, I published a small book by the poet and novelist Janet Lewis. We printed a very long and complex book called **The Animal** by a dear friend of mine, Ted Hamilton. The project was way too large for the one-car-garage studio operation we had; it just about did in both of us. I also printed **In Celebration: Anemos**, a *festschrift* for Denise Levertov's sixtieth birthday. It had a pop-up title page and was designed to be a surprise package for Denise, which it was. Writers like Alice Walker and Robert Hass contributed work. The book was edited by a group of writers and Stanford University co-published it. The third largish project I did at this time was called **Women Writing Poetry in America**. This was a broadside suite in which I paired printers with poets. I co-published this with the Center for Research on Women at Stanford as part of a large conference they put on at the university.

*Are you still printing and publishing?*

I slowed way down after the Levertov and Hamilton projects, which probably had something to do with working and raising three children. Last year I made a book called **Science? Imagine!** for an exhibition in Berkeley. I consider it a prototype for an edition I may someday produce. It's about the way my younger daughter Claire's life—she was eight then—naturally intersects with fundamental scientific activity in fields like physics and biology. I made it as a way of thinking about why girls lose ground in science as they grow older. The book includes commentary on the pathetic lack of women Nobel Prize winners (there have been eleven, if you count Marie Curie twice, since she won two Nobels).

I find myself wanting now, perhaps late in the process, to connect with my kids through the medium of the book. I'm making a tunnel book about them called **All Under Heaven**. But everything takes me years to finish now.

*You had decided early on in your career not to teach and then found yourself doing just that. Did you enjoy it?*

I loved it, probably for the reason I still do. Teaching is very selfish in a lot of ways, you have to constantly learn and change.

*Over the twenty years you've taught at Mills, the status of book art has changed within the college. How has it developed?*

When I began, I was the only faculty member with no departmental affiliation. I had no office, no colleagues, nothing. Within five years I went from teaching a half-unit class to running the first degree-granting graduate program in book arts in the U.S. There was one other program starting at about the same time out of the library school at the University of Alabama, but they had a totally different take, a sort of European apprenticeship model, where the students weren't allowed to do their own work in the first year. I believed students needed to find their own voice. I also had no interest in preserving the tradition of letterpress: I love letterpress, but not in the sense of turning it into a living museum.

Although the first and really only skill I had to offer Mills at that time was my experience as a letterpress printer, I think I brought a healthy dose of curiosity and a willingness to branch out. I began to learn about typo-graphic history and more about its practical application. I got interested in book structures and worked a lot on the issue of book arts in the gallery setting, which was where these books were finding themselves more and more. I curated an exhibition with a friend and colleague, Janice Schopfer, in 1976, which explored in a timid sort of way how books and broadsides could have a presence in the gallery. We put the books on open pedestals and incorporated poetry readings into the exhibition, among other things.

*What about the graduate program?*

When we started the graduate program at Mills we were moved from the humanities into the department of fine arts, which accepted us reluctantly. During the six years of the program the idea of what book arts meant in the book culture of the Bay Area changed enormously. The entity that called itself the book arts community became very broad based and couldn't easily define its constituency any more. The book arts of the mid-1970s began to move from the literary fine-press tradition into something that looked like visual books, but without actually getting there, without marrying itself to what was obviously a separate thread of an artists' book movement. The structural stuff was beginning to happen, but it wasn't as powerful as it became in the 1980s.

Trying to grasp at a definition for all of this was very difficult. It all ended up in a big stew and it still is, as far as I'm concerned. It's not resolved, but it was and is a very interesting struggle. When you start an institutional program under these circumstances, it is difficult to define the basis on which to choose students, particularly when students lack under-graduate book art training. Students came to the graduate program with lit-erary backgrounds or fine arts backgrounds in a variety of mediums. Some had lots of previous letterpress experience and only really wanted us to stamp their diplomas so they could say they had earned an M.A. Some were in the end more interested in doing some printing or binding than in pur-suing graduate-level work. In the beginning we didn't understand that we couldn't be all things to all people and that we needed to define our pur-pose a bit more. I don't fault us. There were no models, and the whole book arts community was tackling these questions; at least we weren't iso-lated. Mills finally killed the graduate program in 1989 for internal political reasons, and the book arts as an undergraduate curriculum—it couldn't be called a program at that point—was shifted back to the humanities, and I became an assistant professor of English.

*What does the Mills course offer now?*

When I was asked in 1989 what the book arts needed, I said that I thought we needed to be left alone for a while. I wasn't being facetious. We needed to get things in motion again without having to write a million memos and justify our every action. We initially stayed with our model of calling the classes printing and binding; I also introduced some book culture classes such as a class on the history of women's literacy. In 1994 we moved to a new studio, with lots of natural light, very high ceilings, a seminar room, and a dark room.

In the fall of 1998 we're going to be starting an entirely new set of courses, along with reinstituting the book arts minor. We're introducing a more integrated and sequential set of classes that will allow a student to develop a significant portfolio toward graduate work if she wants to. We are incorporating relief and experimental printmaking, which was also killed at Mills several years ago, and we will offer an introductory class in book arts that combines all of the fundamentals—letterpress, hand bookbinding, basic printmaking. There will be a theoretically based class, and we will continue to have classes with a historical definition.

I was very aware up until about two years ago that if I left Mills there would be no book arts program, not because I think anyone is indispensable, but because my position was not institutionalized. Although I still don't have tenure and never will, the program feels stable. It would be tough for someone at Mills to have it eliminated at this point, which is a nice feeling; there is a certain vindication in that.

*Are you at all anxious about the idea of book art being institutionalized?*

Of course. But there are trade-offs. The institutionalization inevitably will lead to a certain restriction and loss of spontaneity, a certain inability to have this massive amount of material just "out there." At the same time, it means that the work will be taken more seriously, that people will want to pursue it professionally. I'm very uptight about the idea that "you, too, can learn book arts in two hours," and the way that leads to endless overdone little structures and then a search for some content to go in them. If we're going to move away from that, the enlightened institutions are the places where it's going to happen.

*Lessonsfrom the South,*
offset, accordion fold,
single panel 10¾" x 7",
edition of 500, 1986

# susan
# king

Susan King was recorded by Cathy Courtney at the artist's studio in Los Angeles
on December 18, 1997.

Susan King, 1998

Photo: Allwyn O'Mara

• 113

*Many of your books draw on personal material, including the one on which you are working at the moment. What filtering processes do you go through?*

The book I am currently working on involves the letters my father wrote in the Second World War and, although some of them are quite boring, reading them is also highly emotional and I work in spurts. I have some of my mother's letters, too, and as she's alive I'm hesitant about reading them. With this book especially, because it is somebody else's material, I am still more careful than if it were just my own. The process of actually making a book helps me decide what's too personal or not for public view. By the time I've taken it through writing and rewriting, typing it out and putting it in manuscript form, and setting the type—by computer or by hand—it starts to transform itself, and it's clear to me as I go along what's to be left in or out.

*Are you talking about things private to yourself or some invisible standard that applies to an outsider's eye, some external editorial standard?*

Both. The way I came into books is that I started in Los Angeles, where the literary community wasn't very visible. We were experimenting and there was not the self-censorship that was going on even up in San Francisco. Up there, there were writers much more experienced than I was who I've since discovered were afraid to put anything out because it would be so heavily criticized. Because I was down here at the Woman's Building in this other context, we were just trying things out.

*Did that coming together of energies at the Woman's Building have a different impetus than we have today? Recently there's been a flood of interest in book art that is imitative, people making books because they've seen other people's, often just a pouring out of diaries without much editorial awareness.*

That's what I taught, developing ideas for books for those who have no experience and trying to get personal work transformed in some way. There is tremendous power in being able to see your words in print. That's what hooked me in the beginning. I couldn't believe I was allowed to do this, that somebody wasn't going to stop me, that I was being given tools and being encouraged. It seemed subversive in some way.

If you squelch the beginning work, you're cutting off a thing that's extremely important. I've looked into my own past and my beginnings as an artist and I've seen that I stopped doing certain things that were important to me. For example, I realized I had stopped doing photography about the time I started making books because somebody I respected said, "Oh, you don't know what you're doing." Everything got cut away and I just stopped. All these years later, I'm going back to photography.

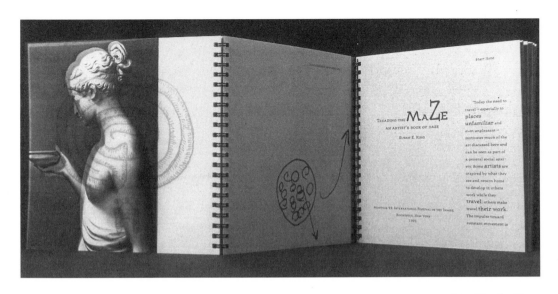

*Treading the Maze,*
offset and photocopy, double spiral binding,
single panel 7⁵⁄₁₆" x 8¼",
edition of 800, 1993

*How were you able to progress in terms
of honing your writing skills?*

It was self-correcting. I became more concerned about the quality of writing in my work and got myself to a workshop with a bunch of poets. I had to start focusing on that part. Artists' books were fairly new—nobody was paying much attention; I could do it in a natural way. It was when I was working on a piece on Georgia O'Keeffe, *Georgia* (1981), a prose poem in nine parts. It had been sitting around for years and started as an art history project when I first came to L.A., and I realized I needed a form that was not formalist art history. I figured out it could be a small finely printed book. (It is my most conservative typographic book, and I intended it that way.) I needed to know how to clean up my writing and the writing group helped. Poets take out everything—they would start throwing words off the page and everything got tightened up quickly. It was terrifying at the beginning, but I soon loved it. The group was all women, and they were really critical even if it was done in a kind way.

*Treading the Maze (1993) is a highly personal book, grounded in your experience of
being diagnosed with breast cancer. How does the telling of that story in the book differ
from the kind of communication you might have talking to a close friend?*

The book is much more artificial than storytelling. You can do a lot with the timing and pacing, so that as you turn the page the world changes or you are taken to a different place. It seems much more impersonal because it's type on a page but in fact, at its best, it can be more personal because it's considered.

*You've said elsewhere that the roots of your storytelling instincts are in growing up in the American South?*

Yes. I was born in 1947 in Lexington, Kentucky, and my father's family had been in that area for generations. I had a sense of going back in history. My grandmother, who lived in the country, would not set her clocks forward for daylight savings time, so when I went to visit her as a child not only was I going back into the rural past, but even the clocks were slowed. Lately I've seen that my storytelling comes directly from hearing my grandmother talk, sitting on the front porch of her house on what used to be a main road. She would see people coming down the road and tell stories about them and, over the years, you'd start to hear the same stories and notice how they'd change. One thing I became aware of as I started paying more attention to my writing is that I can hear how the voice sounds as I'm writing it. It helps me to know that.

My grandfather, Newton King, was also very influential for me. He had been a Methodist preacher and was the last of that generation of Southern gentlemen orators. He would give long prayers at dinner in a big voice, and for me he represented Southern language and that aspect of oral tradition. Because both of my parents' families were religious, there was a lot of focus on the church, and the Southern Methodist Church was dramatic. There was pomp and circumstance and it was theatrical and exciting. Also, I was given so much printed material that came out of the church, things that were given to kids as rewards for learning Bible verses. It was printing done between the wars that got carried over into the 1950s. I would be given highly colored pictures of Jesus put onto wood or paper, or a Bible in which certain words were printed in red, and I can remember trying to figure out how they were printed. My grandmother gave me a New Testament with my name stamped in gold on the front of it, and again I wanted to know how it was made. It was all part of the world that my grandfather inhabited. Image, music, Southern religion, and printing merged for me in a funny relationship by the time I was four or five.

Another important element in my childhood was looking at the postcard collection that had been kept by my father's family. There was a trunk full of these albums of cards from family members and I would pore over them. There weren't telephones in those days and if you went five miles out of town, you sent a postcard back. For me, it was a combination of loving the way they looked and liking the family history. And it was in a book.

*How much were you aware of the wider history of the area in which you lived?*

You could not be unaware unless you were comatose. The Civil War history was all over everything, very present. I was absorbed by it and started to be aware of how racist it was. Even the schools weren't integrated until I was a senior in high school. It seems unbelievable that it didn't happen until 1964. I was in a lily white school in the suburbs and they closed the school down to integrate it and then they bussed a few loads of black kids into our school. I went into a typing class and nobody would sit next to this black kid, so I went over and did. I was outraged.

*Your own family wasn't racist?*

My mother's family came from the North, and I think that had some influence, but I found out a couple of years ago when I was looking at the family history that my great-uncle was in the Klan. When he died in the 1930s, the Klan turned up at his funeral in robes, and there was a picture in the paper. I was horrified. But it's the truth and interesting.

*Wasn't the religious element in your upbringing oppressive?*

Both my parents had suffered growing up in strict religious communities and they did not want that to happen to me. I had a split down the line between the grandparents and my life in the 50s. We lived in a suburban house built right after the war—my class was part of the baby boom, we were the ones that busted out of the school buildings. We were in a new house that had no history of its own, but on the walls were my dad's photographs of the war. I'm much more aware at this point of how much the war was part of our lives. It certainly changed my father in a negative way, and he had a hard time adjusting when he came back. My parents were married the Christmas after Pearl Harbor, and although my father had a deferment because he was teaching school, he wanted to go to war—my mother says they didn't even discuss it. He was in the medics and his letters home are his fantasy about what life was going to be like when he got back to America and how wonderful it was going to be. Of course, it wasn't wonderful. We were living this life of normality, but underneath was the whole trauma of war.

My father's photographs were memorials to this time in his life that had been so terrible. There was one of an old German woman carrying a bundle of sticks that looked like something out of Hansel and Gretel. There was a photograph of the cathedral in Malmedy, Belgium, before it was bombed. He had taken a lot of "before and after" photographs. Over the years the photographs gradually got taken down, but my father finally gave me a box of negatives about six years ago. I wanted to go back and look at them. My father and I had had terrible arguments when Vietnam happened, and I needed to go back and figure out this other time that was so influential before I was born—and I can do that through him and see what he was looking at.

*You've had an ambivalent attitude toward your roots. Having moved away in 1971, you've recently started to go back to a base of your own there?*

Since 1996 I've moved back to Kentucky for part of the year and am living out in the country, where I have a neighbor who, although she's younger, reminds me of my grandmother. I don't have any printing presses there but I've been doing photography and writing. Eventually I hope to have more of a studio and maybe a small printing press. It's hard to believe that Los Angeles and Kentucky can exist in the same country.

I knew by the time I was eight that I would leave Kentucky. I left school at eighteen and went to the University of Kentucky between 1965 and 1971. My art education there was surprisingly good considering where I was. The sculpture school was incredibly macho and I was told I couldn't do sculpture because I wasn't strong enough, so I ended up going into ceramics, lugging around hundred-pound bags of clay and forty-pound kiln shelves. I was making ceramic sculpture and textile sculpture and fell in love with the process of ceramics, which has a lot of the same qualities as making books—you transform material, go through a lot of processes and changes. I stopped ceramics the first year I moved out to L.A., 1974, just before I started making books.

*How did you come to choose Los Angeles?*

I went to graduate school in New Mexico, a cowboy school, where they gave me an assistantship so I could afford to go. Another grad student and I ended up teaching a class on women in art. It was early in the women's art movement, 1972, and there was very little written on the subject. We scoured *Art Forum* and elsewhere and started to put together a course showing women's work, mostly in black-and-white slides. We discovered there was a grant to bring in visiting artists, and among the artists we invited was Judy Chicago, who came for three days and was recruiting people to come to the new art program, the Feminist Studio Workshop, the educational part of the Woman's Building, which was starting in California the following year. She was astonishing because she voiced so many of our unspoken desires. Everything she said was in relation to herself, and it was the first time I had ever heard any woman do that. Her work, her world, were amazing to us. She had confidence. We had hoped to change the world, but she had learned how to have a place in an imperfect world and to operate in it.

Going to L.A. was daunting—we had cable TV in the desert in New Mexico and it showed L.A. as parking lots with freeways; it looked like we were moving to hell, but the plans for the Woman's Building sounded like the graduate program we had not gotten. There was a brochure about the Woman's Building, explaining that it was inspired by the Woman's Building from the 1893 Chicago World's Fair, which had art and handicraft by women from all over the world. Our version was to be a public center for women's culture and an education program, and the thirty women on the graduate feminist art program were to be involved in a complete way. How could you not throw your whole life over and move there? I moved to California in 1973.

*What did you find when you got there?*

We got there and there was no building—it was all fantasy at that point. The group started meeting in Sheila de Bretteville's house. Sheila was a cofounder of the Woman's Building. I believe she grew up on Coney Island. She ended up going to Yale, and then to Italy, where she worked for Olivetti as a designer before she and her architect husband, Peter, came to California together to teach at Cal Arts. Cal Arts was a progressive art school that had been established by Walt Disney and was funded from his foundation.

We found Chouinard, a vacant art school, near downtown Los Angeles, founded by Mrs. Nelbert Chouinard with her First World War widow's pension. It was a perfect site for a school and cultural center. The big painting studios became galleries. It had a lovely interior courtyard. The fact that it had been built by a woman fit with our sense of uncovering women's history. We all helped prepare the building. I learned to hang sheet rock and did a tremendous amount in getting the co-op gallery, Grandview 1 & 11, ready. Afterward, I worked there as a gallery sitter.

*Were artists' books part of the activity at the Woman's Building from the start?*

Before the building existed, I remember Sheila de Bretteville talking about posters and printing and books in the meetings we had at her house, but I remember more vividly sitting on the stairs of the Woman's Building and having Helen Alm, the first director of the Women's Graphic Center at the Woman's Building, hold up an Ed Ruscha book and one by Jane Grabhorn.

Jane was a wacko printer from Northern California, who died about the time I arrived there. She was married to Robert Grabhorn, who did fine printing, but she used the Jumbo Press to poke fun at the pomposity of it all. When I first started printing letterpress, I looked at her work a lot.

*How did her work relate to Ruscha's?*

It was all presented as artists making books and it didn't matter that one might have been made in 1937 and another in 1963.

*It is often said that Ruscha plays a pivotal role in the history of artists' books. Is that how you see it?*

He hasn't been physically part of the current scene, but his books are. He's been out of sight, but he's put conceptual books and Los Angeles and a certain way of thinking on the map. But it's fascinating how many extremely interesting things were being done by the old guys at the same time. They were printing beautiful books by day and suddenly took it upon themselves to do something else that was much more involved with aspects of the book in a creative way. You don't discover that in an art context; it's in the history of Los Angeles fine printing. For instance, there is a book by Will Cheney, now in his nineties, that I found in a book fair. It's his idiosyncratic printer's memoir, with several miniature errata sheets that book people all over town started printing to correct his work. They had this game going back and forth across the city.

*You've drawn from a broad sweep of traditions in your own approach to books?*

Yes. I didn't see that many livres d'artiste when I first began to make books because I didn't have access to them, but I was reading everything I could get my hands on, including printing manuals from the 1930s for high school boys. Later, when I got more interested in letterpress, I started looking at the history of fine printing in California, because, via the libraries, I did have access to that material.

*You felt what you were doing overlapped with that tradition?*

I was taking from it. I longed to be connected with that tradition, but they wouldn't let me in. Women who came after me were let into all the printing clubs, but I was never asked. I think they had no idea what I was doing. I wasn't in a social position where I was being a nice girl and effecting a relationship with the older guys who would invite me to the printing clubs.

*Did you begin to feel part of a "book scene"?*

Right as my first book was coming out, Sheila organized a show called Women and the Printing Arts, which had work from people like Frances Butler and Joan Lyons and a lot of the San Francisco people. That was when I became aware of the activity at the Visual Studies Workshop; the kind of photographic experimentation that went on there was something we'd not seen any place else. There was a conference in San Jose in 1977, and then a big book show in Los Angeles at L.A.I.C.A. (Los Angeles Institute of Contemporary Art) in 1978. I saw books by Betsy Davids and Jim Petrillo in San Jose and met them after the L.A. show. I thought their work was incredibly wonderful.

*Your work was editioned. How did you distribute it?*

The Women's Graphic Center had a catalogue, but it was the catalogue which sold rather than the books! Judith Hoffberg was starting to list new work in *Umbrella*. My second book, **Passport** (1976), sold well in Printed Matter, and there was a bookstore in Chicago that took it too.

**Passport** *brings in the travel theme, which has been a steady element for you?*

It's a passport-size book. It started out with early childhood and how at that stage you know everything in your immediate world, every weed in the front garden, every car in your street. That section was about leaving home to go to school. It had a middle section about a trip I took to London in 1969, and it ended up with driving in L.A., the more mundane travel of everyday life, travel through dreams.

*You had a break from the Woman's Building after* **Passport***?*

The third book I did was **Pacific Legend** (1977), which was about living on the edge of the ocean, because at that point I had moved out to the beach in total burnout from arts administration. I had quit/gotten fired from my job and was completely fed up with dealing with all the politics of the Woman's Building. I swore I would never go back to the Building, but in the end I was lured back to teach a letterpress class, barely knowing what

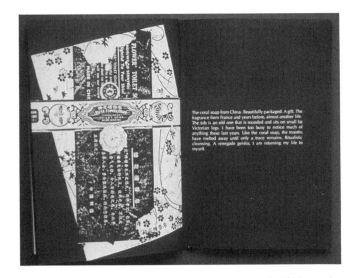

*Pacific Legend,*
diazo print, 8"x 6", 28 pages,
unlimited edition, 1977

*Women & Cars,*
offset, accordion fold, 8½" x 5⅛" unopened,
edition of 500, 1983

I was doing. Once I started, I kept wanting to buy more and more presses. We got a big Vandercook 219, and Frances Butler came down from San Francisco to teach me how to run it. Kathy Walkup came to help and I went up to San Francisco to visit Five Trees Press and received a lot of encouragement. The work that was going on in San Francisco was different from the L. A. activity; the connection had more to do with being women and trying to produce work.

*Were you making books exclusively by this stage?*

Yes. I had gotten hooked again. I began **Always a Bridesmaid Never a Bride** (1978), wanting to write a small book I could set by hand and print. It was a combination of wedding ritual and art ritual and was printed on a wedding invitation, with a double envelope, tissue paper, and little recipes, all sewn up with silk thread. It was mailed off as a wedding announcement, a collision of Southern hospitality and mail art. I ordered a wedding cake and had a publication party. It was with this piece that I became aware that my historical interest was really in cultural history. I hadn't been able to find an outlet for my interest in history at college, but in the context of a group of women talking about women's history and culture, the route I wanted to follow finally hit me.

*You had by this time begun to call yourself Paradise Press?*

It was a "serious joke." California is always called "paradise," and it seemed ridiculous to live somewhere with that name. It took me a while to get over the shock of living the reality of what we'd seen on TV in New Mexico, but after about three years, I knew I wanted to stay here.

*How long did you work at the Woman's Building?*

A good ten years. In 1983 I got a grant to go to the Women's Studio Workshop in Rosendale, New York, where I made **Women and Cars.** At that point I felt I had to make a choice between fine-press publishing and artist's books. I had been trying to do my own work between hours spent in arts administration and teaching. I was starting to do more in the field of fine printing, publishing poetry books for other people and trying to stay alive. It was a failing proposition.

*How did you evolve the structure for **Women and Cars**?*

It was based on one of Hedi Kyle's accordion books that she had done with a series of business cards glued in and that moves as it opens. I saw a show of hers in New York and invited her to L.A. to do workshops. She is wonderful at adapting traditional bindings into something changed and new, and she is exceptionally generous in giving them away to other people to use. My background is sculpture and I'm interested in books that can stand up. The structure for **Women and Cars** informed the content.

**Women and Cars** *was rooted in your Kentucky experiences, which were also the jumping-off point for* **I Spent the Summer in Paris** *(1983)?*

Before I left Kentucky, I spent one summer stuck on Boonesboro Beach by a muddy river reading a book about Paris in the 1920s and realizing how limited my choices were by comparison. I first went to Paris in the 1960s, and was startled by how much I liked it. I remember standing on one of the bridges and thinking how beautiful the light was and how much it explained the history of French painting. I began going back in the 1980s, after I got married, since my husband had access to a place to stay there.

*Paris plays an important role in* **Treading the Maze.** *How did you come to make that book?*

I had spent from April to early August 1989 in Europe and was working on a book about the experience I had had of medieval history—tapestries, windows—and even the Neolithic sites I had seen in Ireland. I had also seen a lot of manuscripts while I was away and had the idea that there would be a way of incorporating a strong image/text link in a way that reflected them. I came back with a lot of material, and all of it was swimming around in my head. It was a strange time and I never quite came out of the experience of traveling before I was diagnosed with breast cancer.

*At what point did you realize the illness was going to be part of the medieval book?*

I was desperate to have some normality in my life. I was spending all my time in doctors' offices and clung to the idea that I would feel better if I could do some work that was important. I started carrying a little notebook and also saving every slip of paper from my medical stuff. I still wasn't connecting it with the European material, and it was a couple of years before the two themes merged. If I had still been battling cancer, it would have been a very different book. I had gotten over the physical trauma but I experienced a lot of grief after the fact of the illness, even though the doctors considered me cured. I was going through that part of the process when I was starting work on the book, reliving those feelings.

*You make a very literal analogy between the red lights of the laser radiation treatment and the rose window at Chartres?*

When you go for radiation therapy, they line up your body with lasers on the wall, almost where a crucifixion might be. I was forced to look in that direction—as I put it in the book, "placed in a posture of devotion"—and I finally connected it with an image I had seen in Europe, the window at Chartres. **Treading the Maze** is full of circles—the map of the city of Paris, the rose window, the maze on the floor, the medical diagrams of breast cancer diagnosis.

Back in the studio, I was looking at a souvenir of the stone maze from the crypt gift shop at Chartres and figured that the structure of the book needed to be the maze. I realized that was what I needed to make the ideas fully converge. I then understood that the two stories were not separate, but two stories that were together. I remembered a remark Betsy Davids had made looking at some of the same sites I had seen, something about staring at preliterate sites in a pleasantly subliterate condition. In Europe, I'd been standing in front of images in silence because I'd often been alone, a singular being, and the trip through illness was a similar thing, with its own images, whether of doctors' diagrams, or lasers, or whatever. I wanted the reader to walk through these mysterious images, where the connection wasn't completely obvious, before they came to the text.

*What was the role of the Visual Studies Workshop in **Treading the Maze**?*

The Visual Studies Workshop was crucial in two ways: first, that I was invited to print a book there for the Montage International Festival of the Image, which gave me a really strict deadline—I had been dragging my feet because the experience of breast cancer was difficult to write about. Second, whenever I've worked outside my own shop, I've always responded to the equipment of the press I'm visiting—for example, the scale of **Lessons from the South** (1986) was determined by the size of the press at Nexus, where it was printed. I would never have undertaken a book with as much text and so many pages as **Treading the Maze** had I been working with my own equipment.

*What are the differences between the VSW version and the trade edition that Chronicle Books published?*

The VSW version of **Treading the Maze** has a piece of mat board in the middle, with two bindings, one on each side. The block of pages on the right has all the text, the one on the left all the images. The structure of the book as it comes from the press directs the reader to turn though all the images before reaching the text, and then turn the text block over and read back through text and image. The idea is that you walk into the maze to the middle and then read your way out again.

With the trade edition, the binding immediately changed back to the standard codex format. Chronicle had an experience of publishing a book with the same binding as the VSW edition and said they would never do it again. I could live with that. The trade edition is prettier, it's got more colors and some of the graphic design is cleaned up. The text is a lot more open, although I feel some of the typography is a little arbitrary. It's an edition of ten thousand and it's reached a wider audience than the other books because of the cancer issue. If I go to a book art conference, people come up and tell me what I should have done at Chronicle. I feel I've been to another planet and back again. What they say has no relation to reality—it's total fantasy. I tried to hold on to as much of the book as I could. I did the best I could and I'm happy.

*Do you remain as committed to book art as ever?*

No. I'm not as committed just to that. I've gotten to another place with what I'm doing. I don't quite know where I am. For a while I thought I wouldn't make books anymore, but I don't feel that way now. I'm exploring my interest in photography again and it's coming back into the book form, but I'm not quite sure how.

*Willow-herb,*
leaf prints on tracing paper,
8½" x 2½",
edition of 2, 1974

# helen
# **douglas**

This interview with Helen Douglas was recorded with Cathy Courtney
in Scotland and London on October 8, 1997 and January 21, 1998.

Photo: Telfer Stokes

*In 1975, you moved with Telfer Stokes from London to the Yarrow Valley, near the countryside in which you grew up. The landscape of the Scottish Borders plays a part in your books and is obviously deeply part of your world.*

Yes. My family has been farming in the area for generations, actually centuries. I was born in 1952 in Galashiels Cottage Hospital (about a mile from the Scottish College of Textiles, where I later taught for nineteen years) and grew up on Glendearg Farm, where my brother still lives. The fields are very green because they've all got stone drains underneath them with wonderful stone walls—dykes—built in the 1850s. None of the land is flat, it's rolling and steep, so the dykes create contours following the line of landscape. Beyond the dykes you often get more marginal land, which goes into wild countryside. There is a rattling burn on the farm, with small waterfalls and brown pools, which runs through the meadow fields, fields that were pastures for the cows and full of flowers because they were never ploughed. As children we used to guddle trout—fishing with our hands under the stones—in the burn. There is also an indigenous wood called the Fairy Dean, a magical place, mainly hazel, birch, alder, and elm. Thomas the Rhymer, the Scottish poet-seer who lived in the area, said that the Queen of the Fairies lived in there and Robert Graves (who knew my mother) related the Queen to the White Goddess and, through that, to Isis (whom I later found in Egypt); somehow, I always felt this was very important. As a child I used to feel a sense of connection with imagination in the Fairy Dean. My mother, who trained as a painter, would go there and draw the trees and, until quite recently, I've felt that it was her material. It's not long ago that I went back to the wood for the first time in years and years.

*Why did you go back?*

Because I'm interested in trees and would love to do a book with them. It's a theme that keeps recurring. I began to dance in 1992 and, recently, have been doing Authentic Movement, and I've consistently found a link with trees, particularly the hawthorns that are seen a lot in the Border landscape. They are twisted but very beautiful. I have a sense of twist within myself that I want to open up, and working with trees would do that. I would like to get the energy and twist and turn of a tree into a book and have been thinking a lot about scale and how one could embrace such a thing.

*You helped on the farm as a child?*

Yes. There was a sense of upkeep, of running things well. It was rather like in the Sienese painting by Lorenzetti, *Good and Bad Government*; bad government shows things awry, but good government is depicted by people harvesting beautiful fields, living in good houses, with everything in order. For my father it was not just good farming and produce; there was also a sense of beauty that went with it, not just outward appearance but things working well.

*Presumably there was a complementary sense of anxiety if a harvest failed or something else went wrong?*

There was a lot of anxiety inbuilt in achieving. "Stealth" was a word my father would use. "Stealth" and "knack" and "style"—knowing how to do something well as quickly as possible. "Stealth" has been an important word in my life. I was born not long after the war and although I didn't realize it at the time, I can see the effect jungle warfare had on my father (as a Chindit), coming back and then having this family. There's something pent up in him and I've often felt it was to do with the war. Stealth was about how you went about doing something. A bit like creeping up on the enemy.

*It does presuppose an enemy.*

I've thought a lot about "collaboration" and what that word means. In war, people "collaborate" with the enemy. Working with Telfer, I never thought about collaboration like that, but I've come to realize there is a way you work with the enemy from within. I don't think I've ever verbalized this to Telfer. He would be absolutely horrified if he looked the word up in a dictionary—I don't think he's ever done that.

*You first left the farm to go to boarding school in Yorkshire and, in 1969, did a foundation year at Carlisle School of Art, where among other things you learned printing and etching. Was the term "artist's book" current at that time?*

No, not at all. My awareness of book art began in about 1971, by which time I was studying art history at the University of East Anglia. I found out about it mainly through magazines, such as *Studio International* and *Art Forum*. I had an awareness of Lawrence Weiner and Richard Long, whose *From Along a Riverbank* (1971) I had been given. I knew about Jan Dibbetts and Ian Hamilton Finlay. My understanding was that books were part of current practice and I saw them in relation to conceptual art, land art, performance, and happenings rather than in relation to narrative. "Narrative" wasn't talked about at that point and had become a derogatory term.

*Were you aware of Ed Ruscha?*

I wasn't so aware of Ruscha until I went to live in Telfer Stokes's house in 1974. I first encountered the books of Dieter Rot there, too.

*Did you know about livres d'artiste?*

I knew about Matisse's *Jazz*. More than livres d'artiste, I was aware of the fine art book tradition through William Morris, and I was certainly aware of William Blake, whose work I love. Aubrey Beardsley was important because of the notion that his main form of work existed in the book, and also because he took on new forms of reprographic processes. His books weren't deluxe editions like Morris's Kelmscott Chaucer and in that way he was taking on the question of reproduction.

I was also aware of the tradition of twentieth-century Russian books, of people like Tatlin, Goncharova, Lissitzsky, and Rodchenko, and I was very interested in the crossovers in Russian art and figures such as Diaghilev. I've often argued with Clive Phillpot that the book art tradition began with those Russian books—the way they unified image and text through the textural mark and used rubber stamp lettering to spoof the livres d'artiste tradition. The multiple cheap edition really came about from that time. And in France, Sonia Delaunay was making a point of sending things through the post, so there was a sense of mail art going on even then.

*You tend to refer to "book" rather than "the book." What is the significance of that and how conscious or political a decision was it to use the term like that?*

From quite early on I felt it wasn't just a book, it was a practice in relation to book. If you can talk about "painting" and "sculpture," you should be able to talk about "book." I was wary of the idea of an artist's book because it presupposed you were an artist. Telfer and I used "book" consciously in writing because often editors tried to put "the" in front of it, but otherwise it just evolved.

*What was your own involvement with making books before you began collaborating with Telfer Stokes?*

I kept a five-year diary, starting when I was about fifteen or sixteen, but there was a point of opening in my life, during my first year at university, when the diary no longer worked for me as a form. Because I was studying art history, much of it through books, I felt there was something incredibly satisfactory about art that was in a book yet wasn't secondhand like an art book is. I could see it was a place where art itself could reside. I got notebooks to work in and started to put objects inside as well as text. I started to get a sense of an "object text" or an "embodied" text, that a visual image in a book was a way of putting my story down in some way. I made a series of books using leaves, feeling an identification with the leaf (**Beleaf, Be leaf**), that it was something to do with me. For example, for one of the leaf books made in 1972 I covered the leaf with green ink and then put it between two sheets and printed it with a roller. I did the same with the next two pages and so on, printing the same leaf but without re-inking it, so gradually the print becomes more and more faint, until there is absolutely no print on the paper. At the very end of the book, I placed the actual leaf. Another book I did was **Willow-herb** (1974), where I took the whole plant and printed a journey through it, right from the top little leaf through to the bottom leaves, printing on tracing paper. The paper leaves were finally gathered in a perspex box. **The Bread and Butter Letters** were done in this early period too. The first book I published was **Threads** in 1974. I threaded a book with black thread and took it to a printers in Galashiels and asked them to print it. It was an edition of two hundred, cost forty pounds to print offset, and I sold them for twenty-five pence.

*Without either of you fully realizing it,* **The Bread and Butter Letters** *and their "embodied text" were the beginning of your collaboration with Telfer Stokes, even though you'd barely met at the time. A similar idea occurs in his book Passage (1972), doesn't it?*

I had been printing using slices of bread on the left and right sides of pieces of paper, spreading the bread with butter—the ink—and leaving the knife print showing. The "jam" went on top and then I folded the spreads to make a sandwich. They weren't books, they were one-offs, a bit like letters. What I was doing was inspired by Richard Wollheim's discussion of "seeing" and "seeing as" in *Art and Its Objects* (Pelican 1970) and I related it to Jasper Johns and the devices he used—"Is it a target or is it brushwork"? Through Martin Attwood, a mutual friend, Telfer heard about these, although he always says that the bread and butter in his book was inspired by a student he was teaching at Corsham who had made a loaf out of pottery. When I saw *Passage,* I had the definite sense that Telfer had picked

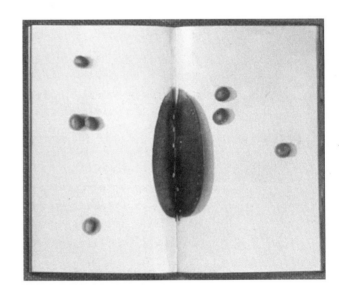

*Chinese Whispers* (with Telfer Stokes), offset, 7"x 4½", 176 pages, edition of 1,000, 1976

up on what I had done and, although I had a mixture of reactions, I felt at that time that ideas were free and was quite pleased that it had been picked up and used. I was intrigued by *Passage* because, by then, I was definitely interested in the book.

*After a period of working with performance artists at Richard Demarco's gallery in Edinburgh, you came to London in September 1974 and rented a room in Telfer's house in Kentish Town?*

Yes. I had loved *Spaces*, which Telfer published after *Passage* and *Foolscrap* (1973), and we began to talk more and more about **Loophole** (1975), the next book Telfer was going to do. We were sharing a kitchen and would talk over meals, and soon we began to work together. I suppose, because we were talking, wordplay—often an implied wordplay embodied in the images—became a continual part of making both **Loophole** and **Chinese Whispers** (1976), the next in the paperback series.

*What had you liked about* Spaces?

My approach to books up to this point had been through printing directly with objects—the slices of bread, bricks, or leaves—and the images tended to be quite flat. I was interested in the way Telfer used photography to create tonal rendering of objects and a sense of the space that the objects exist within. For example, the perspective of the New York loft that Telfer used in *Spaces* created a wonderful punch because of the way he had placed the photograph on the page. I knew it was a flat photograph sitting on top of the page and I loved the play between the surface of the page, the photograph, and beyond that, of course, the illusion of space within the photographic image. He also used the device of including hands holding the photographs within the image of the whole page, so you got an illusion of space coming out from the page in front of the book. I hadn't accessed the levels of photography he was using and it interested me very much. For example, when we came to make **Loophole**, I had no idea how we were going to achieve the scripted view of the billboard—a real one out in the street—seen through the hole in the section of brick wall we had made inside. In fact, Telfer, using the camera, was able to show me how to create the illusion back in the studio.

*How was the world of* **Loophole** *created?*

We built sets, like small film sets, which was the method Telfer had used before. The wheelbarrow pages that begin the book were the biggest set he'd ever made. We had poles marking the edges of the page and we knew where the center line was; we positioned our cameras side-by-side for left and right page (we had identical Pentaxes), so that there was a little overlap over the spine.

*You were dealing both with the illusion of reality within the sets and also with the illusion of reality within the book?*

I thought I was making a narrative that existed within the book, which is what we were doing. Telfer always talked about connecting things. I didn't know how to connect things. Although I had made a book as a child (a story about a hedgehog and a cupboard, both of which came into **Chinese Whispers**, which I did with Telfer), as an adult maker of books I tended to keep things separate. For instance, **Threads** had a single idea running through it. The idea of creating a stream of consciousness was something I wanted to be part of.

*Was Telfer the leader on **Loophole** or was the collaboration more equal?*

I certainly wanted to learn how to put a book together and there was a sense of apprenticeship. I had sharp eyes and learned fast, including how to do layout. He had control in the sense that I fed into the format he had set for his previous books, for example their shape, the edition size, and printing technique, but in another way there was an equality because I strove for the material to put into that form. I piled in ideas, particularly for the Furry Tail section, but also extending the ideas to the concept of the loop form within the book, which he had initiated. Nowadays, I work from a different place, where I gather material and look for the form that is right for the material, but then I was happy to let the material feed into the form and book format.

*What was the thinking behind the format?*

It was the size of a Penguin paperback. Telfer wanted to make a series of books that had an identity. He wanted them to be put on shelves in normal bookshops; even the cat, Woody, which appears on the spine, was like the Penguin. By the end of **Chinese Whispers** I began to question the format because of the confined space. It's small and falls short of camera film proportions.

*What qualities were you trying to avoid? The early books are very much not glossy paperbacks.*

We never retook photographs in those days; it was a kind of bravado. The camera work isn't fantastic quality, but it wasn't something to get hung up about because that sense of quality wasn't what we were after. For instance, if there were hairs on a negative—any photographer's nightmare—Telfer didn't worry too much. I used to get worked up and try and paint them out, but Telfer didn't. In **Chinese Whispers**, when we were working up in Scotland, we used water off the hill for developing film and it had grains of silt which the photographic chemicals combined with to cause pinhole marks in the film, but we still used that film. There was, too, an acceptance of the offset litho process, which wasn't as good then as it became in the 80s.

*But Telfer didn't actually add hairs or pinholes to achieve that effect?*

He didn't do that but he certainly contrived a dog-eared feeling and he quite liked a certain dirtiness. At the time we made them, we thought that group of five paperback books had a nonexpressive aesthetic. Looking back, they had a quite definite expressive aesthetic which is found in that nonexpressivity, in their uniform, all-over gray tonal mechanical look.

*Did you mean the uninformed reader to be disconcerted?*

I never mean the reader to be disconcerted. I don't want to make people feel uncomfortable, but I do want to engage people and make them realize they have to work at the books and can't skim through them and hope to get the ideas. There's a purpose in holding people back so that they realize that the book works on many different levels and can see that this is part of the aesthetic, the enjoyment of looking and making connections. In **Real Fiction** (1987), for example, encouraging people to think about the processes of finding places within the book is very much part of the story, but there is also a story to do with the inner and outer within the book too. It can still upset me now when I see people look at the books and feel bewildered. For instance, people are unnerved by my latest book, **Between the Two** (1997), because there are no words. Even at the London Artists' Book Fair I noticed a feeling of tension when people were looking at it.

*What do you think the fear of there being no words is about?*

There's an assumption that, to find ultimate expression, one needs to put things into words, but I don't know that I believe that. I've thought a lot about words. I feel rather let down by words. I use them a lot; I talk a lot; when I did my Ph.D. my whole expression became words. But I've also used words as a very good way of keeping people at a distance; I've put words between us. When I started dancing, amazing emotions and feelings welled up in me and I realized there was a whole lot of deep expression that I'd kept a blanket of words over. In the early books words played a big part in stringing the narratives together and, as two people working together, Telfer and I needed that. At first we scripted the whole book through little sketches and words we did in each other's notebooks, talking across the table before we started. By the time of **Real Fiction** it was done more in the making, constructing sets, one double spread leading to the next. Now that I'm working on my own the process is very different, much more nonverbal.

*What was the subject of your Ph.D.?*

It is about the development of texture as an aesthetic quality. I was looking at the desire for nature and naturalness constructed through the picturesque—the fascination with texture and how it was developed in architecture and within the interior. I researched one particular textile firm that began in Dundee in the 1830s and was linked to the jute industry, making rough canvas for sails and sacking. I traced how this firm moved into the decorative market with furnishings for the British and American Arts and Crafts interiors and how they created an aesthetic with rough fabric worked on the machine. I was comparing handwoven cloths with craft developed within the factory. In Britain there was more of a split between the idea of craft and the use of machines than there was in America.

*You've also printed your own fabrics?*

After **Chinese Whispers**. I had the distinct feeling of wanting to move further into a more natural imagery and it didn't seem possible to bring that into books. A lot of artists' books tend to be very urban—a quality of street collage—and, if I were to be absolutely truthful about my expression, I had to recognize that parts of me were being left out. I wanted to make something with a more direct appeal, in a sense a reaction against the conceptual procedure of stringing things together in books. The fabrics were a way of moving to a larger scale and engaging with a more sensual approach. It meant working with color, for which I felt an enormous need. Also, I became very interested in illusion at the same time as Telfer was working on *Young Masters and Misses* (1981), and that fed into the fabrics where I used photographic imagery to create a sense of depth and illusion. For instance, I did a tablecloth with a grid of squares and used photography to render cherries sitting on the cloth with their shadows printed too.

*What was Telfer's response to the fabrics?*

I think he felt betrayed that I had gone out of working with books. In 1979 he made *Back to Back*, the first book he did after we stopped working together. (My engagement with printing fabrics was also important for our engagement with printing books in a hands-on sense. Telfer got a Vander-cook proofing press at that time, and after that a Multilith Offset 1250.) He was uneasy that I used the word Weproductions for the fabrics, but I felt that they and the screens I was making were part of it. I realize decorative-ness is a quality that is important to me and it is something Telfer doesn't like and hasn't space for.

*Was the imprint Weproductions formed at the time of your collaboration on* **Loophole***?*

No, Weproductions was formed when Martin Attwood suggested to Telfer that they make a book together in 1971. They were searching for a name and Martin said, "What about Reproductions?" which Telfer misheard or replayed as Weproductions. In the end Martin was too busy to make the book and *Passage* came out with only Telfer's name under the Weproductions imprint.

**Mim** (1986) *explores ideas of texture and decoration. Was that acceptable to Telfer because it was in the context of a critique?*

Yes, that's right. Through my teaching I was looking at pattern, texture, and the importance of mimicry in both architecture and fabrics, and we decided to do a book around that. The different papers in **Mim** add another level. They are mostly cheap wallpapers and have a tacky feel, one surface imitat-ing another, so although the book was rich texturally, it was very far from using beautiful, handmade papers. **Mim** was an attempt to combine image and texts and different sorts of texts in a continuous way.

**Mim** moved us away from the idea of the constructed book form and, for some reason, we felt it was important to reestablish that and did so with **Real Fiction**. It was a time when Telfer and I were coming together cre-atively in a very happy way and there was a sense of familiarity with the material and that we were adding another twist to it. The sets for **Real Fiction** were much smaller than for **Loophole** or **Chinese Whispers** and, unlike those two, the ideas of the book developed in the process of constructing it. In this book the ideas of construction and of creating a space within the book feed into the text that itself is floating in its own constructed space, throw-ing shadows against the page. We created a double spread of card and liter-ally strung up pieces of type on film at angles and lit it so that the words cast shadows on the card behind. It created an integrity between the image and the text. **Real Fiction** was an important book for me. I felt I had gained real control over the concepts that we were dealing with in the earlier books and had also refound an expressive narrative place within book. Our collaboration on **Real Fiction** was very equal and distinct and, afterward, we decided amicably to work separately, that Telfer would work on his next books—*Ajar* and *Desire*—alone and I on my Ph.D.

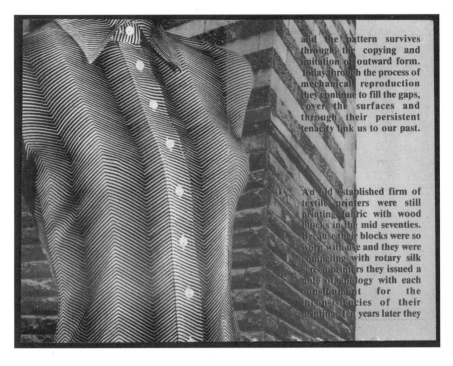

and the pattern survives through the copying and imitation of outward form. Today through the process of mechanical reproduction they continue to fill the gaps, cover the surfaces and through their persistent tenacity link us to our past.

An old established firm of textile printers were still printing fabric with wood blocks in the mid seventies. Because their blocks were so worn with use and they were competing with rotary silk screen printers they issued a note of apology with each consignment for the inconsistencies of their printing. Ten years later they

*Mim* (with Telfer Stokes),
offset, 7½" x 5", 120 pages,
edition of 1,000, 1986

*Although you were still collaborating on the books after your son, Laurie, was born in 1983, you've said you felt this was a period when your public identity with them was less apparent.*

I was a very organized mother and had definite routines so that I could carry on working. I managed to keep my lecturing job at the textile college as well as work on the books, but there wasn't time for anything else. I wanted to be with Laurie and to bring him up, so I wasn't able to be out and about talking about the books and representing them with Telfer at book fairs or wherever. Part of making books is looking at them after they are made and interpreting them, and in this period Telfer would do the looking and interpreting. In that way, I didn't "take the book back in" after

I'd made it, which is an important part of the process in finding the path to the next piece of work.

*Yarrow Cooks* (1992) *to an extent united your life with Laurie and as a bookmaker?*

We made that book with Laurie's school as part of what was expected of parents, fund-raising and being part of a community. **Yarrow Cooks** is intentionally domestic; it was very clearly a cookery book, with recipes contributed by other mothers and drawings by the schoolchildren, but it's a visual book more than an illustrated book. Working with children on the drawings enabled me to come back to an earlier enjoyment that I'd had myself as a child and it fed directly into **Water on the Border** (1994), which developed the graphic linear quality.

*How did **Water on the Border** come about?*

**Water on the Border** was always about the sense of a continuous line flowing through landscape. The idea came on a clear, snowy day when I was up in the wood and looked down at the Yarrow River below, silvery and sparkling. I noticed how Chinese the trees looked, dark against the light, and that

*Water on the Border* (with Telfer Stokes),
offset, 7½" x 5⅘", 124 pages,
edition of 600, 1994

there was a sense of flow in their shapes, too. It occurred to me that, using the theme of water, we could work with children in China and Scotland and that it would be a wonderful way of bringing the two cultures together. The Chinese feeling for the essence of flow in T'ai Chi and in their poetry and painting was a crucial part of the development of the book. Another important aspect was the inclusion of Chinese drinking poems both in their original form and in Old Scots, translated by Brian Holton.

I had been photographing water for about fifteen years and thought the children could draw it, but actually it was almost an impossibility for them; whereas for **Yarrow Cooks** they animated the utensils, their drawings of water became unanimated. In Scotland, because we were looking at water on the border—the margin between land and water—it was easier to give the children the theme of the riverbank, and we would just sit down beside the Yarrow River and find things to draw. In China we based ourselves at the Zhejiang Academy of Fine Art at Hangzhou, because of its famous lake, and worked with children there.

Along with the drawings, I was photographing the water. In China I wanted to trace the surface of the lake and its reflections, using the camera in a more tactile, sensory way rather than trying to freeze an image. Unlike the burns and waterfalls in Scotland, the lake was very languid, and it was we who became the movers as we cycled on the causeway. The sides of the causeway are planted with trees and, as we moved along on our bikes, the trees became markers, metering the water and suggesting a sense of flow. I began to understand that to express flow, one has to be able to meter it. That led to the device in **Water on the Border** where we placed tramlines of black film about an inch from the top and bottom of each page and downward lines to create square or rectangular shapes within the wider page, an echo of the metering we had sensed on the causeway. Where the photographs and drawings were different shapes, we allowed them to cross from one square into the next. The device was also linked to Chinese books, where the image is often contained by framing lines and wraps around the edge of a page. With **Water on the Border** we broke away from the idea of left-hand and right-hand pages completely.

*After collaborating with Telfer on* **Water on the Border**, *you produced* **Between the Two** *alone?*

I was at a crossroads. I had my Ph.D. to finish, which I did by February 1997, but I also knew that I wanted to go on making books that would allow me to develop the expressive way of working and living that I had found. I wrote every day in my notebook for about half an hour, using a pencil, not wanting to make the distinction between writing and drawing. From 1994 to 1997 I carried on working with the camera, gathering material. (I remember Ron King talking at the Tate about being a hunter, but I'm a gatherer, drawing in material.) I knew what **Between the Two** was going to be about: the sense of opening in a more sensuous way which I had begun to feel with my body through dance and massage. Authentic Movement has a lot to do with trusting and following your body impulse, the sense that one thing leads to another, and that was how I had begun to use the camera and wanted to put my book together. I felt that I had come through the

*Between the Two*,
offset, 5¼"x 5¼", 168 pages,
edition of 1,000, 1997

very center of my life. A large element in the earlier books was a sense of intellectual play linked with a conceptual period in art practice. At the time I made them I don't think I would have been able to express what I now can, because I had, for good reason, cut so much off within myself. In that sense **Between the Two** is an autobiographical book.

**Between the Two** is entirely black and white and all the images are natural ones, plants, insects, and a butterfly, photographed in Scotland and in Italy. There is what I call "the white section," snow white pages worked with fine black lines that are developed from photographic images and appear to be almost like drawings of grasses and plants on the page. The middle section is tonal and dreamy, and then there's a third section worked as white line emerging out of black, a kind of arabesque dance of interlacing plants as they loop over pages leading to the flowering within the book.

*Over the past few years, you and Telfer have found a way of staying together as partners in Weproductions while working independently?*

In 1994 we were asked to write for the catalogue of an exhibition at the Minories in Colchester. It was an important turning point. I was analyzing how and why I made books and I began to separate myself and to realize I had come to books in a slightly different way from Telfer. We wrote separately for the Minories and later, in *JAB*, used the phrase "the two I's in We," that is to say that there are two separate beings in Weproductions. Claiming my separate part in the books, both privately and publicly, and standing firm on this made it possible for me to find and expand my own area of bookmaking. Weproductions is our imprint. It still stands for us in partnership in our shared commitment to making books.

*Through Light and the*
*Alphabet,*
letterpress, 13"x 13",
24 pages, edition of 50,
1986

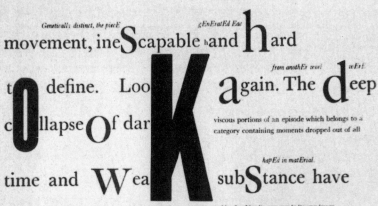

# johanna
# drucker

Johanna Drucker was interviewed by Cathy Courtney at Camberwell College of Arts, London, on July 9, 1997. In the autumn of 1997, Johanna Drucker became professor of art history and director of graduate studies in art history at Purchase College, State University of New York.

Johanna Drucker, 1998

Photo: Brad Freeman

• **143**

*You were taught by Betsy Davids at California College of Arts and Crafts. Are you from California?*

No. I was born in 1952 in Philadelphia, Pennsylvania, where I grew up. My mother was a scientist and my father is a commercial cartoonist. They wanted me to be a scientist so, after college, I went to the University of Rochester for a year to study science, but what I really wanted to be was a writer. I decided to go to art school because I knew I had enough graphic ability to learn to do illustration or wallpaper design and I figured that I could make a living and be a writer. Since I hadn't studied graphic art as a high school student, I didn't have a portfolio, and California College of Arts and Crafts (CCAC) was the only art college in the country at the time that you could get into without one. I went there in 1970. That's how I met Betsy.

*Did you find it easy to adjust to life in California?*

No, I couldn't speak the vernacular. I found it deeply disturbing. California is completely different from the East Coast and was very much a flower-child, hippy environment in 1970, whereas Philadelphia is basically a Quaker city and very proper—it feels Puritan and there is a sense of repression. I was at an age when I thought wearing a bun and speaking elaborate English sentences with many compound clauses and qualifying terms was normal. I had very little social contact as a teenager and was withdrawn and intellectual, so to encounter Californians my own age was like meeting a different species. It was Betsy who helped me move through my language into some point of social connection. She was an ideal figure to me. She was thirteen years older than I was, a beautiful, Pre-Raphaelite–looking young poetess.

*If your spoken sentence construction at this time was complex, was your writing the same?*

My writing was extremely dense. It still is. The first manuscript I gave Betsy was about dreams. She said that the way it was written interested her and that was terrific affirmation for me that I was, indeed, a writer.

*What was the content of your course at CCAC?*

It was very broad. The first year was a foundation course, so I was doing color theory, drawing, painting, sculpture, printing, printmaking. I only stayed two and a half years while I got my degree and in that time I moved pretty quickly into printing and printmaking as my focus. When I first knew her, Betsy was teaching creative writing and literature but it was also the time when she acquired a printing press, an extremely fortuitous moment for me.

*Did you know what an artist's book was at this time?*

No. I was not aware of the term until the 1980s.

*Did you see the creative writing and printmaking that you were doing as separate activities?*

I didn't see them as separate, but what I had in front of me as a model was the small presses and independent people who were doing poetry books or literary books in the Bay Area as an alternative publishing mode. There was an established tradition there and a huge amount of interest in printing. I didn't know the work of the people involved but I knew their names. In retrospect, I see artists' books drawing on a whole number of traditions, and one of those is independent publishing and literary publishing and the fine-print tradition, which are not always distinct.

There was a sense of a publishing environment, but I didn't know how it worked. Then there were younger people involved—Clifford Burke, the women involved at Five Trees Press. Around March 1975, Alastair Johnston and Frances Butler got the Poltroon Press going and that's when I started working for West Coast Print Center. By then there had started to be a scene of people making things and a critical mass.

*When you first see an artist's book, does your eye go to the text or to the images?*

My critical judgment comes immediately into play with language. If I find the language inane without it being deliberately inane, then I lose interest quickly. I probably have more patience with inane images than with inane language. In some ways I'm a language person, but images are always so seductive. I don't see as well as I read. One of the interesting things about being involved in a domestic way with another artist, Brad Freeman, is that it makes me aware of how much more visually literate he is than I am. He sees things immediately, whereas I'll sometimes just have missed the point of an image completely.

*When did you make your first book?*

The first was while I was at the University of Rochester, where I did one for a boy I had a crush on. It looked rather like a Beatrix Potter book and was handmade, watercolored, and bound, and I made two copies. The next book I made was in Betsy's class. **Dark, the Bat-Elf Banquets the Pupae** (1972) had little stone lithographs of pupae characters, like nasty, sexualized children. It's a kind of *Goblin Market* meets the *Water Babies*. I hand cut the paper and bound it in red velvet. There were thirteen copies.

*Were you beginning to think in terms of the architecture of the book?*

I thought in terms of the architecture of the page. I understood the page for a long time before I understood the book. I knew how to make an arrangement on the page of typographic and visual elements to make a structure where these components played with one another and where there was a space and sense of interaction and a sense of color. I didn't understand the architecture of the book or the notion of the whole. I didn't understand the notion of sequence, finitude, the turning of the page, any of those things. You can get a gestalt on a page, but to get a gestalt on a book takes a lot more.

*What do you feel about **Dark, the Bat-Elf** now?*

At the time I loved it. I was so happy it was a real book. Now I see it's juvenilia, silly. It's this weird voice with its own sense of self. I still have two or three copies. One is in the Getty because they wanted to buy as full a collection as they could. There's a whole bunch of juvenilia from those years which, in its own terms, is fine. It's just not what I do now.

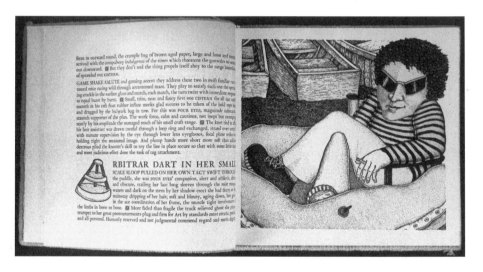

*As No Storm or the Any Port Party* (with Rebis Press), letterpress with photo-engraved plates, 8" x 10", 32 pages, edition of 320, 1975

*Did you already know that the book form was going to be the path for you?*

Yes, I was hooked immediately. After CCAC, I lived in the mountains in Santa Cruz for two years and didn't have access to a printing press, so I made one-of-a-kind books. The advantage of that period was that I was hand drawing the lettering and spent time looking at type and, in some cases, trying to imitate type in the drawing process. **Light and the Pork Pie**

(1974) is an example of one of the books from this period. I was writing things that had to do with direct observation and lived experience, but I edited them into a poetic fantasy language. At a recent literary conference in Edmonton, a graduate student from Stanford who's been writing about my work made the observation that there's no individual subject in the works, that they tend to have a diffuse subject voice. I'd never thought about it—it's like one's own blind spot—but he was absolutely right. The fantasy voice was a screen, a way of diffusing. It was also a way of constructing, it had to do with art and artifice.

I was also working on a couple of novels in Santa Cruz. I've been writing fiction ever since I was a small child. The year I was twelve I wrote five novels, one of which had four hundred pages, a great many characters, elaborate plots, and so forth. It was handwritten.

*What is the relationship between the novels and book art?*

I don't see them relating to book art. I would never self-publish long fictional works. They're meant to be published in a very different format and in a standard way. In a longer, literary prose text, the things I'm interested in have more to do with storytelling than the materiality of the text or its visuality, whereas with book art I want to explore certain possibilities of the book format and language format. One of the projects I've been working on recently plays with the intersection between the novel form and book art, but the question then is who would publish it and who would read it? I don't know if there is an audience for that.

*Where do you feel one-of-a-kind books fit in?*

Although it's a point of contention among book artists, I don't have a strong feeling about it. As a maker, I think art shouldn't have any rules and that if a one-of-a-kind book is the way to make the thing you want to make, you should do it. I've often made them, particularly when I haven't had access to a press or when I want to make a gift for somebody. When I went to do **The Century of Artists' Books**, however, I didn't write about them because it was so difficult to get access to them and form a sense of what the field was. I would have had to simply pick the ones I happened to know and I felt more comfortable writing on editioned works because I felt they were more representative of certain areas of activity.

*What brought you down from the Santa Cruz mountains?*

Betsy had gotten a grant from the NEA to do a series of books and had put me down as one of the people she would like to work with. I wrote the text for what became **As No Storm or the Any Port Party** in Santa Cruz in the spring of 1975 and we then spent a summer together working in her garage every day, extremely hard. The experience was terrific. I learned a huge amount from Betsy because she is a very careful craftsperson, so I was able to perceive the production values she attended to that I wasn't even aware of. Compared to Betsy, I'm a little bit sloppy because I always want to see the book and get it done and that tends to make me hasty. I have a wider tolerance for error than Betsy. If the production levels are such that it looks consistent and makes the effect I want, I'm satisfied. This is definitely self-criticism. For me, "good enough" was sufficient, whereas to Betsy it's really, "How good can it be?" Everyone has to learn their own aesthetic and their own ways. For example, I am constitutionally ill-suited to achieve tight registration—therefore, I don't construct things that need it.

**As No Storm or the Any Port Party** is a pun on "a snowstorm" and the expression "any port in a storm." Again, it was taking something lived and transforming it through language into something coded. It was about a New Year's party I went to that was in an outdoor swimming pool in Philadelphia—there was a huge snowstorm, and it was a disaster as a party. The book has canvas covers and is bound Japanese style with grommets and rope. It is printed on Rives, which we damped, and it measures about eight by ten inches. The monotype pages are single sheets, printed on both sides, and the images were printed on long sheets, folded so there was no show through. The images were from pen-and-ink stipple drawings that I had done and were put on engraved plates. It was an edition of 320 and published under Betsy's imprint, Rebis Press.

I was apprenticed to Betsy and Jim Petrillo, who was her partner in the press at that point, and I learned a lot about the profession of being an artist from them. I did secretarial work for a bit after **As No Storm** was done and it was invaluable experience. We did circulars and put mailing lists together—Rebis did a lot of their own distribution. That was a time when there was grant money—which there isn't anymore—and I learned about grant proposals and how to promote yourself and to approach galleries. I also learned how to deal with people who sent in proposals if you had a press name.

*Were you involved with the Woman's Building in Los Angeles?*

No. I wasn't involved with that and I didn't know much about that work until much later.

*This was the time you began to work at the West Coast Print Center?*

Yes. That was a printing facility, established in 1975 under the aegis of the NEA, whose mission was to provide low-cost printing to the literary community, primarily in the Bay Area, but not exclusively linked to it. My job was as the staff typesetter, which meant I typeset everything that came across the threshold and got exposed to a wide range of literature and people. That was a terrific education and lasted two years, during which I made friends with a whole community of literary people. Within the group there were many different points of view about what constituted a contemporary poetic. I began to perceive that you didn't just write but that you were supposed to understand why and how you were writing. I wasn't capable of doing that at that point, but I began to understand it. It became clear to me that the kind of fiction I wanted to write was no longer seen as acceptable within a critical framework. I was deeply disappointed. Nineteenth-century romantic novels had been my model up until then; I thought that form was what I was destined to write.

I made a bunch of books in this period. One was **Twenty-Six '76**, an alphabet travel book of private letters to Jim Petrillo and Betsy based on a trip we took to Los Angeles, where we were doing performances. Another was **From A to Z**, which I consider a maniac monument to juvenilia. I had forty-eight drawers of type and I used every piece once and only once to make a book in which everything made sense. It was a nasty, mean-spirited book about all the people I had met in the poetry world, parodying their style, giving them a typeface that suited their literary mode, and talking about the gossips, the intersections, the social interactions, the politicking and self-importance of these people. I finished the book a few hours before I left for two years in Europe. I thought everyone would be furious but, in fact, I had changed people enough so that no one recognized themselves.

*Did you continue to make books in Europe?*

I printed two in Amsterdam. **The Experience of the Medium** (1978) was about printing and minimalism and language. It was a big portfolio and I sold it and was able to live on it for a bit, which inspired me to think I could make a living as an artist. Then there was a poetry book. When I returned to California I printed a couple more little projects before working on a big book, **Against Fiction**, which I printed in 1984. It had been written over a period of five or six years beginning in the late 1970s and was about the conflicts I had had in recognizing that the form of fiction I had been intending to write was regarded as totally outmoded. Speaking in 1997, I feel there's a place for that fiction again.

*The Word Made Flesh*,
letterpress,
10½"x 12½", 24 pages,
edition of 50, 1988

*You also began graduate studies at Berkeley in 1980?*

Yes, at that point I became much more interested in theory problems in relationship to language. **Through Light and the Alphabet** was printed in the summer of 1986, after I had finished my Ph.D. Like **The Word Made Flesh**, printed three years later in 1989, it was informed by critical and theoretical discussion of language as material and of the visual materiality of the text. This was also the subject of my dissertation so that at that point the creative projects and scholarly projects were feeding from one another in a happy synthesis. The two letterpress books, **Through Light** and **WMF**, are counterpoint works. In the first, which I think of as a typographic fugue, a new typographic element is introduced on each successive page while all the existing elements are maintained. The linear format of the text becomes split, and the typographic complexity allows alternative paths to be formed in the process of reading, undermining any single linear path. In **WMF**, there are visual chunks of type that almost obstruct reading or meaning for the viewer, forcing attention onto the physical, visual quality of the language.

I was interested in learning about the history of printing and the book, and thought that if I could combine the studio expertise I had with a critical and historical perspective I could be an effective teacher of practice with a historical dimension. In the course of that study, I became initiated into critical theory, into semiotics, structuralism, psychoanalysis, fields I had never understood before. I became very excited about them and their possibilities. It led me to finishing a Ph.D. in Ecriture—an ad hoc interdisciplinary Ph.D. I was looking at writing as a visual form in terms of historical, critical, and theoretical perspectives. I did no creative work as part of that degree, it was all academic, but I continued to teach studio practice as part of my student teaching.

When I finished at Berkeley, I got a wonderful job at the University of Texas at Dallas, where I taught art practice, art history, and art theory. It was an ideal job, but Dallas wasn't an ideal environment. I realized that a degree in Ecriture wasn't terribly viable and that if I wanted to have mobility, I needed to be more mainstream. Twentieth-century art history became my focus. That's how I moved into writing critically about the visual arts and, eventually, into writing around artists' books.

*When did you first start writing about book art?*

My dissertation addresses aspects of book art because all four of the people I focus on—Guillaume Apollinaire, Filippo Marinetti, Tristan Tzara, and Ilia Zdanevich—to some extent address the question of the book. But I didn't pick up the issue of the book directly within that work, I concentrated more on the page. Partly through the work I did on Zdanevich, I began to realize that the book is a much more complex and larger structure than a page.

*Is there a conflict for you in being a critic of artists' books as well as a book artist yourself?*

The only time there is a conflict is when I'm giving public lectures and the question then is, Does one speak about one's own work or only about other people's? My tendency has been not to include my own work when I'm giving a critical presentation. Otherwise, because I was a maker before I was a critic, it gives me the advantage of being able to sense how a book's production was achieved and what the relationship of production to conception is. That doesn't mean they have to be integrated—sometimes discrepancies are as interesting as integration and synthesis.

*Your critical thinking underlies the artists' books you have done over the past decade?*

All of my books have certain things in common, no matter how they are produced. I have been concerned with format decisions—the arrangement of text on the page and through the book—as a way to structure meaning in a poetic text or narrative in a fictional one. I have been interested in exploring the ways the visual representation of language can be manipulated in a print format without losing legibility and while serving to expand the possibilities of nonlinear readings. My writing is experimental in nature and concerned with abstract or critical issues: text as image, memory and history, subjectivity and narrative, and feminist themes. For instance, **Simulant Portrait** (1990), **History of the/myWor(l)d** (1989), **Otherspace** (1992), and **Narratology** (1994) are all engaged with the tropes of genre fiction in relation to women's literature and lived experience. By contrast, **The Word Made Flesh** (1989), **Through Light and the Alphabet** (1986), and **Prove Before Laying** (1997) are more clearly focused on the manipulation of visual conventions and the critical or theoretical implications of this activity.

*How did you come to write* **The Century of Artists' Books?**

I wouldn't have done so had it not been for Brad Freeman and Steve Clay, both of whom encouraged me to do it. Steve is the founder and publisher of Granary Books and Brad is an offset printer and book artist who has been making books for about fifteen years. He was at the Visual Studies Workshop for a while as their printer and production consultant and then he was at Pyramid Atlantic, which is where I met him. Betsy had helped me facilitate a project that was printed at Pyramid Atlantic, **Simulant Portrait**.

**The Century of Artists' Books** was partly a response to Riva Castleman's exhibition, *A Century of Artists' Books*, at the Museum of Modern Art in New York. It was an important event for artists' books in that it put them in a mainstream venue and said they were works to be taken seriously in the context of twentieth-century art. However, to the perception of many people active in the artists' book community, it seemed to leave out precisely what we would call artists' books in the broadest sense. It focused much more on the tradition of livres d'artiste. I don't care if someone wants to look at livres d'artiste, but I do care if they're called artists' books. Also, her title was *a* century and I felt that the twentieth was *the* century of artists' books.

*Did Riva Castleman respond?*

I don't suppose she knows of our existence.

*What do you see as the dividing line between livres d'artiste and artists' books?*

Putting it crudely, the livre d'artiste, in spite of providing conceptual and aesthetic opportunities to experiment for many of the artists and writers who worked in that genre, was nonetheless largely publisher driven and the production values for those works are within certain set parameters that are clearly defined. Within the realm of artists' books there is a wider range of possible production values and the work is much more artist initiated and driven. The books tend to be more wide-ranging in terms of the degree of self-conscious investigation of the book form—ranging from the most usable, ordinary banal object to examples that ask the question, "How sculptural can a book be?" The artists' book seems to be about experimentation, breaking boundaries.

*Would you agree that there are certain books being produced now that have a strong relationship to livres d'artiste but are also very sensitive to the book form and have, perhaps, interwoven the two pretty firmly?*

*Simulant Portrait,*
offset, 8¾" x 7¼", 48 pages,
edition of 350, 1990

That happens sometimes at its most successful. It would be foolish to exclude the livres d'artiste tradition or the idea of high production values, but one could go out on a limb and say that it tends to be that the higher the production values, the lower the conceptual values. If I have to make a choice, I'm less interested in something that has perfect production values but is only representing something I've seen before than in something imaginative with an interesting conceptual premise, even if it isn't terribly well achieved in production terms. A livre d'artiste tends to have either an interesting text or an interesting image but it's a little bit the framing problem: you can take the worst drawing in the world and put it in a terrific frame and it will look important. I'm afraid that happens with book production as well.

*If a book was beautifully produced on fine paper but also interesting conceptually, would you then let it back into the category of artists' book rather than livre d'artiste?*

I would let it back into the artists' book world if it were interesting conceptually.

*What did you seek to cover in* **The Century of Artists' Books***?*

My intention was to establish a series of conceptual frameworks within which the specificity of the book form—historical, critical, and aesthetic—could begin to be discussed with a critical meta-language that arises from the book form itself. My sense was that I should look at a lot of books and extract from the field the ways in which people had thought about the book and let that give rise to the conceptual categories rather than start with the categories and find books to fill them.

*Were there revelations?*

I found books I'd never seen that I adored, such as *In the Crack of the Dawn* by Lawrence Weiner and Matt Mullican. I didn't know Gary Richman's work well and I loved that; it's super-smart and interesting. One way that I discovered new work was through looking at all the online entries in the New York Public Library. There were some surprises. I didn't know the work of Stephen Willats and I really liked it. I didn't know Telfer Stokes and Helen Douglas's books well, but Brad Freeman turned me on to them. I drew a lot on Brad's expertise and also on the artists' book dealer Tony Zwicker, who was a terrific asset, generous with her knowledge and a good, strict disciplinarian.

*What were the reactions to the book?*

The reaction of artists depended on whether they were in the book or left out. People are doing a lot of hard work and they would like to be recognized and were understandably piqued if they weren't. But I couldn't write about everyone who was working in the field. There was also some confusion, which was partly my fault because the title makes it sound like more of a survey than it is. I hope it will give rise to other writing that will pick up on the issues it raises.

*What do you feel about the level of critical discourse on book art in America?*

It's sparse. There's so little—one could put together a list in about five minutes that would cover the field. There's no other art field in the twentieth century where this is so, except maybe video. It's similar to video in that it's had difficulty finding its niche. Nancy Princenthal's work has been steady and responsible, an insightful contribution to the field. Joan Lyons's *Artists' Books: A Critical Anthology and Sourcebook* had pieces by varied people and continues to be useful. Buzz Spector, Renée Riese Hubert, and Judith Hoffberg have been writing about artists' books also and helping the critical discussion.

*Is there a danger that the books will become overloaded by critical discourse?*

That's always a problem. It can become a means of making false class structures in academic institutions; there are the people who have crit speak and the people who don't.

*Where do you want things to go, in terms of critical developments?*

I don't so much want things to go in one place or another. I'm not dogmatic about what people make. I would like for there to be enough critical discussion for work which is sculptural and object work to be called that and not lumped in with artists' books. And for work that is really about finely produced editions to be able to be about that, and work that's conceptually based to be about that, and so forth. Just as we wouldn't talk about painting—we talk about the traditions of abstraction, figuration, minimalism, and so on—I would like the book field to be able to differentiate between the areas.

*Since working at the University of Texas, you've had experience of a variety*
*of academic institutions?*

I taught history of twentieth-century art at Columbia, in New York, for five years. I'm now teaching contemporary art history and theory in the department of the history of art at Yale, a post I took up three years ago. I'm an associate professor.

*You've also been involved with the periodical JAB. How did that come about?*

I'm on the editorial board and have produced a fair amount of writing for the journal, but it's Brad Freeman's project. He is the publisher and editor. He felt strongly that there was a need for an arena for serious critical debate. The acronym *JAB* was chosen to express its editorial policy, which is a little bit "gloves off," spiky and aggressive. From its conception we've encouraged controversy and diverse points of view. Brad has not been hesitant to publish points of view that are completely in opposition to his or mine. He and I don't see the world exactly the same way either, although we're probably closer than not.

We've been working hard to make it international. We've brought in people like Simon Cutts and Erica van Horn, Telfer Stokes, Helen Douglas, and the poets Steve McCaffery and Darren Werschler-Henry. In the next issue I have translated a piece by Didier Mathieu in France. We're hoping for a report from Australia—there seems to be a lot going on there. There have been seven issues so far. It was deliberately contentious and it's been successful in that. For instance, one of the pieces I wrote was a description of several conferences I'd been to. The first version was descriptive and

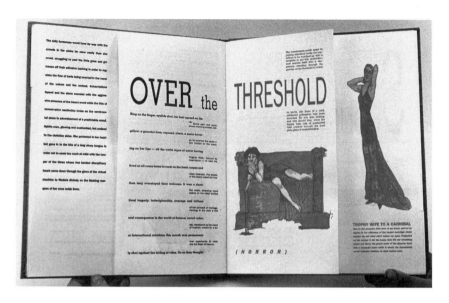

*Narratology,*
letterpress from polymer plates with watercolor,
10"x 12", 40 pages,
edition of 70, 1994

mild. Brad and someone else said, "punch it up." I did and, of course, got into all kinds of trouble.

*How did you feel about that?*

It was useful for the field. But I lost sleep over it and didn't enjoy it. It's not my general mode. I have a mouth, but I tend to be more conciliatory in general and don't see myself as a conflict figure. To realize that I had done these things in print which had indeed generated conflict that would have real-life consequences was a little bit uncomfortable.

*You've now been making book art for twenty-five years and have produced about thirty editioned works. What are your concerns now?*

The most recent book was **Narratology**, which is about the intersection of debates about the notion of lived experience versus narrative fantasy in women's genre fiction. It picks up some of the issues of **Simulant**, which was about the making of a female subject through historical discourse. **Narratology** reflects a moment in feminist critical debate in America in the early 90s when the concept "lived experience" was being raised as a banner against theoretical language. There was a sense that the lived was authentic and the theoretical was somehow too abstract. I started to analyze my own experience in those terms and realized that my sense of the lived was already completely permeated with all the ideas about the narrative that had come from genre and traditional fiction; trying to peel the two apart was almost impossible. The book is about that intersection and integration.

**Simulant** was the first book I did on a computer and I wanted it to look generic, as if it had been done on a Mac, whereas **Narratology** was an opportunity to take advantage of what digital technology could bring to letterpress printing without looking digital. I wanted to preserve the letterpress aesthetic, which for me means a discrete use of each space of the page rather than the densely layered feel of photographic digital imagery. The book was designed and set in Quark, output as film, turned into polymer plates, printed letterpress, and hand finished with watercolor.

*Why letterpress?*

I chose to print my books letterpress because it was affordable to me—and because it was a simple technology that I could learn and use without needing access to expensive equipment or highly technical skills. I didn't have a photography background, for instance, so I didn't gravitate toward offset printing, although I did have exposure to it during my years (1975–77) at the West Coast Print Center. Letterpress books sell in a higher-end market than offset books—even though they often cost less to produce in terms of materials, equipment, binding, and even labor. It's always difficult for an artist to get paid for their labor, especially in a field as plagued by distribution and identity problems as artists' books. No one quite knows what market they should be in, whether they should sell in bookstores or galleries, be in libraries, special collections, museums, or should circulate in the world at large. All of my books have recovered the costs of their production through sales, except for the offset book Brad and I did with Nexus Press, which was a "subsidized" project. Nexus provided low-cost printing services and we provided film and paper and paid for the binding, with Brad putting in most of the 1,200 hours in prepress digital work we did on the project. We'll never make back the costs of that project, which was largely supported by sales of my letterpress books.

*Do you still write fiction?*

All the time. I've sent some out to agents recently. I still intend to pursue that.

From the series
*My Father's Coat,*
etching, 20"x 14", 1996

# paul
# coldwell

Paul Coldwell was interviewed by Cathy Courtney at Camberwell College of Arts,
London, during 1997.

Paul Coldwell, 1998

Photo: Mike Beddington

**Freud's Coat** (1996) *was your first book. It was triggered by the Art of the Book research project at Camberwell College of Arts, where you teach, but the book is strikingly well integrated with your art practice in other disciplines. Had you thought in terms of making a book before?*

I'm a sculptor and printmaker but I had been toying with the book format for a number of years. I'd been making prints where it was important that they were part of a series and sequence, so the book became a natural progression from that. I needed a catalyst to go from the notion of thinking about a book to doing one, and it took a specific project to spur me into investing the time to overcome the practical barriers.

*Can you give me a thumbnail sketch of your background and training as an artist?*

I was born in London in 1952 and grew up in Rochester, Kent, going straight from school to Canterbury College of Art for a year before going on to Bristol Polytechnic to do a degree in fine art between 1972 and 1975. Then I went to the Slade for two years as a postgraduate in printmaking. I felt printmaking was seen as a marginal activity and, as I disliked that, I was quite a rebellious student. Then I had a year off and was invited back to the Slade as a research assistant for three years, working with Stanley Jones and Peter Dalgleish. To a certain extent, I feel that's when my education began. I liked teaching and the responsibility that went with it. I felt I was allowed to start afresh and I began doing work that was very different from what I had produced before. I was also looking at things that weren't necessarily art; I'd spent part of my year off working as an ice cream salesman in Soho and at a number of similar jobs, and suddenly felt I had permission to look at both popular and high culture without prejudice. At the same time, I was beginning to make some sculptural pieces at home, very secretly, and they were incredibly important to me.

*Why was the sculpture private?*

As a child I was brought up making things. At a certain age you become self-conscious about things that are important to you. The sculpture was so crucial to me that I couldn't bear to do it in public. When I was at Bristol, Anthony Caro was the predominant influence and you measured the quality of a sculpture by its weight and, at the Slade, it was said you could distinguish a sculptor from a painter by his boots. I've never been interested in such a male view of an artist and my approach has been almost feminine in terms of materials. The overall climate for sculpture was very much heavy metal, welding, and abstraction, and abstract art has never held that much meaning for me when I've made it myself. The kind of sculpture I wanted to make seemed very out of fashion. I was like a seed waiting for the right conditions to germinate.

It was wonderful to start making sculptures again in 1978. I carried on for about three years without showing the pieces to anyone. I worked in a room at home, a reaction against the idea that an artist had to have a studio. The things I made were very small objects that were quite domestic and often were fitted onto the wall. They were fiberglass or even laminated paper and they involved a lot of drawing: drawing has always been central to my activity and I see both sculpture and printing as ways of taking drawing into other forms. The sculptures all had figurative elements. For example, one was a wall piece that used the head of Hypnos, the god of sleep, and a snooker pocket. It was a metaphor for the depth of sleep (I liked the weight of the ball in the pocket) and was triggered by the fact I had been playing a lot of snooker and by the idea that when you get the ball in the pocket it is the end of an action. I wanted the sculpture to be a small piece that the viewer discovered, and I enjoyed the idea of almost concealing sculptures, a very different approach from the monumental pieces that were prevalent then. For instance, I did some wedges holding grapes just above eye level, a decorative element that seemed almost to have been pinned on the wall. I was beginning to build a language of my own that had a degree of humor. A lot of surrealist objects were important to me, such as Meret Oppenheim's fur cup and the Duchamp objects that I had seen in the collection in Philadelphia.

*Were you making prints during this period too?*

Yes. My wife, Charlotte Hodes, and I had an etching press in the kitchen. There is a point where you need your own tools so you can think more privately. We called ourselves the Culford Press because we lived in Culford Road and I wanted the name to be matter-of-fact, intentionally blunt and unpoetic. One of the people we worked with at the Culford Press was Paula Rego and, in 1989, I printed her nursery rhymes, which affected me in three ways. First, it was a very intense time working with her, and we had endless wonderful conversations. Second, I received considerable praise for my part in making these prints, which helped my confidence; and third, I had a little bit of money for the first time in my life and it bought six months' of studio time. I rented a large studio.

Another marking point at this time was the fact that I had become a father, which gave me an amazing kick up the backside because you realize you are on the way out and that if you've got something in you, you'd better get on and do it. A big breakthrough came when I was watching my son use some building bricks and realized that making is about playing and being at ease rather than being self-conscious. I scavenged tons of wood from a warehouse and built mountains of one-inch blocks. Then I made structures that were like slices through a building, made out of lots of different layers with different elements trapped between the layers. At the same time I was making simple, direct prints using hard-ground etching.

*When did you first show the sculptures?*

Mel Gooding, the critic and writer, brought some members of the Arts Council to my studio and, to my surprise, they bought two. Then, in 1993, Emma Hill offered me a show at the Eagle Gallery. I've always loved the idea of sculpture in domestic settings rather than in vast galleries, and the Eagle was the perfect scale for me. I made all the work in about six months, specifically for the space and planned it very carefully. The show contained both prints and sculptures, acting as counterpoints to one another.

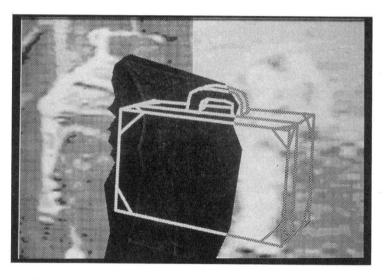

*Freud's Coat*,
lithography, 12½"x 18⅛",
23 pages, edition of 100,
1996

*Some of the sculpture there relates very clearly to the images you later used in* **Freud's Coat**?

There was a piece called Journey with a suitcase and a hanging shirt. One of the things about family life is that it pins you down; it's both a voluntary state and yet one in which you are aware of a tension in knowing that certain freedoms have gone and certain responsibilities have come. I wanted to make a work that articulated these conflicts, a visual way of presenting that tension. The suitcase was made up of small blocks of wood, cut as if a segment of the interior had been revealed to show the objects inside—a house, a chair, a letter, a bunch of grapes— almost carved into the suitcase. It suggested that if another section had been cut away, a number of other objects would have been revealed, just as a slice of bacon reveals one configuration and the next slice another. On top of the suitcase was a bottle and a little picture frame. These represented the things you need to sustain you on a journey, sustenance and a sense of where you have come from. Tied to the suitcase was a leather shirt. I didn't want a dramatic struggle, but I wanted to suggest the tension of being prevented from leaving.

*What dictated the choice of things in the suitcase?*

I've always been interested in articulating time passing and also in forming a symbolic language for the significant components of one's life. Morandi's etchings, for example, were important to me in that very simple objects become imbued with a presence and, perhaps, introduce a sense of the past. The chair was a recurring image in the prints and sculptures at the Eagle Gallery. I've always thought of chairs as being important because they indicate that you're going to stay somewhere, even momentarily. Also, the chair has other connotations. When my father died, the presence of his chair without him was haunting. The sense of absence and the figure leaving have been ongoing concerns of mine.

*Your show at the Economist Building in 1994 developed from the work you made for the Eagle Gallery?*

It was a very different space and, again, I made a family of prints and sculptures especially for that environment. There was a piece that was a bed, which gave me enormous problems because of its size. I wanted it to be halfway between a child's bed and an adult's, seeing it as looking both back and forward. The base was made from slats of polished brass with photo frames drawn on them as if the bed were reflecting back memories. It reminded me of the way in films you see someone come into an anonymous hotel room, unpack a suitcase, take out a photo of their loved one, place it beside the bed, and by doing so change the room into a place with a connection with who they are.

All the pieces in the Economist show relate to the **Freud** book because they were about trying to make images about past and present. Another sculpture was *Belongings*, three objects, a huge photographic frame about five feet high, a chair, and a spade. They were made as wooden cages in the shape of the objects, as if the object had been inside them and had been transported. I was thinking of a man arriving on a beach in a new land with the three essentials for setting up his new life. He had a chair to say, "I'm here now," he had a spade as a sign of work, and he had a picture frame to remind him of where he had come from. Another piece, *To Come and Go*, was made out of small wooden blocks, a suitcase, on top of which a little boat and an iron were balanced. They were wedged so that the piece was wonky to give the sense that if any part was removed the whole thing would collapse. I wanted to express the way all the strands in a person's life are held in balance.

*The iron appears often in your work. What does it represent to you?*

The iron and ironing board represent a sense of domestic dignity. It's the way even poor people prepare themselves to look their best in the outside world. It's also a kind of domestic sculptural activity. An iron has a weight to it. It's a dangerous object. There are all sorts of connotations to it.

*In 1995 you and Charlotte were invited to go to Madrid as artists-in-residence at the Fundación Olivar de Castillejo. Was this an important period for you?*

In the light of what happened later at the Freud Museum, going to Madrid was prophetic. I was able to see a lot of religious relics in the back rooms of monasteries and convents, an enormously good preparation for the Freud Museum, which itself has qualities of a reliquary. There wasn't much money, but we had free accommodation and free entry to the Prado, where we went almost every day, so I was able to see Goya, Velázquez, and Zurbarán until the paintings were coming out of my ears, which was glorious. The Zurbarán paintings always interested me because they are so devoid of anything gestural.

The other marvelous aspect of the residency was that I was able to focus on my own work—mainly drawings and collages—without any other distraction. Just before going to Madrid I had been invited onto the Computer Research Project at Camberwell College of Arts by Tristran Humphries, who was leading it. I had enormous difficulty in getting my head round the computer, but I'd had just enough experience that I could take something with me which fed into the drawings that I did in Madrid. I was all the time thinking about how I might use the computer, how I could utilize the anonymity of line, the cut and paste, and the layering, so, although a lot of the drawings worked in their own right, I was also thinking in terms of developing them on the computer when I got back. In these drawings I was acting a bit like a computer myself, but with a pencil and scissors.

*In what direction was the work going?*

It was increasingly getting away from any notion of gesture and expressionistic mark making. I wanted something much cooler, quieter, and reliant on a different kind of expression, more controlled and slowed down. I made about forty drawings, many of them using the motif of a jacket or coat, which was very much a metaphor for my father. It carries the idea of something protective but that also knits into life. The jacket was often combined with images of books and bones.

*Was it a natural transition to go back to the computer screen when you returned?*

Yes. One thing that worked well in Spain was that, because of being away from home, I had limited tools to work with. When I started back at the research project I realized that I needed to close down my options in a similar way and to avoid the ability that the computer has to change everything at the touch of a button. I just drew with the mouse using the imagery I'd developed in Madrid with other elements scanned in, like the pattern inside an envelope that I used as a background and that had a feeling almost of cloth that I could weave in and out of.

*You often use the word "weave." Why is it important to you?*

I'm a great believer that one's life is a whole package and that all the bits count. The interesting thing about a fabric is that you only need one fiber to go wrong and you've got a hole.

*Did the computer alter the way you drew?*

It gave me confidence to look more closely at the notion of drawing as carrying an emotional weight without necessarily being gestural. The computer separates your hand from the event on the screen and, for me, the attempt to make gestural marks with it is false. All the decisions you make are conscious in that you decide the size of the line—its character—whether it is going to have a round or square end. In addition, because the image on the screen is virtual—it has no size, scale, or texture—one of the things I needed to do continuously was to output proofs in order to have something tangible with a specific size, proportion, and weight. I was working with George Whale, the research assistant on the project, who helped me understand the technology. In order for him to help me, I had to articulate what I wanted to have happen, what I was trying to achieve. This working relationship that we established was crucial to the making of **Freud's Coat.**

*What were the images you produced at this stage?*

I made a series called **My Father's Coat** (1996), seven prints that took the motif I'd begun in Madrid and wove it in with suitcases, bones, houses, flowers, books. Often the viewer had to unravel them visually in order to see one element, to disregard other elements in order to focus on one in particular. I was interested in hiding things without concealing them. Instead of putting something in a dark corner, I would place it there openly but within a visual complexity.

*They were printouts from the computer?*

No. They were seven large etchings, each one very different. Photo positives were made from the images worked on the computer and then these were etched in a conventional way. The output from the Inkjet printer seemed to me very bland and to have no physicality. My prints were very deeply etched, a little like braille if you ran you finger over them, so it was almost in direct opposition to the virtual reality of the screen.

*You said that the **Freud** book was influenced by doing prints and drawings in sequence. What made them a sequence?*

It was the realization of not trying to get everything out in one single image, of spreading the ideas around. Although each drawing or print works in an autonomous way, when you see them all together they resonate differently, elements weave in and out and notions are established between them. But they're not a sequence in the sense that you have to read them in a particular order. A collection of work is probably a better description. Prints work in a more poignant way in series; you have a chunk of something that can hold its own against a painting or a sculpture.

*How did **Freud's Coat** come about?*

I was invited onto a committee looking at potential outcomes from Camberwell's Book Arts Research Project. There were a number of venues being discussed, and when the Freud Museum was mentioned I said I would love to do something there. Professor Eileen Hogan made the arrangements and things were signed and sealed in a couple of weeks. I'm a great believer that if things happen quickly that is a good sign.

*Had you thought much about book art up to this point?*

Patrick Caulfield's *Laforgue* (1973) was one book I bought and have enormous affection for. I'd always hankered after making a book. I like the democracy of books and the fact that they can occupy a different kind of world than things that hang on walls. There's an aspect of me that likes not to be center stage, and I relate to the book not having an exclusive space but just being one more with the rest on the shelf until it's pulled out and referred to.

*The Freud Museum itself was the starting point for your book?*

Yes. The outer building is a typical red brick Hampstead double-fronted house in Maresfield Gardens, north London. Inside there is Freud's study on the ground floor, with his desk, his chair, and his couch, and it was this room that my work revolved around. Although there are gardens, the shades are always drawn and, consequently, the room is rather somber. Because of the world-class collection of antiquities that Freud amassed and that are all piled on top of one another, it has the atmosphere of an antechamber at the British Museum. Almost every wall surface is covered in engravings, bookshelves, and cupboards full of statues and objects. Freud was able to flee Austria with his possessions in 1938 to avoid persecution by the Nazis. He lived in the house in London for only one year before dying of cancer.

Having spent time in the museum, I was overwhelmed by a sense of inadequacy. I realized I knew little about Freud, and it seemed presumptuous of me to try to proceed. However, I began to try to educate myself by reading a number of Freud's works, talking at length to Fiona Barnes (a Jungian analyst) and to Dr. Matthew Hodes (a psychiatrist) about Freud's fundamental ideas and influence. I realized I was getting nowhere fast, and it was a chance conversation with Paula Rego that turned the key. She said, "Remember your feelings when you first walked into the museum and trust them." When I had first walked in I had written down a line from T. S. Eliot, "an atmosphere of Juliet's tomb," from his poem "Portrait of a Lady." There was something incredibly oppressive and funereal about the house. The Egyptian antiquities and the heads staring out from the numerous engravings give a sense of an Old Testament God who is unyielding and judgmental.

The museum's curator, Erica Davies, talked to me about the objects and gave me access to everything. I started to read transcriptions from Freud's diaries from the last five years of his life and certain phrases stood out that were interesting in terms of the intertwining of his private life and the public, political context of the time. His flight from Austria was a final journey in more ways than one and he was reconstructing his life carrying the knowledge that he was ill with cancer. He talked about wanting to die in freedom, which I found a tragic notion.

*How did you begin to relate what you found at the museum to the book you were to make?*

I began to feel there were some possibilities, but the break came when I was talking to Erica and mentioned my set of prints, **My Father's Coat.** She said, "I've got Freud's coat upstairs." She came down with this strange old woolen coat with no lining. It was very small and looked like a Joseph Beuys multiple. In one pocket was a handwritten note by Mana Friedman, who had helped collate all the material after Freud died, saying that the coat had been bought by Freud for his emigration to London and that Anna Freud used to wear it after her father died. In the other pocket was Anna Freud's plastic rainhat.

The skies suddenly opened and I knew I had found what really interested me. The fact that Anna had wrapped herself in the coat after Freud had died had incredibly erotic overtones. It also connected with my daughter wanting to be in my coat—when she was very little, we used to carry her in a pouch on our fronts as if she were a little kangaroo, and even when she was much bigger than the pouch she would ask to go in my coat and be held as a baby. It was important to her and also to me. Suddenly I felt a connection with Freud as a man rather than as one of the three or four most important figures of the twentieth century. I took a lot of photographs of the coat and focused on parts of it that I thought had an erotic charge, the bits where the flesh comes out—the cuffs and collar—or the openings, the buttonholes. As well as simple representations, I cut up bits of the coat images and shaped them as if they were petals or flowers.

*Were you using the computer from the beginning?*

Yes. For some reason making the book and the computer research project were locked together in my mind from the outset. This work was new territory, unlike anything else I had done with the computer, but I couldn't think of any other practical way of being able to manipulate the images and manufacture the book with the freedom I wanted and within a specific budget.

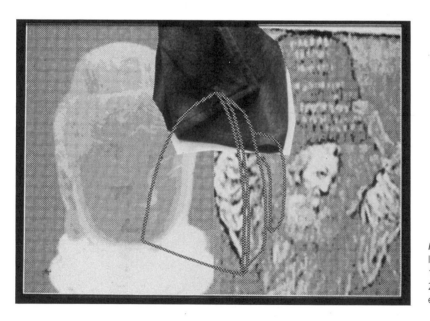

*Freud's Coat,*
lithography,
12½" x 18⅛",
23 pages,
edition of 100, 1996

I scanned in the images of the coat alongside video images I had from filming Freud's study. One of the book's themes was the sense of an unyielding past which I had felt in his room, and I videoed all the heads I could from the engravings and from the numerous figures on his desk. I felt that the head and what goes on inside was such a fundamental image for Freud. To these I added elements that would suggest a life under construction, introducing objects such as books, irons, suitcases, knives and forks, a diagram of a house, a cameo picture frame, and a glass. Some of these were drawn with the mouse on the computer with an intentional deadpan quality, others were photo-collage.

*Were those things you saw in the museum?*

No, they were from my own world. To me, they represent fundamental aspects of one's life, and I wanted them to act in a symbolic way in the book. The book is, after all, my response to Freud and the museum. I was, however, very surprised by the reaction to the book and how some people felt that I had touched on issues around Freud and his work. For instance, a number of people saw my use of the sense of the past as a critique of Freud's own thinking that the answers are always in the past and that if you go back far enough you will always find an answer. For me, that is like going forward dragging your grandmother with you, quite an oppressive way of living and, as a person, I'm not like that at all, nor am I a hoarder and collector. Similarly, people found the texture of the book evocative and perceived an aspect of tragedy about the upheavals in Europe of the time, and I was very pleased that came through.

*That period of history chimes well with the thoughts behind pieces such as* **Journey**?

Yes. Also the fact that being happy is a very vulnerable state, just as having a degree of security is a vulnerable state. (As a child I often had a dream of being an orphan and owning nothing and, because I had nothing to lose, being able to move only forward.) The fact that things in my life were good and secure and that I was healthy made the thoughts I had about Freud all the more poignant. There is a notion of narrative running through the book, which gradually darkens, and I had in mind ideas of a kind of Passover, where preparations are made for a journey. As you travel through the book, things get more somber and it ends on a note of absence.

*How conscious of the narrative were you from the beginning?*

I did a quick dummy to start off with, but that was just to enable me to begin. It was a very practical process. I was proofing the images, laying them out on the floor, feeling an order for them and, if I felt there were gaps, I would make another page as a link. The order of the images became very important. Everything had to be subordinate to the whole. Occasionally pages were pieces of work in their own right and those I had to strip down or leave out.

*There is no color in the book?*

I didn't see any reason to use anything other than black and white. Economics came into it, because the price would have gone sky-high if I'd used color and I wanted it to sell at an accessible price, but there was such a range of color within the black and a sense of silver in the halftones that I was delighted with it as it was. The background for the images is a halftone dot that runs throughout and, for the heads, I used a very large dot so that they seem almost like exaggerated newspaper photographs. One of the reasons for choosing the large dot was that I didn't want all the information to be given away at once and wanted to suggest that there was something back in space that needed attention. I wanted viewers to have to hold the book away from themselves in order to read the images. For similar reasons, the pages are long and thin, to slow down the experience of opening the book and turning the leaves.

All the pages of **Freud's Coat** are cropped to the edge, so there are no white borders and it appears very functional. In the same way, the typeface is simple Times, factual and unemotional. I wanted a robust book that didn't need to be approached in a reverential way with white gloves, and I chose a plain gray cloth for the binding. If I could change anything, it would be to have the book open in a flatter way. It's an edition of one hundred.

*Was this the first time you had used text in your work?*

I had used words in some images I'd made about fifteen years before. Words have always been important in the process of making for me in terms of using phrases to cement ideas. I generally make verbal as well as visual notes when planning work, often a poetic phrase. For **Freud's Coat**, it seemed appropriate to use words from the start and in the end I included about five lines from Freud's diaries and letters. They were lines that resonated on a personal level but that could also be seen within a wider context. For example, the last phrase in the book is "how impossible it is to flee one's fate," which was Freud writing about the inevitability of getting flowers on his birthday, but which can also be seen as the inescapable fate awaiting the Jews at this time, or his own approaching death.

*Giacometti's coat also appears in the book?*

There is a wonderful photograph of Giacometti crossing Paris in his coat and a very interesting essay by John Berger about him wearing the coat, which I was reading at the time of making the book. However, it is not necessary to know that it is Giacometti's coat—people will register a hung coat.

*How was **Freud's Coat** launched?*

It was launched at the Freud Museum on an apocalyptic day when a major water main flooded the whole of north London, so there was an Old Testament feeling to the evening and many people arrived much later than expected. The book was seen on a podium I had built as part of an installation alongside a glass cabinet, inside which were small, pure white sculptures made of wood and plastic: books with objects set into them. I wanted them to be clinical—a reaction to the earth colors in Freud's study—and to suggest the medical side of his life. Most of the imagery inside the book sculptures—a globe or a picture frame or a house—came from **Freud's Coat**. There was also a large floor sculpture that consisted of a set of traveling cages, one to hold a house, one a suitcase, one a book, and one an ironing board. These were felt lined as if they were transporting items to set up a new life. I intended the imagery from the small sculptures, the floor piece, and **Freud's Coat** to bounce off one another and for the images to be interpreted differently in the context of the other works.

*Several important institutional collectors purchased **Freud's Coat** after the launch?*

The Tate, the Victoria and Albert Museum, and a number of art colleges—Winchester, Dublin, and Camberwell—bought it, as did the Museum of Modern Art in New York and the New York Public Library.

*Will you make more books?*

Yes. The format suits the way I think and the fact that a book is a traveling item appeals to me. I like the density of the form. I am at present working on a new book, **With the Melting of the Snows**, which is a response to Martin Bell's final BBC radio broadcast from Bosnia.

*Has your role at Camberwell College of Arts changed recently?*

Yes. I'm now subject leader in printmaking and leader of the research project, "The Integration of Computer Technology Within Fine Art Practice."

*Hermetic Waste,*
text by Hildegard of Bingen, Parcelsus,
and government fact sheet on nuclear waste,
7¾" x 12", letterpress text
with 7 intaglio collagraphs,
edition of 40, 1986

# susan
# johanknecht

Cathy Courtney's interview with Susan Johanknecht was recorded at the artist's home in London on August 29, 1996. The interview began in front of Johanknecht's CD-ROM, of science & desire, so the conversation was punctuated by whispered text and movement on the screen. of science & desire is available in book form. In September 1997, Johanknecht became course leader of the M.A. in Book Arts at Camberwell College of Arts, London.

Susan Johanknecht, 1998

Photo: Mervyn Arthur

*This is the first CD-ROM you've made?*

Yes. It started out with the book artist and curator Les Bicknell approaching me about an exhibition that was going to be at the Glynn Vivian Gallery in Wales in 1995, looking at the relationship between the book, the page, and the wall. I'd already been working on this project **of science & desire** for a while and began thinking about the relationship between the text, which was to do with science, and the process of investigation in science and how that could happen on a wall. The first idea was to use blackboards, almost like a projection of thought, and then I got more interested in the idea of projections and asked a graphic designer, Everol McKenzie, about how I could make the piece work using computer technology that could be projected onto a wall. He suggested that I make a CD-ROM because it would be an interactive piece as well.

*of science & desire,*
CD ROM disk and book, letterpress text with relief prints,
6"x 6", 32 pages, edition of 150, 1995

*You liked the idea immediately?*

Yes. Because to have a CD-ROM that was an actual object, that was marketable at the end, was quite an interesting relationship to a book. They're very related forms. A CD-ROM is intimate, you're sitting almost the same distance monitor-to-eye that would be hand-to-eye for a book. It's glowing, when the sound comes up you could have earphones on, a very intimate experience. You're deciding how you want to go through a piece, clicking on different parts, the same as you can follow a book in a linear way from beginning to end or flip through to relevant sections.

*What do you think the differences are?*

The thing people say upsets them most about CD-ROMs is that you've got the monitor, you're not holding it in your hand so you haven't got that tactile contact. If you look at the same page in the book, you've got the softness of the rubber and paper to turn, a very different kind of experience. I used rubber for the book cover because it had that combination of being sexual and sensual but also clinical. You could imagine rubber in a laboratory, being used in a scientific way; it had that dual reading.

*Did you do all the drawings for the CD-ROM?*

Yes. There's something so magical about having your drawings move. The images are the same as in the book but the icons are different. I wanted the movement to be slow. In most CD-ROMs the animations are whipping about with lots of color, but I wanted this to be much more contemplative. When we scanned in the drawings the shadowy acetate shapes around them came up on the screen. It was possible to get rid of them but it was so exciting to have that quality of accident and discovery with electronic media, and I left them in. That's not something I would have predicted; I had imagined them quite pristine. That's another thing that has drawn me to the medium, that element of accident, the same as with printmaking.

*What do you think the relationship is between printmaking and books?*

Printmaking is sequential; you're making multiples, that's the essence of printmaking. There's nothing more satisfying than working on a print and getting all your different stages spread out on the table as you're printing and seeing them drying. A logical next step is to start putting them together in a book. Especially if you're making images that are not "beautiful" and not those you would want to live with on the wall. In a book you can put them on a shelf and come to them when you want to have that experience.

*What was the origin of* **of science & desire**?

My work often comes out of what's going on in my life and, having children, you're constantly brought back to your own childhood. Working with them on their science homework brought me back my own experience at school and those 1960s science books with their diagrams. It brought back the way you were taught an experiment as though "this is the rule, this is the ritual. Everyone in the class is going to see this ritual and understand one fact from it." That always seemed silly to me as a child because, depending on how you perceive it, you might be looking at the color that happens to be reflected on one of the objects or you might be listening to the sound of the bubbles when something is evaporating. There are different parts of the experiment that would capture someone's imagination.

*When were your children born?*

One in 1986 and one in 1992.

*And you?*

I was born in Toledo, Ohio, in 1955 and then lived in Syracuse, New York. It was suburban America, very isolated. The kind of childhood where you were just told to go out and play every day and left to your own devices. The love of objects and of manipulating them and making up my own kind of narrative with them comes from fairly isolated play as a child.

*What kind of play in particular?*

I had lots of dolls and we'd make clothes ourselves with anything we'd find. A lot of the sewing implements that found their way into **WHO WILL BE IT?** (CD-ROM and boxed book, 1996) are ones that I had as a child or that my grandmother left me. Haberdashery and kitchen objects have their own worlds and a kind of violence of their own as well, innate in what they do. But they're beautiful objects and have a lot of resonance for me. Both my grandmothers were into mending. In those days you darned socks, and they'd have wonderful wooden nobbles that you put the sock over and big, shaped needles and lovely yarns and threads. Even threads for mending nylon stockings, all different flesh tones.

*Something like a nylon stocking texture would attract you?*

Yes.

*Were your grandmothers near you as a child?*

One was in New York City and the other in upstate New York, which was fairly close. Both were Swedish and had made the transition from Swedish culture to American, so there was an air of mystery because they had all these wonderful recipes and things they could make that my parents didn't want anything to do with because they wanted to be as American as possible. So there was that European mystery to it.

*How was it they were both Swedish?*

Random function in life!

*What was on the walls of your house as a child?*

The only thing that comes to mind was a very interesting oval mirror that distorted everything that you saw in it. Otherwise probably family photographs and nondescript things. It was very middle-class American suburban aesthetic, the kitsch of the time.

*What were your childhood books?*

A lot of them we've still got for my children, so it's quite interesting having a second go-round with them. It's more the images than the texts because the texts of American children's books really annoy me—*The Little Engine That Could* and all that "get going, you can achieve, everyone can achieve." It's the images I remember—that limited color range and lithographic crayon quality. There might be be black, green, and yellow through the whole book, yet the artist would achieve a wonderful colorful feeling just from that limited range. Which I suppose was one of the things that led me to printmaking.

*What did you read as a teenager?*

I was obsessed with Russian novels and worked my way through those. And I read a lot of poetry. I did English literature for my first degree at the University of Vermont.

*At what point did you become consciously aware of galleries?*

I didn't have access to them until I came to London, really. As a child I can remember going to the Everson Museum in Syracuse and seeing Yoko Ono's exhibition there and being amazed by it and my parents being horrified. I remember a maze and a loo at the end. I don't know if that truly was what it was.

*Had you been aware of a visual hunger?*

I think it was latent until I got to the university and then I signed up immediately for art courses and for lithography because I love that quality of crayon mark. I can remember going and begging to be taken in on a very high-level art course and they said, "Oh, no, you've got to do drawing one, two, and three beforehand." But because the man who was teaching it was going on a sabbatical, he did take me on the course. The person who was taking over from him turned out to be Claire Van Vliet of the Janus Press. Claire was very interested in the images I was drawing and kept saying, "Where are these coming from?" and I said they were from poems I'd written. At that point Claire said, "Do you want to make a book?" and I went to her studio in northern Vermont at Easter to make one. I wrote a text, a series of three poems to do with my relationship with my mother, and did a lithograph of a fist holding a horse chestnut and a cord running down from the horse chestnut along the vein. It was called **Birthcords**. It was the first book I did and I was hooked. Learning to set type and to actually see words you'd written have that authority in type was amazing.

*Up until that point you didn't know such books existed?*

No. I think that's true of students now. They often don't.

*Had you drawn before?*

I've always drawn. Not much painting, because my brother and I weren't allowed to make a mess at home.

*The first book was autobiographical in its roots. Your work is no longer overtly autobiographical? Is there a personal subtext?*

I think there always is. There's a personal impetus to deal with an issue and to understand it better. There's an element of mystery in exploring something. With the photo-animations in my second CD-ROM, **WHO WILL BE IT?** I set objects up and I moved them around until they found their own way to express the text. I was learning something from it. I was setting up the conditions under which this transformation happened and because it had a link to things I felt strongly about and was thinking about in my personal life, it had a magic. If it had been just a design project for somebody else I wouldn't have had the same passion about it.

*Do you think women approach books in a different way than men do?*

Books are a good format for dealing with personal imagery because they're a step off from a diary or journal, but I don't think it's necessarily that women treat them differently than men. I know there are lots of examples of books that women have made that seem very personal compared to men's, but it's just a different use of language, a different way of feeling comfortable expressing yourself. Men's books are just as personal, but they may be less direct.

*Tell me more about the first book.*

We're in 1977. It was very straightforward image as an illustration of and separate from text, which is something I've worked steadily against ever since. Perhaps with the CD-ROM it's the ultimate point where you've got image and text at the same time. If you're hearing the voice and looking at the image, you can't really perceive them separately.

*WHO WILL BE IT?*,
letterpress, 3½" x 4" in archival box,
edition of 50, 1996

*What was Claire Van Vliet
like?*

She is incredibly ener-
getic and a devoted bookmaker. I've known her
since she was working with lithography and
texts from Kafka. Then she started making paper
and pulp paintings. That was at the point when I was living there and
working as an apprentice. And as I was leaving and after I left, she became
more and more interested in book structures.

*What was her environment?*

The way she lived and worked was totally integrated and the press was part
of the house. That's had an influence on me in the way that my press is part
of my house. When I did my formal apprenticeship with Claire she lived in
an old house that had been built in the 1800s and renovated. She had a
simple, small Vandercook. The studio grew to have a larger Vandercook. She
then moved to a larger house that she'd designed herself, a cross between a
Vermont farm house and a Scandinavian house. That house had much more
papermaking equipment, an etching press, several different letterpress
machines, and space to put larger work up. Her wall work is very important to her as well.

*When you were an apprentice at the Janus Press, what did you learn?*

I was there for a couple of years; we got a National Endowment for the Arts
grant for me to be her apprentice. I learned typesetting, printing, simple
bookbinding skills—taking a book from start to finish. I was working on
Janus Press books, some by Peter Schumann and the Bread and Puppet
Theater, whatever happened to be coming through the studio at the time.

I formed Gefn Press at that stage. I had a second book ready and was going to print it and needed a press name very quickly and wanted one that wasn't going to pin me down later and that I could live with through my life. I wanted a name that visually looked good and picked Gefn more because I liked the look than the meaning. In Scandinavian mythology Gefn is a goddess who turned her sons into oxen and ploughed the land that separated Denmark from Sweden. In retrospect, the ploughing links with my last name because "knecht" is a ploughman or farmhand, but I didn't realize that at the time.

*What was that book?*

A short poem, **Notes to K**, that I wrote after reading Kafka's diaries. The image was a photocopy of an image of Felice Bauer, whom Kafka was engaged to. I wasn't confident in my image-making at that stage, which is why, later on, I decided to go to art school. But at that stage it was very much the text and the writing. My interest in materials grew later on.

I carried on making more books, texts I had written or come across or poets I met. Then I went and lived in New Zealand and met a poet, Mollie Ames, who'd written **Pegasus Pete**, which I wanted to print, so I did some woodcuts to go with it. The woodcuts suited the poem but I was frustrated with their naïveté. From New Zealand I applied to Central School of Art in London—they were the only ones that sent me a prospectus and an application form after all my letters, and I was lucky enough to get in. I came in 1981 to start the foundation course.

When I arrived at Central they said, "You've got to be open-minded, you can't just think you're going to do printmaking and books. You might end up doing sculpture." I remember laughing and thinking I'd never do sculpture, but of course that's the one thing I really did enjoy the most and have carried on. Even in terms of **WHO WILL BE IT?** which is, in a sense, moving sculptures.

*What sculptures were you doing?*

Papier-mâché, low-relief pieces, using a lot of found objects. That led quite smoothly into making sculptural books using heavy materials and attaching them at the spine. At one stage I was using found materials and making relief sculptures across the wall that I thought of as books (no one else did) because all the different objects became like characters in parts of a narrative that went across a wall.

*I remember seeing your degree show. Tell me about some of those books.*

I made painted ones that are on mill-board that's hinged and constructed, maybe two feet tall and several feet wide when they open out. They were intensely to do with color and changes of color sensation as you turn the pages. Then I did some books where I used *Vogue* magazine and *Harpers & Queen*, looking at the way fabrics were reproduced in glossy magazines, lush and sensuous, bits of fur coats and silk dresses. I would cut all those bits out and use them in terms of their texture and color—or their illusion of texture, which is what was interesting about them. They got collaged onto some of the heavy board, sculptural books. I made cutouts so that you would see pages several layers down.

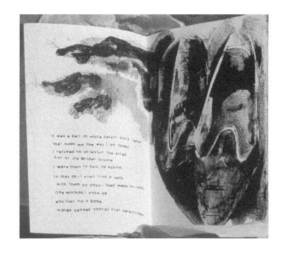

*Well-Heeled,*
text by Julie O'Callaghan, lithograph with 7 lithographs on 8 folded sheets, packaged in shoe box, edition of 30, 1985

*I remember one about shoes.*

That was just as I finished at Central. I had to get a part-time job to support myself and was working at a shoe shop in Covent Garden. It was very, very expensive, they were designer shoes, incredibly beautiful. I wanted to deal with shoes and obsessions with shoes because of the experience of the visitors to the shop and the people who just looked forward to *Vogue* magazine coming out every month. It was a world I hadn't known existed before. It would have been easy just to condemn it as luxurious and ridiculous, but it was also fascinating.

*The text is by Julie O'Callaghan?*

I wanted a text about obsessions with shoes but I didn't want to write it myself; at that stage I wanted to be dealing with imagery and book design. I discovered a poetry book about obsessions with food and wrote to the author, Julie O'Callaghan, and asked would she write me a book about obsessions with shoes. It turned out she was American, about my age, working at Trinity College in Dublin. She sent me back the text for

**Well-Heeled** in just a few months' time. We've subsequently done **Jasper the Lion Heart** together (1990), a text about my son's fear of lions.

*At this stage, what was the artists' book scene in London as far as you were aware?*

I knew Ron King and had worked for him for a while at Circle Press. It was while he was still based in Guildford and we were working on the knitting book, **Neighbours We'll not part Tonight**, which I was helping to print and set the type for—I made an American typo, which he'll never let me forget! How people integrate their life and work is always very interesting when you're working in a place day after day. Ron's workshop was separate from the house, although he tends to make domestic environments within his workshop. And he enjoys the business side of it and it was useful for me to learn about that. There was always a feeling of lots of different projects going on and lots of people coming in. The fact that presses like Circle and Janus have survived so long has made it possible for people to come after them.

*Who else was important to you at this time?*

Mike Peel was important in looking at the relationship between text and image and the link between the personal and the political. Ian Tyson was also important. I remember him talking about his concept of laying out books on a grid structure. It was totally different from the way I was thinking at that stage but in retrospect—even in terms of mapping out a CD-ROM —it's an interesting concept.

Meeting up with Pella Erskine-Tulloch, Jane Rolo, and Rob Hadrill at Book Works was very important. Book Works was hard to find. You'd get out at London Bridge Station and wander around for a while; for an American it was like going into a Dickens novel, trying to find Green Dragon Court in the damp and the puddles. There was a wonderful gallery space and workshop and there were trains rattling overhead. I remember installations by Pavel Büchler and Langlands and Bell. The Book Works people were from a bookbinding background, but they were totally open to all uses of the book and to making it accessible. I had a show there in 1985: double-elephant-size collagraphs with images of books lined with bodies, legs, and parts of bodies, big black-and-white collagraphs with the text below. It dominated the room right round the walls, as if you were inside a book.

*You did an extra year at Central?*

I had access to the presses but not to type, which is why the books during that period are all different solutions to that problem. That was an important phase. If I'd had type I would have been less innovative. I had to use things like rubber stamps and transfer them onto lithographic plates—then I saw how wonderfully they integrated with the drawn image.

When I did **Eat Book** (1990) I wanted the look of a hand-stencilled Victorian children's book, and I did the entire text by hand to look like a typeface and then had it printed offset litho. **Eat Book** was done with Katharine Meynell, whom Book Works put me in contact with. That again was a very important aspect of Book Works—they were able to put people together. I had approached Jane Rolo saying I wanted to do a book about the experience of birth but looking at the moon and seas on the moon. My first child was probably a month old. Jane put me in touch with Kate, a video artist who was dealing with motherhood in her own work. I gave Kate a list of the names of the seas and we put together **Mare Fecunditatis: Seas of the Moon** (1988).

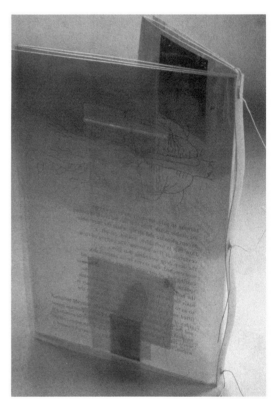

**Eat Book** came about because Kate and I wanted to do a book about the violence of nurturing a child. She used a lot of nursery rhymes, chopping them about, and the momentum comes from the violence of the language. I interspersed them with images of utensils I found in Brixton market and blew them up big and sharp and printed them letterpress at Book Works. There were also large photographic images that we took in a squat that Kate was living in at the time, exploring rituals at the table.

**Emissions** (1992), *also made with Meynell, was an important book for you?*

**Emissions** was right in the middle of all the AIDS panic. It was a response to that as well as to various medical things that Kate and I were going through at the time. It was an interest in the body generally and, because of AIDS, the fear of the body. I had also wanted to make a plastic, see-through book.

*Emissions,*
text by Kate Meynell,
9"x 6", 20 pages, edition of 150,
1992

*You'd used plastic to a lesser extent in* **Hermetic Waste** *(1986)?*

Yes. **Hermetic Waste** had a builders' grided plastic cover and was interleaved with plastic in front of each collagraph and had a plastic slipcase. That was at the time of Chernobyl and I was thinking about nuclear waste and had also been reading a lot about alchemy and science and wanted to look at the links between all three. I also wanted to play around with the idea of different voices, so I had a nuclear fact sheet, Paracelsus (the alchemy voice), and Hildegard of Bingen, the abbess who had visions. Hildegard's visions were totally cinematic and to do with oneness in the environment. Imagery was also so important in alchemy as the experiments were handed down though engravings, very richly drawn with cross-hatching, but they were diagrams. The images for **Hermetic Waste** were worked out by making papier-mâché sculptures first and then they became collagraphs.

*Plastic was used differently in* **Emissions***?*

It was a transparent book and we used translucent ink so that with the body prints you could see your own hand straight through but you had the sense of the body print the way you do when someone leans their head against the bus window and you get a kind of greasy impression of skin. The text was very gushing and I wanted it to be like another illustration and not to dominate; for example, the line tracing the immune system, that drawing is of equal weight as a line of text. You initially come across the text backward and see it as an image and a texture, then you turn the page and can actually read it. As you turn the page again, the text superimposes itself on the page before and becomes a texture again.

*What about the samples of body secretions that appear in* **Emissions***?*

There's an element of transformation, of one thing giving the illusion of another, so they're not as literal as they seem. There's no actual spittle or semen in the bags. Or blood. I wanted it to stay the way it is and if it had been actual semen or spittle it wouldn't have carried on looking like that. I'm not interested in literal documentation. Transformation is more what I'm interested in, it has more resonance. **Emissions** was displayed on a light box with light shining below the plastic. Everyone who looks through it leaves their fingerprints on it. They see their own hand through it. A lot of things that were sparked off in **Emissions** will carry on in the work.

*Some of them are there in* **Crevice/Map** *(1994)?*

That was about landscape and the body and underlying landscapes within the body, flows and circulations that happen inside. The drawing of the immune system in **Emissions** was important to me and needed to go further. That lead into the maps and the drawings inside the body. I did a lot of drawings at the Royal College of Surgeons in preparation for **Crevice/Map**, drawings from the inside of bodies, mostly lungs and torsos.

*How did the landscape and the map become merged with the body drawings?*

At first I did book constructions based on the landscape in Brittany and was playing about with incised marks from the rocks there. Then I decided to collaborate with Jenifer Newson (a printmaker who trained with Ian Tyson at Wimbledon School of Art), and we went to the Royal Geographic Society and looked at a lot of old Ordnance Survey maps bound and backed in linen on delicate paper with folds that had become part of the map. Those old maps were important to the birth of the book and the structure it was going to take. The mark-making on them was important. We blew them up on the photocopying machine until the marks were almost deteriorating. Jenny was going walking on Ben Nevis, so we blew up a map of that area, drew into it and superimposed body drawings on it. When she got back she talked through her journey and I wrote everything down and from that built a text for the typographical side of the book. The other side of the book was a poem I had written about the body and landscape and a journey through the body.

*You were always going to use both sides of the surface?*

In some ways that came from **Emissions**. We wanted a paper that would not be transparent but see-through enough that you would have a sense of both sides. It's a Fabriano paper with a strong layline, which was important in the sense of a grid. It's two pieces joined on the sewing machine. It was very difficult to print and eventually was done by Shelley Rose, a technician at Central who had printed Michael Rothenstein's work.

*Your show at the Hardware Gallery represented the ideal way in which you would like* **Crevice/Map** *to be discovered?*

We had a group of books hanging so that they made a landscape you had to walk through. They were at different levels and different planes and you perceived different aspects as you would walking through a landscape. Small areas of the book were projected onto the wall, into corners and onto skirting boards, so there was a sense of response to the environment and the body/map being projected onto the physical space. It was an interest in taking the book into the environment but in an illusory way as opposed to literally drawing or painting onto a wall.

*What is coming up in the future?*

A piece looking at the vulnerability of architectural structures and another collaboration with Katharine Meynell, **Erosions**. We'd like to do a book that's in volumes, so there's a CD-ROM, some floppy disks, some printed pages. Thinking about how to carry on this dialogue between electronic media and more tactile materials and incorporating it into one. The actual disks themselves are lovely objects.

*You now have most of the equipment you need in your home?*

I got a Vandercook two years ago. The first thing I printed on it was **of science & desire**. The press came by sea from Chicago through the Northwest passage—I had tried for ages to get one in England but never had any luck—

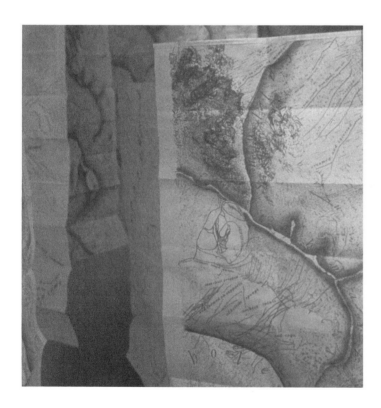

*Crevice/Map* (installation view), screenprint and hand coloring, 7"x 12", unfolds to 24"x 57", edition of 80, 1994

and I got the type along the way from different places. The press is down-stairs and the computer equipment is in the room above so the dialogue between them is implicit in the house as well as what's happening in my work. That dialogue is always there, alongside domestic day-to-day life.

*Teachings of Sourgrass,*
book two of three, from
"Garden Variety Book,"
letterpress,
5½" x 3½", 12 pages,
edition of 39, 1995

# alisa
# golden

Cathy Courtney's interview with *Alisa Golden* was recorded at her studio in *Albany,*
*California, on April 10, 1996.*

Alisa Golden, 1998

Photo: Val Simonetti

*When were you born and where did you grow up?*

I was born in New Jersey in 1962. We moved when I was four, so I've lived in California since then. I spent most of my school years in Santa Monica.

*What books do you remember from childhood?*

We had a lot of kids' books, a lot of Jewish kids' books. I don't remember books before I could read. I learned at about four-and-a-half. When I was in second grade, my favorite book was *Arm in Arm* by Remy Charlip, which is beautifully illustrated, whimsical, with wordplay; those are the things it turns out I'm still interested in. It has tiny watercolors, cartoonlike; each page has a separate pun. There's a picture of two octopi entwined: "Two octopuses came down the aisle, arm in arm, in arm, in arm." Another was "It was a dark and stormy night. The Captain said to me, 'Tell me a story,' so I began, 'It was a dark and stormy night.'" The typeface was black and white, sans serif, the watercolors were a subtle blend, very magical.

I always made books myself. Once I learned to write I felt very freed. In my second grade we wrote lots of poems. We took a piece of construction paper and stapled it around the edge and I thought, "That's neat. I like that." There was also a place in the room where there were book jackets and you could use these as the starting-off point for your own stories. The first story I wrote was called "Up, Up and Away," and I wrote poems and stories ever after.

*Were you taken to galleries?*

My parents had a membership to the L.A. County Museum so we went a lot. I clearly remember the Oldenberg ice pack, which was out in the courtyard for a while in the late 1960s, early 1970s. I was told that it moved and I was interested in that.

*Did television play a role in your childhood?*

Although I liked many shows, I was against television on principle. I hated walking into a room when it was on and seeing my family staring, not talking to one another or listening to me. I even wrote poems about the experience.

*Were you solitary or sociable as a child?*

Very shy. I have a younger sister who is very outgoing. I was the passive, quiet child who pretty much stayed inside and read books and did crafts.

*Was it a religious household?*

Definitions of "religious" are all relative. We were American Reform Jews who celebrated most all of the Jewish holidays and kept the Sabbath on Friday nights, never ate pork, but did not observe many of the mitzvoth, the commandments, such as keeping Kosher or not turning lights on and off on the Sabbath.

*When did you first see an artist's book?*

*Arm in Arm* started me thinking about mixing words and images in an interesting way. I didn't come across any artists' books until Betsy Davids's class.

After Santa Monica High School I went to U.C. Berkeley for almost two years. I couldn't pick a major so I dropped out twice. I kept trying to go back but I found certain things were closed to me. When I took art classes I found I was supposed to mix egg tempera and I didn't really want to do that; I didn't even know that I wanted to paint. I felt the requirements were so stiff before you could get to anything you might want to do. I wanted to sit in on the creative writing class and I was told it was closed. I said, "I'm out of here. I'm done with this." I took a year off and sat in cafes and wrote poems until I looked in the catalogue of California College of Arts and Crafts (CCAC) and it said, "Letterpress printing and creative writing. Merging words and images." I thought, "That's what I'm supposed to be doing." I signed up for the class in 1983.

I had done letterpress printing in junior high school but I didn't know people had presses and type and could make their own books. In high school I had had a calligraphy class, too, with Kitty Maryatt (who now teaches book art at Scripps College in Southern California) and I learned my first bookbinding from her. By the time I discovered Betsy Davids's class I was experimenting with rubber stamps and on my journal pages the words and images were mixed together but I don't think I saw them as a book. I started keeping a diary as a child and I would have a drawing book too. They merged when I was about eighteen and I thought, "Why don't I just put it all together, try not to write any of this corny, awful stuff and try to do some writing work and visual work in one place?"

*What was the content of Betsy Davids's course?*

There was letterpress in the morning and the afternoon was the creative writing part. You could take both classes and for the most part there was a core of six or seven who did both. We were introduced to the type cabinet. We had a little printing history. Some book structures. Betsy showed a wonderful range of artists' books and that suddenly made everything very accessible.

*Can you remember what books you saw at this time?*

I was very struck by Shelley Hoyt's work; there was something very clear about the printing and the colors. I don't think there was ever any text but I liked the images. I wasn't influenced by other people's books at that time. I later went and looked at Califia Books when it started in San Francisco in about 1985 and I liked Walter Hamady's assemblage type and rubber stamps, but I never consciously thought, "Ah, I like this person's style, I'm going to go after that." I've always liked Dada typography but I haven't made use of it as much as I even would like to. There are all these things that are very appealing to me but somehow don't seem to be needed in whatever book I'm working on.

*What was your first book?*

**never mind the crowd**. Betsy said, "Set one page." I did something where whatever didn't fit in one line just migrated to the next; there were no hyphens or anything. It was set in eight-point type. Then I set a poem (it was all my text) in twelve-point or fourteen-point Universe. When I saw it printed I decided it would be the cover of a book of poems. I started writing poems furiously and hunting photographs I had taken over the years and which I photocopied and put in with photo corners. I used too heavy a paper and too heavy thread but it's not bad for my first book. I'm fond of it. **never mind the crowd** generated never mind the press, so I had the title for my press straight away. The first colophon is "never mind the universe 55 type or the archival poster paper or the king james cover or the letterpress . . . in fact go feed your dog or something." That set the tone for all the colophons; they all begin "never mind."

*What did you do with the book?*

It was an edition of thirty. I gave it away mostly. Then I went to a bookstore and said, "Hi. I have a book. Who do I talk to about carrying it?" He thumbed through it, a big guy, and said, "I'll pass." That was my first brush with merchants!

Then I decided I would transfer to CCAC. I started doing silkscreen. I took some art history classes. I pretty much did six books a year for two years. I made a book myself in the summer after that. It was all I was doing. I was thinking books, writing constantly. I know the process now, having done it for thirteen years, so I don't remember exactly what it was like at that time.

*Tell me about some of the early books.*

The second book was **R:I,P. Reason: Independence, Privacy**. It was about a man who wanted his privacy and happened to have a little daughter. It was based on a composite of people I knew who very much wanted to keep their privacy. I did two editions. The third book was **Brief Ground**, which

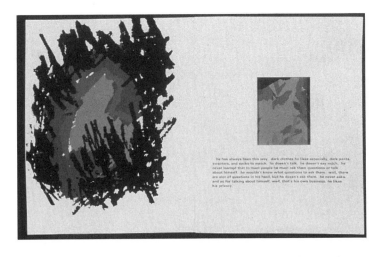

R:I,P. Reason: Independence, Privacy., die-cut letterpress with silkscreen prints, 9½" x 8", 26 pages, 2 editions, approx. 30 of each, 1983

has photo-silkscreens of meat carvings taken from an encyclopedia. Inside there are three vignettes, a poem about expectations and meat. It was on craft paper.

*Were you trying to stretch yourself technically?*

I still try. At that point I hadn't done a binding other than the pamphlet stitch. **Landmind** also had the same stitch. For **Out Out** I silkscreened the background and I was consciously trying to change the process because I wanted to print type over the images; I did a collage and a bit of photo-silkscreening of the collage and then cut the paper out irregularly because it was about misfits in society. The cover was cut on a diagonal so it almost looked like a sandwich the way the papers were different shapes behind it. It was very, very visual, probably the first nontraditional book I made. It was still fictitious. I was writing fiction and short poems and vignettes.

*What response were you getting to the work?*

The response I was getting from my printmaking teachers was very good. When I showed it to people who had no clue, it was, "What is this? How do I read it? Do you mean me to do this? Is it published?" All kinds of questions that are only now in this country and in the Bay Area being a lot more accepted in terms of "Ah, I know, this is an artist's book."

*Did it depress you that people didn't know how to react?*

Not at all. I just had to keep doing it. Occasionally I would think "I'm a writer in an art school, I'm a this and a that, I should be doing this instead

**alisa golden • 193**

of . . ." It was difficult to merge the two parts at one time. There were certain times when I could just draw and certain times I could just write; the drawings would come out terribly if I was in a writing stage and the poems wouldn't work at all if I were in a drawing stage. Either I'm hearing words in my head or I'm visualizing. That was more frustrating.

*Somewhere inside you they're very separate?*

They are.

*Do you feel your drawings are incomplete if they're not involved with words? Are some drawings independent?*

At this point most of my drawings had been on linoleum blocks and carved for books or prints. I had not carried on the idea of drawing just to draw. Currently I've got this notebook that's just for drawings and I'm going to work on them. I've got some ideas about what medium I'm going to use. They probably won't have words.

*Is the writing ever complete without images? Do you always want to put it in a book?*

Probably. I need the text first or a very clear idea. In general I'm always searching for a text. It appears one day; I hear something in my head and I can just start writing. The drawings are a little bit easier to manipulate into what I want to do. Some of the books have illustrations in them that aren't necessarily very strong because of that: I'm always looking for the strong piece of writing and the other stuff comes later.

*When you look at other people's work, does your eye go to the image or the text first?*

It's natural to get a sense of the whole book and look at the images first and then go back and read the text. I'm starting to wonder if there's a better way to sequence things. Maybe you should put the illustrations all at the front—but no, because then your eye won't want to read all that text at the back.

*Tell me more about the early books.*

There were some that I felt less strongly about, some that I did more as therapy than for other people. Often artists will take autobiographical material or their feelings about a certain thing and it's more therapy for them to make this piece—it may not be strong but the fact that they are exposing themselves may be enough for them. I don't like that particular style. If the piece is going to do what I want, it has to be strong and I want it to move me and be well crafted. The tendency right now is to be very slanted toward autobiographical work and I do some of that but, I hope, in a more universal sense.

In my last semester at CCAC I learned papermaking. I don't make paper pieces because that didn't work for me at all. I made batches of paper and a couple of books, including **The Sky Is a Working Color**, a small book with a pinkish cover which is an accordion-fold with pages glued to each of the little folds, so there was a lot more handiwork involved, it was more sculptural than what, maybe, would be called a fine-press book. There was another one, **The Waiting Letter**, which had a letter sewn in the middle that was sealed but you could look through the envelope and see my jury duty notice and a poem. Various people asked "Can I undo this envelope?" and I saw one where the envelope was slit, but you really could see through it.

*Do you have strong feelings about the way your books are treated?*

Probably, yes. I want to know that they've been handled; if they're ragged because they've been put under a pile of *Newsweeks*, that's another thought. The day when book art is accepted for what it is, then it'll have a place on the bookshelf, a special spot or a special table where you can look through the books. Maybe then the artists will be better treated. I don't know if that will ever happen in this country.

*Are you talking about in a bookshop or in a person's home?*

A person's home.

*In England a lot of people don't want to be known as book artists.*

There has to be a link because if we're all separate no one can . . . it's like William Morris's socialism: if everybody bands together to make an army to make war, why can't they band together to make an army to make peace? It has to be a group of people to get taken seriously.

*When you make a book how much do you think about how it will be handled in the outside world?*

I try to think about that. I noticed years ago that if I picked up a book and it had thin pages and was big, I would think how poorly it handled and the likelihood of it getting folded or damaged. I try to use materials that are somewhat durable. Unless there's a purpose in not doing so—I have one book, **Paper Wings**, that has very thin Mulberry paper and a tentative quality; it was my decision to have a cover that was going to bend eventually, because that was what the book was all about. Usually the materials are durable enough so that people can handle them, because that's the point of a book; otherwise you could just frame it and have done with it.

*Do you stay interested in the books once they're done?*

They're pretty much done. I have too many ideas, I can't keep up. I don't see the books as a link to one another but I do see them as a continuous path for me.

*What is the path?*

At this point it's exploring new structures, new media, new ways of sequencing or putting the type together or new ways to make people think.

*What happened when you left CCAC?*

I had a few years on borrowed press time, then I got my own. I had initially gotten trained as a computer typesetter by working on the school newspaper and I got a job doing that and then that business folded away. I went to an art supply store and worked there for a year; they put me in the graphics department, which sold Letraset and rub-on letters. The good part of working in the store was the discount on the supplies and access to the paper cutter and whatnot. And I had to look at these type books all day, helping people, so I got even more familiar with a whole other group of type, which is now the type that is used in the computer. Then I worked in a bookstore for a couple of years. I tried to sell some of my books there but I saw how people treated regular books—it would be picking them up and saying, "Gee, it doesn't weigh very much, why is it so expensive?" I realized a trade bookstore is not the place for artists' books. So I learned a lot about that and all this work in retail helped me overcome my shyness.

Then I quit there and took off a year because I knew we wanted to have a child so I wanted definite art time for at least a year with nothing to get in my way. Luckily, my husband has a good job. So I printed. I wanted to see what it would mean if I did that full-time, what would happen.

*You had your own press by this stage?*

Yes. I got it in 1988, the same press as now, the Challenge 15-inch cylinder press. That was the one that was available. I looked for a Vandercook and there weren't any. I ended up putting Vandercook rollers on the press because I was having trouble with the mechanical parts. What books I did that year, I don't remember. In terms of a career, it only started to feel more solidified two years ago when I started teaching book structures and I also started doing programs for the Pacific Center for the Book Arts, so now there is a link to the general public and to the book arts community.

*You didn't find that until recently?*

I wasn't ready to. I was terrified. I was still terrified the first class I taught, I was very nervous. Now it seems very natural and I enjoy it.

*Do you teach what Betsy Davids taught you?*

Her class was all-encompassing—I just teach structures. I initially started teaching the basic structures I learned from Betsy and now I'm learning more from other book artists and I'm teaching myself some so that I have a range. Sometimes people I'm teaching ask me questions and I say, "Well, this is only the second one I've made, but I know how it functions." I know how to read a manual that tells me how it goes together, whereas I would have been lost if I hadn't had the previous training and seen such a variety of structures.

*Tell me about your subscription books. They are usually in groups of three?*

I've found three is as many as I can handle in one subscription. The first one was **The Hand Correspondence** (1990–91), then there was **Catching A River** (1993), which also had three words in the title. So does the **Garden Variety Book** (1994–95). It just turns out that three is a workable number to commit to. You get paid up front and then your deadlines are already there. The latest subscription is **The Lending Library** (1996), with an ink-washed cover. Inside it are library pockets glued to a concertina and each one has the date when the subscription is due stamped just as a library pocket might do—March 15, July 15, November 15, 1996—which is when each of the books will arrive. They're all about borrowing and lending in some form or another. The first one is about whether you can borrow wisdom; it's called **The Mirror Business**; the second one's called **The Local Desk**, and the last one's called **Fishcake**. The subscription is currently sixty-five dollars for the three books, the prepublication price. The price goes up when all the books are done. Each subscription is an edition of about forty books. Once the whole book is done I can sell it through Califia Books and they take a cut. I've done subscriptions every other year because it's a major time commitment to do three books in a year. Sometimes it takes up as much time as doing one of my regular small editions of what I would call a "forty-dollar book" anyway. I'm going to take a break from the subscriptions. I did it two years in a row, and it's too much.

The sets in the subscription series loosely relate to each other, but they're a way that I can explore materials and maybe some of the writings that I don't feel to be strong enough to be a book on their own. For the

**Garden Variety Book** each part is a pseudo seed packet, one says **Lemon**, one says **Helianthus** (which is a sunflower), and one says **Oxalis**, otherwise known as sourgrass and a weed around here. All of these have to do with gardens and with my daughter, Mollie. Gardening is something I am interested in, something I do when I'm not making a book.

The first book in the series, **Lemon**, is called *A Book in the Garden* and has handmade paper and some collages and a color photocopy. The paper also has some lavender in it, and I've shaped the type appropriately to the page. For the second, called **Teachings of Sourgrass**, the text is "My job is turning the yard"—a prison term—"into a garden without boundaries." When the yard is full of oxalis, it looks like a prison. Mollie's on the front of this book picking her bouquet of sourgrass; all kids are fascinated by this weed. She wanted me to put it in a vase and it was hard to explain to her that this particular flower was ugly, when to her it was beautiful. The third book, titled **Sunflowers in December & Sunflowers for Sale or Rent**, is about people's assumptions about what belongs to us and what people believe that we don't know about.

Another series is **The Hand Correspondence**; **Mirror/Error** is part of that, using a story I wrote in about 1986 or '87 when I was living in a tiny apartment, and came from the feeling of shadows that you see on the shades. The three books in this series have the same paper for their covers and envelopes. The first envelope says "The," the second says "Hand," and "Correspondence" is on the third. The theme here was communicating and correspondence and I liked the idea of correspondence and art going through the mail. I started thinking it was one book but I got such a good response that I ended up with a subscription series.

*Who was the response from?*

Other book artists. University libraries. Just some generally interested people. In 1990 people were beginning to have seen artists' books so it wasn't a foreign concept. I sold it out.

*What is the little metal hand?*

That's on the tie. It just tied it up for **The Hand Correspondence**—it's from a wonderful bead and charm store in Oakland. **Eight Degrees of Charity** (1995) has another hand, a little copper one. I was initially thinking of using an old coin with a hole in the middle but then I saw the hand and thought charity isn't necessarily about coins. The text is by Maimonides.

*What attracted you to the text?*

The abundance of people on the streets. The question I struggle with every day as I walk by these guys sitting outside the post office. It's the same guys every day asking for money and I don't know how I feel about it or what I'm going to do about it. I saw the text initially on one of the Jewish calendars.

*How important is it to you not to make a loss on the books you make?*

It's important in an abstract way. I was happy when I broke even. At this point I always make a little bit on each book, so I'm happy about that. I never get paid for my time. When you're in a relationship where your partner makes tons more than you do, there is a little pressure in your head—or at least in my head—that says I want to contribute monetarily so I don't feel that's his car or his house or whatever, even though I'm taking care of stuff. Also, I would love to be able to say to students who ask, "Do you make a living?" "Yes. Do it. Go at it with your heart." Initially I said, "No, you've got to go and get other work." Now I say, "If you can do teaching, too, maybe you can if you do higher-end books." It is a business. I'm doing what I love. There are parts of it I don't enjoy, but it's my business at this point.

*You've just done your first collaborative project?*

Yes, **Tidal Poems**. This is a collaboration with Anne Schwartzburg, who was a CCAC student after I was. I met her through Betsy. I've always loved her drawings and I admire her writing as well. She has been doing one-of-a-kinds and I felt that in a collaborative work we could both do some writing and I would maybe carve the blocks and she would do the drawings. It ended up we both carved the blocks and she did three of the drawings. We took a couple of months painting the backs and fronts of about 120 sheets of Stonehenge paper and then we cut those up and printed on them. About half the poems are hers and half mine—we've interspersed them so you don't know whose is whose unless you start examining them. Hers are more personal and about relationships and mine are more public in terms of things out in the world.

What I found was that we made a book I probably could not produce, certainly not in an edition of sixty, by myself. We found as a team we meshed very well. She could do an edition, which she hadn't been able to do because she doesn't have a press and I could have her input in terms of her painting. On the first day we started painting, we brought out the inks and she took a brush and scrubbed here and drew a line there and made a circle here and I looked at her and tried to get a line down; I was a little too careful with my lines and then I thought "Right, I'll do it." I started to scrub and paint a line here and do a circle there and it got to be very free for me, who had been working very, very tightly and carving little linoleum blocks and setting type and making sure it was printing just so and the binding was just so. It loosened me up quite a bit. It was very exciting. Since we worked well together we have an idea for our

*Fly on a Ladder*,
letterpress, 2½" x 2¾" x 1"
in Jacob's Ladder binding,
edition of 40, 1996

next book. Finally in my life I could let there be some other input. In my twenties I would have said, "I don't want you to do it because I think this looks better"—kind of arrogant. Maybe it's a stage that people go through before they can say, "Let's see what we can do together. I'm open to your suggestions," without having to edit everyone else's work in the "right way," whatever that is.

I couldn't have collaborated before because my laundry room where I had the press was too small. All this time I've had just a tiny utility room with a few inches above my head to work in, which was fine for one person. The studio was finally finished in March 1995. I'm filling up the studio very fast, but can fit three letterpress students in there. I even have room to be working on two books at once as well. Currently [fall 1996] I am setting type for **Waking Snakes**, a book of poems, collagraphs, linocuts, and type fragments. I'm printing it on periwinkle-colored paper I just had made at Magnolia Editions. The structure was devised by Michael, my spouse, who said, "I'm going to invent a book structure." When I said, "Why don't you learn some first?" he took that as a challenge and came back a few hours later with a binding that used no sewing and no glue. We call it "Slot and Tab." The book will have all the deckle edges showing and be protected in a small clamshell box in an edition of twenty.

The second book is a Jacob's ladder structure (the child's toy), called **Fly on a Ladder**. I'm excited I finally figured out how to make one. It's about dreams and flying, and involves the retelling of the biblical Jacob's dream in the desert. It will function as the toy and, if you turn it sideways, it will open and read like a "regular" book. The printing will be from a zinc plate (images and text). The binding will be labor intensive. But I want to make a bunch and sell them for cheap. Probably not sell any in shops or galleries so I don't have to mark up the price another 40 percent.

These books are part of my plan to find a way to balance the creation of high-end, expensive, small-edition books with a line of inexpensive but inspiring books accessible to regular folk. The subscriptions are midline books, priced a little too high for a general audience. And I'm tired of doing them. My initial goal was to make art that anyone could afford. In order to do that I think the deluxe books will have to fund the inexpensive ones. Much work is waiting.

*Leavings,*
letterpress and Gocco
printed, 6½"x 4¼"
expands to 51",
edition of 100, 1997

# julie chen

Cathy Courtney's interview with Julie Chen in Berkeley, California, took place by fax and e-mail between in June and August 1998.

Julie Chen in her studio, 1998

Photo: Sibila Savage

*You have lived in Berkeley all of your adult life. Is that where you grew up?*

I was born in a suburb of Los Angeles in 1963 and lived in that area until I was twelve. Then my family—my father, a Methodist minister, my mother, my younger sister, and I—moved to New Jersey, where we lived until I was almost out of high school. We moved back to California, to San Jose, where I spent a year finishing high school, and then I returned to New Jersey to go to college, but eventually transferred to the University of California at Berkeley to finish my degree in studio art. I have stayed in that area ever since.

*Were both your parents religious?*

Yes, both of my parents are religious in the sense that they have both been very active in the church community for most of their lives. Even though my father is a minister, the subject of religion, or religious doctrine and moral beliefs, was not really a focus at home when I was growing up. It was more like the family business, taken for granted.

*What do you remember being on the walls of your childhood homes?*

The walls were covered in an assortment of framed photographs of family members, one dark abstract painting, and many craft projects that were created by my mother and, later, by me and my sister as well. My mother is an expert seamstress and we made quilts and banners. We also got into the popular folk crafts of the times, such as macramé and decoupage. It was an interesting mix of kitsch and creativity.

*What objects were significant for you?*

The one object that was very important to me as a child was a Japanese Kabuki Lion Dancer figure that was kept in a glass case all by itself. He was about eighteen inches high and decked out in a sumptuous costume and had very dramatic features. He was so mysterious, so foreign, yet so sure of himself. The expression in his face and in his body gesture radiated such force, such determination, such a sense of belonging, of knowing his place. The idea of the figure enclosed behind glass is one that sticks with me in my art life today. Almost every book that I have made has been enclosed in some way or another, and that goes back directly to my fascination with the Lion Dancer. The fact that the reader is first presented with a package that can be opened in order to get to the book is a very deliberate choice on my part. I want to create a sense of mystery and anticipation, of having to "go through" something before getting to the heart of the work. The force of the mystery comes not from the inability to see what is inside the box, but from being separated from it physically, and that sense of "otherness" is very important. The separation also helps to create a dramatic tension, like the curtain going up before a play begins.

*Were other objects significant to you?*

Through the collection of an aunt, I became very interested in jewelry and pottery from Native American tribes of the Southwest. Later, I had a teacher who had the class do in-depth studies of ancient Central American cultures such as the Maya and Aztec people. I developed a fascination with artifacts and loved to create fake artifacts to go along with my school projects. I produced several collage books about Native American culture by cutting things out of magazines and adding my own text. They were bound together with twine and tape. I took a long road trip to the Southwest a few years ago and felt comfortable in the desert landscape and nourished by exploring the ruins and looking at the art and artifacts. The starkness there makes the connection between the artifacts and the life seem much clearer and stronger than the connections between art and life in the present day. I still feel drawn to the landscape and culture of the Southwest tribes, especially the Navajo and the Hopi, but the relationship with my own work is not very apparent. It is more of an internal link in how I approach my work, in trying to make it "stand up" to the purity of those ancient artifacts and in trying to connect to elemental truths in what I am trying to express.

*What books and magazines were around you at home when you were growing up?*

I loved magazines such as National Geographic and Arizona Highways that showed other places and cultures. Sunset magazine, with its various crafts projects, was a real presence in the house. Neither of my parents were big readers, and it's hard to remember specifically what I read as a child, but I was encouraged and was taken to the library on a regular basis. My parents bought a set of encyclopedias that we were all very proud of. I read the more standard children's books such as The Little House on the Prairie series by Laura Ingalls Wilder. My mother had many cookbooks and I remember with special fondness one about cake decorating that had color photographs of fabulous creations. My father, being a minister, had many religious books.

*What role did television play in your life?*

I was a total TV junkie from early childhood and watched all the sitcoms as well as cartoons and game shows and, later, soap operas. My family watched together while eating dinner, then after dinner. I watch only occasionally now, except for "The Simpsons," which is the only show my daughter watches regularly. She has very little interest in TV.

*Did you write as you grew up?*

I loved to write poetry. I spent time in the summers writing stories and also went through a period of being in love with the simplicity and rigidity of the haiku form.

*Were you encouraged to draw and paint?*

My parents always encouraged me to be creative, especially in ways that involved making things. I had very little formal exposure to art as a child and, although we went to small craft fairs, there was nothing approaching a museum or gallery. Neither of my parents had any exposure to art themselves.

*What did you do after leaving college?*

I had married very young, when I was still in college. My husband and I would have been content just to live together, and in fact did so for a year, but my family leaned on us pretty hard to get married and make our relationship more legitimate and respectable. I decided I wanted to have a baby the year after I graduated from college, and my daughter was born in 1985. I found motherhood to be very difficult for the first two years. I think now that postpartum depression played a large role in how I felt, but at the time I was at loose ends. None of my close friends had children, and in fact that is still the case to this day. I felt pretty isolated. I hadn't been doing much serious art work since college, but had been planning to go back to it eventually.

*When did you first encounter book art?*

My first contact with book arts came through Kathy Walkup and the book arts program at Mills. My sister was studying there in the mid-1980s, and I happened to visit her on campus one day with my young daughter. On a whim, I got a copy of the graduate program brochure and when I started reading about the book arts program I was completely fascinated, even though I had virtually no understanding of what any of the classes really entailed. I made an appointment to meet with Kathy and as soon as I walked into the studio, I knew that this was what I wanted to do. It sounds like an overdramatization, but when I saw the presses—I had no idea what they were—and smelled the ink and solvent, I was completely hooked. Within four months, I was in the program starting my life's work. It was like the answer to my unuttered prayers. The program got me started on what I consider to be my true vocation at a time when I needed to have my art spirit jump-started.

*What kind of environment did you encounter at Mills, and what was the content of the book art course?*

I was there from 1987 to 1989, and at that time the press room was very cozy with just enough room for two Vandercooks, a platen press, and several banks of type in the main room. In a second room there was more type and a composing stone, and we also had a separate classroom that served as a bindery, but that was in a different part of the building and we had to go through the library to get to it.

The first year of the graduate program was like a boot camp for book artists. You took one whole year of printing, including rigorous typography instruction, and, at the same time, one whole year of binding. For someone such as myself, who started out with virtually no experience in either discipline, there seemed to be a phenomenal amount of technical information to absorb all at once. Learning how to set type, run the press, and sew up a book, I had to use the limits of my powers of concentration just to keep up. We also took a course in the history of the book and some seminars during the first year. Kathy Walkup covered a broad range of topics and had us look at typographical examples from various periods, from the Gutenberg Bible through the works of the Golden Cockerel Press, through Russian constructivism and into the present day. She also gave lectures about such related topics as the history of women in printing. Through it all, we were encouraged to do our own creative work. The technical training was of a very high standard, but the way in which Kathy structured the program to foster creative expression through the book form was invaluable to me.

*Did you come across book art by other people?*

Through Kathy Walkup, I was exposed to the work of Claire Van Vliet and Susan King very early on, and also the work of Ron King, who came to visit Mills when I was there. Those are the three I remember the most. When Ron came I was still struggling to catch up in my general knowledge of books and I was terribly intimidated by him, partially because he made such large dramatic books, such as *The Left-handed Punch*. At the time it seemed completely out of anything in my experience of the book form and the way in which printmaking could be combined with the book. If I had come to his work at a slightly later time at Mills, it would probably have had greater impact. As it was, I felt more comfortable with Claire and Susan's work. I was in complete awe of Claire's Janus Press books because of the level of craftsmanship and the sheer beauty of them. I tried to emulate them as best I could with my extremely limited experience and knowledge and I still look to both Claire and Susan's work as models of a high standard I would like to follow.

*What in particular was important to you about their work?*

Everything in Claire Van Vliet's books—the printing, binding, materials, colors, textures—worked so beautifully together, and each aspect was perfectly executed. Her contents also fascinated me. Books such as *The Circus of Dr. Lao* and *Aunt Sally's Lament* still move me greatly even though I have at this point looked at them over and over with my own students in the Mills library.

Susan King's work I found to be inspirational for slightly different reasons. I admire the innovative use of structure in many of her pieces, but it is the way in which she uses the personal voice that really speaks to me. Even though my work is very different from Susan's in subject matter, tone, and in many, many other ways, there is something about her perspective as a writer and book artist that I responded to as a student, and still do. For instance, in *Treading the Maze*, the courageous way in which she shares her personal experiences is inspirational to me. Also, the way in which she connects different aspects of her experience into a larger pattern is something I relate to in my own work. For example, the image of the rose window in a cathedral becomes connected visually and symbolically with a sketch of a mutating cell drawn by a doctor. Those kinds of subtle connections are something I feel drawn to. Another book of Susan's that I really admire is *Lessons from the South*. I remember being very excited by her use of structure in this book, and the way in which parts of the text were printed on the concertina "spine," and not just on the pages. Also, the way in which the pages were translucent and opened out in a nontraditional way. This book helped to open my eyes to the incredible potential of the form in terms of the artist's book.

*Were Ed Ruscha's books significant to you?*

We did look at his books, I think, but I don't remember clearly. I was probably not that interested in them then because they were offset printed, and at the time I was completely in love with letterpress. My recollection is that we spent much more time talking about and examining the works of contemporary American book artists such as Claire and Susan.

*You Are Here,*
letterpress printed from polymer plates,
4"x 4", expands to 11½"x 15", edition of 100, 1992

*Have your feelings about offset books changed over time? Is it a process you would use yourself?*

I am much more interested in the possibility of using the offset process now. I've only used it indirectly a few times in doing commercial graphics work for clients, but I've seen some wonderful offset artists' books, such as Phillip Zimmerman's *High Tension*. I am very interested in expanding my technical vocabulary whenever possible, but as the equipment I have in my shop is all geared toward letterpress, I'll probably stick mostly to that for a while.

*What were your own first book works?*

My early books seem like exercises to me now. I had very little idea how to start, so I decided to focus on something I knew and, with my religious background, it seemed natural to start with a Bible story. Also, we had been shown some beautiful biblical books, such as the Golden Cockerel Press *Four Gospels*. So I made a concertina version of the story of Creation, **The First Seven Days**.

*Wasn't that quite a sophisticated structure for a first book?*

I knew next to nothing. I had begun at Mills in the spring so did not have a chance to take the binding class, which had started in the previous fall, and I didn't even know how to sew a pamphlet. So I got a minimal amount of tutoring by one of the other students in the program. I had a vague notion that I wanted to make a book that could be displayed, so I asked to be shown how to make a concertina and was taught how to make a simple concertina with nonadhesive covers. It seemed like magic to me. As I began to make sketches for the book, I realized the standard concertina was not quite right for my ideas, so I devised a hybrid structure composed of two concertinas that folded up separately into two halves of a single book.

*How did you relate text and image in* **The First Seven Days**?

I wanted there to be a sense of visual continuation, so that the images flowed from one page to the next and I wanted the text to be integrated within the visual plane of each spread and to become part of the image instead of the more standard differentiation between text and image. It was an idea that came out of a total lack of knowledge and understanding about typography, and yet looking back at it now, it seems to work reasonably well.

*Did you not consider making a book in which the text was your own composition?*

**Origin** (1988) was the first book I made that was totally my own creation. The text is a short story I had written in college about a mystical experience having to do with a river. It was written in response to a short story by Barry Lopez in his book *River Notes*. The structure of **Origin** is based on the flag-book structure devised by Hedi Kyle, something which completely fascinated me, as I had never seen anything even remotely like it before. I knew I wanted to use it and decided that this text would work well with it because of the way in which things in the text are revealed only in pieces as the story progressed. As you read the book, page by page, only fragments of the image can be seen on each spread, and the continuous collagraphic image of a river is revealed only when the book is opened for display. Looking back, the concept behind **Origin** was my first real dip into the realm of the artist's book.

*When did your books cease to be* "exercises"?

Not until I was out of graduate school, where I was experimenting with so many aspects of the book that there's always something that didn't get fully addressed and resolved at the time. Many of them were very "successful" exercises, but I look at them in that way because I really didn't know what I was doing at the time. It was equal parts intuition and putting into immediate practice things I had only just learned about. It was like singing in public after your first lesson; maybe you've got enough talent and audacity to get by, but it's not going to be anything truly meaningful and deep until you've worked at it for a while.

*You used the flag structure again for* **Requiem** *(1989)?*

I was totally in love with the structure then (I still am), so I was always hoping for another chance to use it. The idea for **Requiem** developed somewhat simultaneously with the idea to use the structure. This happens to me pretty often, where I will be working with ideas for a structure, or a new variation on a structure, with no ideas for how to use it, and also, working with ideas for a text or text-image combination with no idea of what structure will house it. Sometimes it takes months for me to realize that these two aspects that I have been obsessing about separately are actually the same project.

I decided to use six flags in a row in the structure instead of three as in **Origin**. I wanted to create a visual tapestry effect that would symbolize the sounds created by the instruments and voices and also to give the book an unusual proportion when opened to present the viewer with a "larger-than-life" effect. The main text of the books comes from the text of the requiem mass, printed in both Latin and English, but the beginning pages contain my own text, having to do with my impressions of the conductor of an orchestra and the concentrated force that seems to radiate from him before the music begins. In a way, this text acts like the prologue to a piece of music, or perhaps like the moment of silence before the music begins.

*An element of sound is built into* **Requiem** *if it is pulled open in a single movement?*

**Requiem** came out of my experience of attending a live performance of the Berlioz Requiem at the San Francisco Symphony. I knew I wanted to use a structure that made a particular noise and could reproduce the sound of the choir rising before beginning to sing, a hushed moment of extreme tension during the performance. The flag book answered the challenge perfectly. If it is opened fairly quickly, the sound of all the flag "pages" moving through space and hitting the adjacent flags is uncannily similar to the one in the concert hall.

*It seems that music plays an important role in your life and in your books?*

Music has a strong influence on me. A later book, **Listening** (1992), was also about listening to live music and itself has an element of performance so that you can wear it as a headdress; I wanted to take the idea of recreating live performance of music one step further than in **Requiem** and involve the reader in a more active way. The hand images in **Listening** refer to the gestures used by the conductor of an orchestra. The text explores the

*Listening*,
letterpress printed from polymer plates,
3½"x 4", expands to 32",
edition of 75, 1992

relationship of sound and silence in a piece of music and how the tension in the silences can be just as powerful as the music itself.

*The map is another theme which recurs in your work?*

Yes, the map is such a rich metaphor for emotion. The idea of having a two-dimensional record of a three-dimensional space, and that somehow the record can relate directly to the space is compelling. Also, I didn't consciously choose to use the map form in an abstract way; it was more that the map form suggested itself to me at a time when I was grasping for a way to express some intense emotional ideas. **You Are Here** (1992) was the first book in which I used the idea of the map. That was an instance where the structure and the content developed independently for months before my realization that they should be combined. I had seen a version of the structure in one of Keith Smith's books in which he mentioned that, although he had devised it, he had never found a use for it. I started fiddling with it just for fun and at the same time  began writing the text for **You Are Here,** which uses the idea of the map as a direct metaphor for emotional life.

I used map imagery again in a later book titled **Radio Silence** (1995). As in **You Are Here**, the text deals with intense emotional experience. In this instance I incorporated strips of found map in order to suggest an actual journey. I made many different models for this book, and ended up choosing one in which the text is on one long continuous narrow strip of paper with layers of concertina-folded maps, and other papers behind it. I wanted the reader to have to take an actual physical journey from the beginning of the book to the end that parallels the journey talked about in the text.

*Some of your books—such as* **Radio Silence**—*address an unnamed "you," who is clearly not the reader and seems to be someone from your private life. How do you hone personal experience for use in your books?*

I am often asked about the apparently autobiographical nature of my work. The "you" that appears changes with each book and does not necessarily represent anyone in my life. While it is true that on some level the work is coming out of my own experience, I look on the material more as autobiographical fiction, with fiction as the operative word. The intimate voice, the first-person narration that appears in many of my books, is sometimes confused with my personal voice, but this is not generally the case. Any personal experience is filtered in such a way that only the essence might appear.

I feel strongly that any direct connection that may exist between the contents of my work and my private life is completely immaterial and does not matter at all to the work itself. It is the relationship between the work and the personal experience of the reader that interests me. I always hope that the use

*Listening*,
letterpress printed from polymer plates,
3½" x 4", expands to 32",
edition of 75, 1992

of the intimate voice will resonate with the reader and help to create a direct emotional connection for him or her.

*Your books often have a sad flavor.* **Leavings** *(1997), for example, is a collection of potentially overlooked fragments, memorialized in a precious container.*

**Leavings** is one of my more recent works in which each page spread contains collaged strips of text as well as a pocket containing a removable tag. There is text and image on each tag, as well as a small glassine envelope containing fragments of various materials. The images that are on the tags also show on the backside of the book through holes cut through the pages. I wanted to use both sides of the book, to fill all the available space with content as a sort of allegory for the process of memory, in which things are rigidly compartmentalized in order to keep them from overflowing into chaos.

One subject in my work that I keep coming back to is that of loss. I'm not exactly sure where this comes from. Looking back, I think one contributing factor comes from my experience of moving many times as a child. Although I grew up in a stable family, we moved a lot, and so in a subtle way, I had to deal repeatedly with the loss of my world: my neighborhood, school environment, and friends. Because my family was always there and because we often didn't move far away from the previous area, there was an illusion that the loss was not very great. It took me until I was past thirty years old to understand how this series of moves may have affected me. This childhood experience certainly does not account fully for the power that the subject of loss has in my art, but my perspective as an artist has probably been influenced by it.

*Have you been able to earn a living through your work with books?*

I had no idea how I was actually going to earn a living after leaving Mills and I decided that since I had my shop all set up at home, I might try going into letterpress job printing. It turned out that I did not need to earn a living for many years, so I decided to run Flying Fish Press full-time, with the intention of one day turning a profit. I decided to publish the work of other artists as well as my own in the hope that diversity would generate sales. I believed that it would also help take the pressure off me of feeling that I had to produce my own work all the time. My goal was to establish a reputation of producing limited edition artists' books of the highest caliber, in terms of content and craftsmanship. I hired a part-time assistant, Chris Rolik, to help with the production work. She's still with me today. Since my change in financial circumstances (I got divorced in 1994), I have a much more urgent need to make a living and I'm happy to say it's finally starting to happen.

*You also have a teaching role?*

I teach bookbinding at Mills. The majority of my students have little or no studio art experience, so we start with the basics and then progress through simple nonadhesive structures into more sophisticated adhesive structures, such as hardcover books and boxes. I love teaching. I have been teaching here and there for years, but my experience at Mills is the first one in which I have been able to work with students over a long period of time. I find that the process of teaching the things that I love nourishes my own creative work.

*Through Flying Fish Press publications you have collaborated with other artists; did this begin when you were a student?*

Yes, I began by collaborating with friends who happened to be artists and writers. Then right after I graduated, I steeled up my nerve to approach Nance O'Banion, a better-known artist I had met when I was a graduate student. Nance has taught papermaking at California College of Arts and Crafts for many years now, and I, along with several other graduate students from Mills, crossregistered for her class. She is a vibrant, giving teacher, able to encourage everyone's individual artistic development. I had a very positive response to her work, which I first saw at a one-woman show of hers. It consisted mostly of large sculptural paper pieces and, even though she had not done much work with books at the time, I felt drawn to approach her with an offer to work with her on a limited-edition book.

I had very little understanding of how a collaboration between a publisher and artist might work, so I just made it up as I went along. Nance almost immediately started envisioning a book with pop-ups and fold-out elements. I started making models based on her general ideas but neither of us had a clear picture at this point, and Nance had not even started making any artwork for the book. It didn't have a title, just the idea of something with a sculptural presence.

We went through a series of maybe ten different models before settling on the one we used. **Domestic Science** (1990) is a two-sided book that can be read in a circular fashion, with two title pages, and the structure is such that you just naturally flip the book over to the other side after viewing its first side. It has five pop-ups on one side and four fold-out chapters filled with text and image on the other. I liked the structure we used because it was

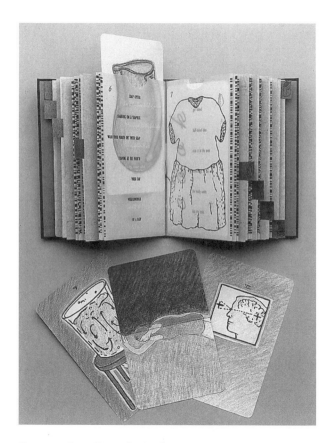

*Correspondence Course* (text and
illustration by Nance O'Banion),
printed letterpress from photopolymer plates
by Julie Chen with 4-color process
screenprinting by Thomas Wojak,
8¾" x 6½", with 48 removable cards,
edition of 100, 1993

compact—one of the rejected versions measured perhaps twelve feet when opened for display and was completely unwieldy—and because of the fact that the chapters on one side fold out in a line of zigzags, which reminded me of Nance's earlier sculptural work. I feel I had a strong influence on the ultimate contents, in that it wasn't until the final model was made that she started filling it with artwork. Even though the text and images are all generated by Nance, I got to determine the physical expression of the piece. The final blocks were not cut until right before the book was due to be released. It was a very dynamic relationship with a lot of trust between us, an intense experience that spanned more than a year of active work.

*You collaborated with Nance again on* **Correspondence Course** *(1993)?*

Nance had been working fairly steadily on the book format since **Domestic Science** and had more solid ideas for our second collaboration. She wanted to work with the element of transparency as well as the element of randomness such as could be had with a deck of cards. Once again we embarked with my making models and her beginning the text and images. The final product is a book in codex form, whose pages are made up of transparent envelopes with text and image printed on them in black and white. Each envelope contains a card, usually with the image on one side and the text on the other, which is removable so that the reader can switch them around or simply take out the cards and play with them separately and maybe view the transparent envelope pages on their own. The cards are coded by color, number, and icon so they can be put in their original order.

*How did you come to work with Lois Morrison?*

Lois is the mother of my first serious boyfriend, and the first artist I ever knew personally. We have remained very good friends for the past twenty or so years. We both started making books around the same time, unbeknownst to each other. She specializes in one-of-a-kind books made of fabric with text done in running stitch or satin stitch, incredibly labor intensive and visually rich. When we decided to work together the first time, I was still in graduate school, still shy of the idea of producing my own work, casting about for manuscripts to produce. She had an idea for what became **Memories of Fruit** (1988) and sent me the initial manuscript for which I created a structure that incorporated elements for several of her more intriguing ideas, such as the man with the fruit phobia. I decided to string the fruit shapes on elastic threads, so that when you open the page the fruits appear to be actively chasing his running figure. It was a fun project to do.

With our second book, **Ste Ostrich in Manhattan** (1990), we decided to make a book using one of Lois's animal characters. I got the idea for the carousel format from a children's book from the 1930s that I saw at the local antiquarian book fair. It was a revelation. It's simply several layers of concertina of varying depths that are nested together and cut through so that you can create a scene spanning several layers. I made a model, sent it to Lois, and she started cutting lino blocks and pretty soon we were in production.

My working relationship with Lois was pretty different from the one with Nance, partially because Lois lives on the East Coast, and we were not able to meet in person at any time during the production. We didn't even have fax or e-mail back then. Also, the individual working styles of Nance and Lois are very different, as was the nature of the projects I worked on with each of them. Nance's have a stream-of-consciousness flavor to them that extended into aspects of production and things were constantly changing and being shifted around as we did the book. With Lois, things proceeded in a much more orderly and predictable fashion.

*In **Octopus** (1992), which you made with Elizabeth McDevitt, you are credited as both designer and engineer. Where do you draw the distinction?*

For me, the role of the designer has to do with stylistic ideas and choices such as the typography and page layout of the book, the choices of materials, colors, typeface, and such. The designer in me creates the look and feel of the book. The engineer role is also very dear to my heart, as I love to experiment with structural and sculptural elements. It's more of a technical role, devising how to make things happen physically with pop-ups, movable parts, and other structural variations necessary for the project.

*How did **Octopus** come about?*

Elizabeth and I were in graduate school together. She is a wonderful poet, and has also served as editor on many of my projects. Her background is literary, and I trust her opinion more than just about anybody else's. She has a very critical mind for text and a great sensitivity about the book form, so we have made a good team on occasion. The text of **Octopus** is one of Elizabeth's poems that compares emotional behavior to that of the mysterious octopus. She made a one-of-a-kind version of this book while we were still in school, and I liked it so much that I decided that I wanted to redesign it and republish it in a limited edition. I love the tunnel book form for its ability to suggest atmosphere. In this instance we were able to create a very watery, shadowy environment that illustrated the text beautifully. The tentacles of the octopus appear illusively deep in the recesses of the back pages.

*What are you working on now?*

At present I am collaborating with Barbara Tetenbaum, a book artist who teaches at Oregon College of Art and Craft. We got to know

*Radio Silence*,
letterpress printed from photopolymer plates,
5"x 3½"x 2⅜", expands to 7',
edition of 75, 1995

each other about five years ago when I taught a workshop at OCAC. This is our first collaboration and deals indirectly with a subject dear to both our hearts—music. I have become fascinated with numbers over the years for reasons that I can't fully explain. Numbers have begun playing an increasingly important role in my books, and they seem to be getting bigger and bigger with every project. I'm not sure where this is leading, but you'll definitely feel their presence in my collaboration with Tetenbaum, as well as in future projects. I am also working on a series on miniature books of my own. When I was a student I often dreamed about making large-format books, to make a large serious statement of some kind, but since starting the press, things seem to be going in the opposite direction. I love to work with books that can fit in the palm of your hand, and since I have small hands, my books tend to be small too.

*Will books continue to be an important element in your working life?*

I cannot imagine living a life in which books were not a central part of my activity.

*How do you spell
a woman?*,
book with metal pages,
magnetized text,
and doll, 7"x 5"x1½",
16 pages,
one of a kind, 1996

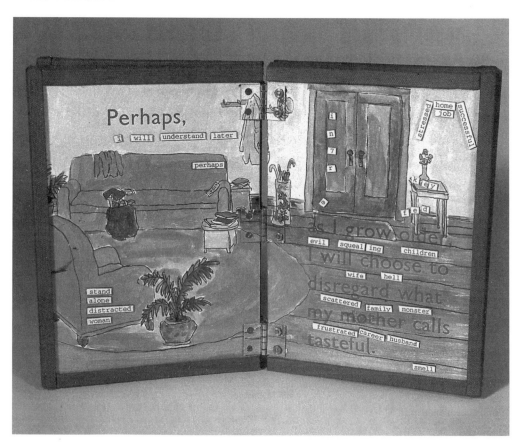

# karen
# bleitz

Karen Bleitz was interviewed by Cathy Courtney in London at Circle Press on March 17 and at Liliane Lijn's studio on May 21, 1998.

Karen Bleitz, 1998

Photo: Celeste Trimble

*You came to live in London to take the M.A. book arts course at Camberwell, but until that time you lived in America?*

I was born in San Diego in 1973. I'm an only child, and my parents divorced when I was about three months old. My father is American and my mother is Vietnamese. They met in the airport in Saigon when my mother was working for Pan Am as an information attendant. My father was a pilot for the same airline, flying cargo to the soldiers during the Vietnam war. After she told my father that she wanted to go to college in the United States, he sent her some application forms and off she went. I admire her bravery. She was the youngest of nine children, all of whom came to the States eventually. She went with only one hundred dollars to her name. It took a lot of courage and determination to take a step like that. Three years later she married my father.

*Did you spend time in Vietnam yourself when you were growing up?*

I've only been to Vietnam once. That was in 1992, when I went to meet my grandmother shortly before her death. It was an odd experience. In the United States, every person I've ever met has asked, "What are you? What is your ethnicity?" Growing up, this led me to believe that I was somehow more Vietnamese than American. When I went to Vietnam, I was shocked to discover that everyone there could only see how foreign I was, how American I was. They could tell by every action and movement and by the way that I talked to my mother. I was a head taller than almost everyone else in the country. It wasn't until that visit that I realized that I really am half-and-half, somewhere in the middle. I fit in neither country and therefore can sort of fit in both.

*What was on the walls of your parents' houses when you were growing up?*

I didn't like the art in my mother's house except for paintings by her brother, a famous artist in Vietnam, who did wonderful eggshell and lacquer paintings where he built up and built up until they became really beautiful. In my father's house there was a koala skin hanging and a couple of pictures of birds by an uncle of mine who did photography. When I was growing up, whenever my father decided I looked bigger, he would stand me against a wall in the washroom and mark it with a pen. The house is rented out now and he forbade anyone living there to paint over this record. A couple of Christmases ago he asked me for some help and said he'd made me a present but had broken it. I went to help him and discovered he'd cut out this big chunk of the wall to frame it for me. Best present I've ever gotten.

*Were books important to you in childhood?*

Very. I had lots of children's books. I remember getting Dr. Seuss books and my father saying they were ridiculous and ending my publisher's subscription, which was crushing. In around eighth grade I started reading fantasy books and couldn't put them down and that's probably when I started to enjoy reading because that was a whole new world, where you had superpowers, that you could enter instantly whenever you wanted.

*Did you draw as a child?*

I drew and painted but I was always more scared to make a mark than not because each time I did, it was as if I had to prove something. I went to do a summer program at a proper art college in Los Angeles (Otis Parsons) and I did terribly there. I was about fifteen. It was disheartening to realize how bad that stuff was, so I went back to books and reading.

*Were you taken to galleries as a child?*

Not at all.

*At what point in your life did you encounter computers?*

In elementary school, where we had Apple IIEs and played games like Lemonade and Oregon Trail, back in the days when everything was DOS and floppy disks were actually floppy. There were Logo turtles instead of mice, and every command had to be keyed in. I remember how tedious it was to make a picture of a super-pixilated unicorn dot by dot by dot. For every dot that was placed on the screen, you had to specify its color and grid coordinates. Later, when I was in high school, I got a Macintosh Classic, which I used as a glorified word processor.

I've always been conscious of having been born at the dawn of the computer era. I've had a cashpoint card from the age of ten. I've always interacted with machines in order to do mundane tasks and, in my ease with them, they become the functional equivalent of forks, something you use and don't even seem to see any more. When you stop and think about it, with the simplest of transactions that you do all day long, you are continually entering the binary world of the computer.

*In retrospect, was there anything in your growing up that related to book art?*

Only the fact that when I started really loving books I began to be interested in collecting earlier editions of them, getting hardbound copies or ones with prettier covers. I began to objectify them. I had a fetish about my library. I was determined that it be huge and perfectly arranged. When I moved across America in 1994, I packed each and every book and filled the entire trunk of my car. I had to have that library with me, it was so much of my identity. All my books were annotated and underlined and dog-eared. My books were me.

*Did you make any books yourself when you were growing up?*

When I was in college taking a Spanish poetry class, I printed poems using rubber stamps. I wanted to have some consistent type so I carved an alphabet of individual letters. They were huge, with wonderful lines, and they became part of the aesthetic of the poem. I was using acrylic paint, rolling the colors down onto a piece of glass and stamping the letters onto that and then onto the paper. I was doing rubber letterpress before I even knew what letterpress was. I took a printmaking class and started playing around.

*Apart from the poetry, did you write much?*

I have never written creatively except in little spurts when I am upset.

*Did television figure much in your childhood?*

It played a huge role. My endurance amazed me. I could probably watch ten hours of TV a day. I think I got such a dose that I'll never be able to watch it again.

*When you stopped watching it, what took its place?*

The American teenager's passport to freedom: the automobile. I went to punk rock music shows and I hung out with punk rock kids and was very involved with that social scene. They were people who had a lot of energy and were playful and fun, yet they had belief systems too. However, most of them were pseudo-political. The biggest issue was contradicting or escaping from the norm—in short, dyeing your hair green and getting a mohawk.

*What publications do you associate with this time in your life?*

Fanzines. Maximum Rock and Roll. Kids were out there photocopying stuff and getting people to buy it, doing reviews of records and other kinds of self-publication. I didn't do any of that. I was put off by the fact that so many of the fanzines seemed to be made by somebody who just wanted to have their name out there and would put a bunch of crap on a piece of paper, photocopy it, and circulate it without it being substantial or interesting.

*When you left home to go to college, what had you gone to study?*

At first I wanted to study animal behavior and I volunteered at an emergency animal shelter but was shocked by the detachment toward the animals of the people who worked there. I applied to U.C. Davis, but didn't even check in with my science adviser and went straight to the literature classes. That's what really changed my life, studying folktales and mythology. It was back to the world of fantasy but with a reasoned, critical view, applying it to how people formed their world.

*When did you first encounter anything you would now think of as an artist's book?*

I remember it exactly. A bibliophile friend gave me a copy of *Griffin and Sabine*. It was on the American top-ten list, a wonderful book. On each page was a printed postcard and you flipped the page over and there was the back of the card and you read the correspondence between two people. Eventually you reached a page where there was the printed front of an envelope and on the back of that was a real envelope and inside that was a "handwritten" letter which you took out and read. I really got the sensation I was snooping through somebody's pile of letters. It wasn't a book telling me, the reader, that I was reading somebody's letters; I felt it and I did it. Suddenly the doors of the medium opened themselves to me. I don't remember who that book is by. I probably discovered it in 1993. I didn't hear the words "book art" until I got to Mills.

*How did you find life at Mills?*

I came to love Mills, and it was a very important place for me. It was small and the teachers were interested in the students and even in learning from them. It was the first time I encountered a teacher who wanted to continue learning. That was thrilling because I loved the idea of being an academic, of being with people who wanted to study for the rest of their lives. I thought I would never leave the safety of this nourishing university environment. I went there to study comparative literature.

*How did that lead to book art?*

Totally randomly. One evening I poked my head round a friend's door to see if she was coming to dinner. She was making this thing. I asked her what it was and she said it was a book. There were no pages. She said she was taking a class in bookbinding and I said, "If that's a book, then I want to make a book too." It all clicked immediately when I started the class. I realized that everything I had done spiraled to it, but that I had had no idea this was what I needed to find.

The class was taught by Gillian Boal, a conservationist at U.C. Berkeley. She was very craft conscious and would grab hold of your book, tug at the covers and say, "Oh, your spine just ripped. You'd better make another one." It was a good foundation because it's very important for me to have something that works. She didn't push us in any particular direction but just stressed that things must be well made and that we must understand how hinges and joints worked and must think about how the structures should relate to the piece we were making.

There were about eight people in the class, which was three hours twice a week, plus we had keys to the building and twenty-four-hour access. There were two proof presses and two clamshell presses and a well-stocked bindery. Gillian taught us a lot of binding structures, a lot of Hedi Kyle's, and things from Keith Smith's nonadhesive-binding book. They were nice, solid structures and we could modify them to suit ourselves. Every time I wanted to do something fun it would turn into something serious. That was the most exciting thing for me, that I wouldn't realize I'd had these thoughts or that these images were in my head until I started making the structure and using the material. The ideas and images would come together and the book would suddenly create itself. The first class was a semester, and after that I took an artist's book class with Kathy Walkup.

*Were you shown any books by other artists?*

We were taken to the Mills library by Gillian and Kathy. I didn't pay attention to who made the books or to the press names, I was just having fun poking around the books. The first book that really caught my eye was *The Softness on the Other Side of the Hole*, which had wood covers and fake pubic hair. The others that stuck out in my mind were *The Left-handed Punch* and *Anansi Company* because they were playful, colorful books. I didn't make the connection then that they were by the same person.

*Were you shown Ed Ruscha's work?*

Not that I remember. I'm bad with names. I'm sure I would recognize his work if I saw it.

*What happened in Kathy Walkup's class?*

She let us experiment. She taught us how to use the letterpress, and we had to do a broadside and a book and another project, which could be whatever we wanted. It was all very relaxed. There were about eleven or twelve of us.

*How had your thinking developed by the time you got to Kathy's class?*

What most excited me was how you could get a person to go through a book in a different way. I identified with something Alice said in Lewis Carroll's book, that grown-up books were no fun, there weren't any pictures and they were totally cerebral and didn't give you a space other than for relating information. I was interested in making people move through a space physically. For instance, I made a book out of perspex in 1996 in which a woman was taken apart in layers—you took off the makeup, you took off the skin, you saw the ovaries and the breasts. At the end of the book she complains that somebody dissected her, went through her and looked at her only in parts. She declares that you, the reader, have done this. And, with each page turning, the reader has indeed undressed her. I was interested in forcing the reader, by the act of reading, to go through a physical process that would really make them guilty of the woman's indictment.

*Why that issue?*

As a child I had never been aware that being a woman could prevent me from doing or being anything. When studying literature at Mills, you are taught to think about where the women's voices were and why their voices had been suppressed. At the same time it was an environment where I was surrounded by strong women. I'd never been so close to women before that and I realized that a lot of women in the 90s are still struggling and that, maybe, I was too without realizing it. It made me more conscious of what I was and what I might face in the years to come. **Lost** (1995) was the first book I made. In it the outline of a woman is stenciled on top of images of the things that are externally imposed on women, for example, extracts from a book of etiquette, collaged fashion plates, or visions of the perfect family. It's easy for women to lose their identity in all of those things. The images close over

*Lost,*
collage and acrylic paint, 9½" x 5",
8 pages, one of a kind, 1995

**karen bleitz • 227**

her and fill in her lines. She is vacant, just a silhouette. It's a concertina book on heavy card so it has a smacky, heavy sense. I don't like floppy, flippy, frilly things. I like heavy things that really turn.

*How do you spell a woman?* (1996) picks up on those women's issues again?

**How do you spell a woman?** is a book with metal pages. The woman in it is a cartoonish character, easy for people to identify with. I watercolored different scenes like domestic and work environments, and color photocopied them, and stuck them down on the metal, and then I made magnetized text that could be moved on the pages. There is some text which can't be moved, which puts forth questions like, "How do you spell a woman?" "Where am I going to live?" "What am I going to do?" "How am I going to create myself?" "How am I going to be sexually?" "How am I going to be as a parent?" Just as in life you're given so many factors—your race, socioeconomic situation, etc.—and it's up to each individual to make choices, to arrange and rearrange them, so the reader has words and scenes that can be moved to create infinite possibilities with the limited resources. You can change the outfits on the magnetized doll and choose an environment for her.

*You did a book questioning the relationship of pornography to art?*

That was the pop-up porno (1995), which doesn't have a title. It is a little red book with a cheap plastic-looking red vinyl cover. I found a funny set of encyclopedias of adult relationships published in the 1960s or 70s with all kinds of fantastic pictures that were a great source for collage. I juxtaposed those with art pictures—say, beautiful Japanese erotic painting—and pictures from a stack of pornos that my friend had collected while working at a "swingers" motel. The book is playful, obscene, and sexy all at once. At the end is a picture of a fragmented woman who must piece together several different perspectives of sex and sexuality in order to come to terms with her own body.

*Were all your books one of a kind?*

Yes. We were supposed to do an edition for Kathy Walkup but I hated what I did. I was working collaboratively with a poet friend of mine and he procrastinated and procrastinated, and it was doom because Eileen Hogan was due to show up in a few days from Camberwell College of Arts and I needed to be ready for that. It was a poem that opened up like doors and the pages began short and got wider and wider—it was difficult to write because the poetry had to work with every combination of doors. In the end we stayed up all

*Untitled*,
pop-up book with color photocopies
and red vinyl, 5″x 5½″x 1″, 22 pages,
one of a kind, 1995

night and my friend fell asleep on the floor while I carried on printing. The situation had become so horrible that I didn't feel the book was mine anymore. I liked the idea of doing collaborations, but that experience was such a burn.

*What reactions did you get to your books at Mills?*

People liked them and I was surprised. I had made them for myself, not as a big art statement. My main task at Mills was to write a huge thesis on contemporary feminist writers who used elements of the surreal or magic in their work. I was just making books as a relaxed way of being creative. When Eileen Hogan came over, I was really surprised that someone from a real art school would look at **How do you spell a woman?** and not want to change it.

Eileen had come over for a book art symposium at Mills that was also in memory of Charlene Garry, in whose name a sister relationship had been established between Mills and Camberwell with funding for one student a year to go to Camberwell to do the M.A. book art course there. My group was the second year that sent a student to Camberwell, and I was the one who got the scholarship.

*Books moved from being a sideline to being your central activity?*

Completely. I love literature and study but if I was going to be a professor I would just have to hole up in a library and do nothing but that, whereas book art is a combination of so much that I enjoy—writing, painting, using hammers and screws, being playful but also intellectual. It is a place where I can do all the things I want and give them real meaning and form.

As soon as I found out I was accepted at Camberwell and had finished Mills, I got two apprenticeships, one with Peter Koch, a printer, and one with Dominic Riley, a bookbinder who also does restoration. Both were wonderful experiences. Peter helped me to understand what an apprenticeship is—training, experience, learning, watching—rather than doing a course and coming away with a piece of paper. He giggled about the fact that I was going off to do an M.A. and said, "Fine. You can come back and teach with an M.A. Or you can come back and work with me for another five years and then say you're a printer."

*What did you learn from him?*

To be super nitpicky. I did a lot of typesetting, a bit of typography. I learned how to run presses and how to tell when something is good and well printed and, when it's not, how to make it good and well printed. I can persevere and will sit and fiddle for an hour to make sure something is square. I'm good at repetitive tasks.

*What was his workshop like?*

It was perfect and neat. All the type is beautiful, everything is put away perfectly, everything is well maintained. It was his kingdom, the place where he could make money from jobbing printing and earn the time to do his own work. When you're on a course like the one at Mills where everything is provided, you don't think about what it takes to run a press and keep it going. It takes a lot of time and effort and maintenance and things that are not fun, like leveling the bed of the press or sweeping. I got a real idea of what was involved.

*What did you learn from Dominic Riley?*

I was mostly doing restoration and it was good to learn what materials there are and how to use them and more tricks of the trade. I worked four days a week for Peter and one day for Dominic. Doing that put me in a mode where I was seriously considering becoming a straight binder or printer. Peter is very much in the crafts camp; he likes things to be either really well made or really well justified. When I came to Camberwell and was encouraged to make use of my freedom, I flowered. It was nice to say, "I know the rules but now I'd like to try something different."

*Were you involved in the Pacific Center for the Book Arts in San Francisco?*

Not really, although I was aware of it. Dominic was involved with *The Ampersand*, the PCBA's publication like a zine for book artists, and through that I realized there was a wider book art community in America.

*Does there seem to be a British book art community?*

I still don't know that much about who is who or what's what. I'm slowly learning but I'm scared to learn too much because I hear so many things that people say about one another and I don't want to get involved. People talk about books being Bibles of book art, and so on, and I don't want to get tied down by that.

*What did you discover at Camberwell?*

Camberwell was a good lesson in how to make do with what you've got and learn to be innovative. It was also difficult because a lot of staff weren't there and you were conscious of the fact that you were in the second year of a program that hadn't sorted itself out yet. Money was an issue and it felt like there were a lot of aspects that we had to face in addition to doing our work, so it was a lesson in real life. I found it hard to work at Camberwell. It was stressful because there was always a fight for the silkscreen bench or to use a computer. I encountered so many frustrating obstacles that it would mess up the way I approached my work.

Luckily, I stumbled into another apprenticeship. Peter Koch had told me to check out Ron King and Ken Campbell—I was supposed to be his Berkeley emissary. My opportunity arrived when one of the other Camberwell students, who was working in Ron's studio, offered to take me along with her to meet him. I walked in and there was *The Left-handed Punch* and *Anansi Company*, which I had not connected with Ron's name at all. I was so happy, I started pulling things down from the shelves. I've worked at Circle Press since early 1997. It's very different from Peter's; Peter is a printer and in his place you find printed matter and books on typography. At Ron's there is an explosion of things—sculptures, giant alphabet posters—and that was very inspiring. In terms of equipment, when you look around Circle Press, you don't necessarily have everything, but you have a bunch of other things that can get you to a certain place if you start to play, and that's what I really liked about it.

*What have you learned from Ron?*

I've learned discipline. All my life I've been a procrastinator. Ron is at the Press from nine thirty or ten o'clock until seven in the evening, six or seven

*Dolly: Edition Unlimited* (with Circle Press),
letterpress with wood and paper, hand-cut on a
fret saw, 8"x 9"x 2",
edition of 17, 1997

days a week. If I'm working there I arrive at ten thirty and leave at seven and I'll have a target for the day and meet it but I will relax at lunchtime. I was killing myself in the way I was working before because I didn't know how to structure myself.

*What did you achieve on the M.A. course?*

It began with crash-course inductions into processes like silkscreen, letterpress, and photography. You had to come up with a project for your final show, and from the first day you had forty-eight weeks to learn whatever you needed in order to achieve it, which was terrifying. It was a countdown from the beginning and every day was one day less. I would have liked another year, which may have been because I didn't come from art school as most of the others did, but I liked having come from a literary background. We all worked really hard.

The first thing I made was **Dolly** (1997). I picked up a magazine that contained an article about Dolly, a sheep named after Dolly Parton because it was cloned from a cell taken from a mammary gland. Cloning issues were brought to the world's attention by Dr. Ian Wilmut, who was trying to find a faster and more cost-effective means of breeding transgenic animals for the pharmaceutical industry. They were taken up instantly by the press and turned into a media circus. Wilmut's original article was completely obscured by talk of resurrecting the dead and women giving birth to themselves.

I decided to make a structure about a sheep that would replicate itself in book form. I spent ages researching. The book looks quite ordinary on the shelf. The covers are made of paper-covered wood that has been letterpress printed. Just as in life you couldn't look at the real issues without being bombarded by the fuss, in the book I spliced boldface newspaper headlines in ironic places in Wilmut's article, which makes his text difficult to read. The surprise comes when you open the covers and see that the text block is actually a wooden block with bound paper sandwiched inside it. In the middle is a jigsaw cutout of a sheep. The reader realizes that the sheep can be pulled out and made to stand up. It looks like a single animal but, when you open it out to 365 degrees, you get a whole herd from the one sheep. The sheep is cute but she is also terrifying—all the blank pages are mindless, identical sheep.

*It's a cloned book?*

It's full title is **Dolly: Edition Unlimited,** but it is actually limited to seventeen.

*Your final show included more magnet pieces?*

Lately, I've been dealing with issues of technology. I began to wonder how the book will find its place in a high-tech future where everything is digitized, where the transmission of information is instantaneous, and the barriers that have separated the author from the public are constantly shifting. I was interested in what John Updike was doing, putting out the first paragraph of a novel on the Net and letting other people add to it before he edits it. There are so many questions of authorship and authority thrown up at the moment. It's a cut-and-paste world and things aren't so tangible. In an information-overloaded society, do we have time or space for books anymore?

I began to explore the bulletin boards on the Internet, where users can manipulate other people's texts and spit their own ideas back into cyberspace. The piece I did for my Camberwell show using magnets sprang from the idea of giving the conventional page the possibilities available to digital documents. I silkscreened different texts onto three metal sheets. The first text was Douglas Coupland's glossary from his book *Generation X*, the next was a marketing report commissioned by the sponsors of the Lollapalooza festival called "Targeting the stoned cyberpunk," which discussed the best ways to approach and sell to a crowd they assumed was emotionally and mentally impaired by drugs. The third text was a rebuttal to the media's labeling titled, "Don't call me Generation X, call me a child of the 80s," in which the author fondly reminisces about a childhood of consumerism. Ironic or not, his comments placed him in the bulls-eye of the festival sponsors' target market. The words of the three texts were re-silkscreened onto individual magnets and placed in their original order on the metal sheets. I decided to take them to pubs, cafes, and clubs where people my age would be hanging out. I left them laying around for people to read, reflect upon, and rewrite. When I went back to collect them, the texts were always rearranged.

The metal sheets were then photocopied and, over time, grew into what became an actual bound book. **Redefining** is a self-contained play box which was constructed from wood, the metal sheets with their magnets, and a ring binding to which people could add new photocopies as they made them. I chose the Coupland text for the top lid and left the bottom lid and insides blank as margin spaces for creating new texts.

*You are planning to stay in London now that your course has finished.*

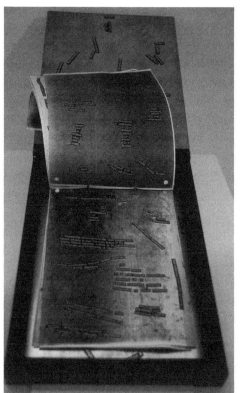

*Redefining,*
metal pages, magnets, silk-screen, photocopies, 13" x 10½" x 2", add-on pages, one of a kind, 1997

*Will you go on making books?*
I want to stay in London for as long as I can. I don't see myself not making things, and they are most likely to be books. Currently I'm working on a series of huge posters that will deal with how human interaction with computers is changing the way we read. I'm also building maquettes of different living spaces made out of binary-code-covered perspex where all the planes are defined by the binary codes of 0s and 1s used for computer signals. I will introduce scaled-down

photographs of people in various actions into the virtual environment and then rephotograph the maquette and make a fairly standard book from the images. Or something like that.

*You've recently begun working for Liliane Lijn as well as at Circle Press?*

I'm helping her print out the second part of the edition of *Her Mother's Voice* (1996) on the computer. It is giving us so many problems. Computer technology requires you to change the way you think in order to overcome the difficulties. It is interesting to go from Ron King's studio where everything is manual and physical—if it doesn't work, you jiggle it a little—to the computer. Ron and Liliane's studios are as different as night and day and the two worlds seem to be totally at odds, yet they produce the same thing—a book.

# Index

Editor and Publisher: Linda L. Brownrigg
Copyediting and Proofreading: Mimi Kusch
Design and Typesetting: Jaime Robles
Typeset in Frutiger and Joanna with old style figures in Adobe Garamond Expert

Photos: Portrait credits appear on portrait pages. Ian Tyson's work by Colin Still; Sas Colby's *Requiem* and *Shrine* by Phillip Kagan; Susan King's color plate *New York* (*My Mother Told Me*) by John Kife; Johanna Drucker's work by Brad Freeman; Alisa Golden's work by Jim Hair; Julie Chen's work by Sibila Savage; Karen Bleitz's work by Celeste Trimble.

Printed by Thomson-Shore on #60 Glatfelter text.